Latin American Monographs

Second Series

Bahia in the
First Brazilian Republic

23

Center for Latin American Studies
University of Florida

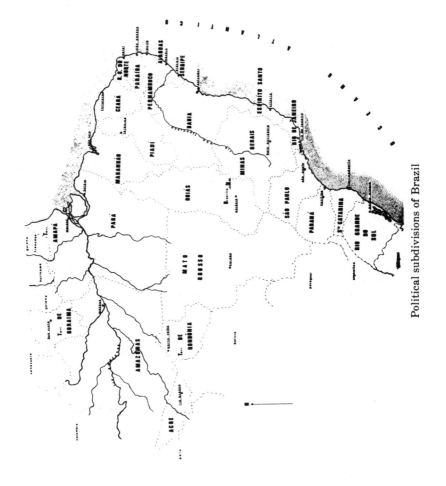

Political subdivisions of Brazil

Bahia in the
First Brazilian Republic
Coronelismo and Oligarchies, 1889–1934

Eul-Soo Pang

A University of Florida Book

University Presses of Florida

Gainesville / 1979

Latin American Monographs—Second Series

Library of Congress Cataloging in Publication Data

Pang, Eul-Soo.
   Bahia in the First Brazilian Republic.

   (Latin American monographs; 2d ser., 23)
   "A University of Florida book."
   Bibliography: p.
   1. Bahia, Brazil (State)—Politics and government.
   2. Coronelismo. I. Title. II. Series: Florida.
University, Gainesville. Center for Latin American
Studies. Latin American monographs; 2d ser., 23.
   F2551.P3   320.9'81'4   78–2682
   ISBN 0–8130–0604–X

A UNIVERSITY OF FLORIDA BOOK
SPONSORED BY THE CENTER FOR LATIN AMERICAN STUDIES

COPYRIGHT © 1979 BY THE BOARD OF REGENTS
OF THE STATE OF FLORIDA

PRINTED BY ROSE PRINTING COMPANY, INCORPORATED
TALLAHASSEE, FLORIDA

Preface

IN POLITICAL terms, the Old Republic or the First Republic (1889–1930) exhibited many inherent contradictions. Its birth owed much to the maturing effects of the liberal, modernizing forces of the second half of the nineteenth century, yet the survival of the political system itself depended on the continued support and manipulation of power by the traditional oligarchies. It was the rapid economic expansion of the central south region that played the pivotal role in the founding of the republic, but the oligarchs of the export economy (coffee, cattle, and minerals) failed to remain united after 1889, pitting themselves against each other for self-aggrandizement. Thus the most salient feature of the politics of the First Republic was the variation in composition and style of the regional oligarchies; only a few were able to dominate federation politics, either collectively or individually, enabling them to dictate their terms to the others.

"Oligarchy" is defined herein as both a system of political domination and rule either by a person(s), representing a consanguine or nonconsanguine clan or group held together by common economic stakes, political interests, and ideological and religious beliefs, or by a collective desire for the personal glorification of a charismatic leader, all to foster and defend the commonweal. "Region" in this study refers to a geoeconomically and/or culturally distinguishable area of contiguous states, when used in national politics, and of several *municípios* (counties) within a state, such as the cacao region and the Middle São Francisco region, when used in the context of single-state politics. At both national and state political levels, a region sought to function collectively, as a unit.

One more clarification of terminology: The Brazilian regional oligarchy was not, and still is not, monolithic; furthermore, it was not necessarily rural in character. The versatility of oligarchic organization is recognized here since it varied widely from region to region. Thus, in the traditional, agrarian northeast and far west, the predominant form was a single-clan oligarchy; in the urban, industrial central south, the membership of oligarchy was broadly based on the mixture of clans, classes, and even several sectors of society. There was no homogeneity in the Brazilian oligarchic structure; its very raison d'être differed from one region to another.

Therefore, the quintessence of the politics of the First Republic was the process of harmonizing the conflicting claims of regional oligarchies, and in order to achieve hegemony, such key states as São Paulo, Minas Gerais, and Rio Grande do Sul sought to integrate twenty federated states through their oligarchic leadership. Such efforts frequently resulted in periodic alliances and "understandings" among regional oligarchies, but these were often thwarted by the differences in social and economic interests among the numerous regions. A close look at the so-called *café com leite* alliance between coffee-growing São Paulo and cattle-raising Minas Gerais reveals that it was in fact *café contra leite*, especially after 1910, wherein the two competed more than they cooperated with each other for the supreme role of the arbiter of federation politics.

Hence, the national politics of Brazil should be regarded as bloc politics of a few powerful states united to pursue common but shifting interests. Seen in this context, a rudimentary comprehension of Brazilian national politics, especially during the First Republic, must begin with a microstudy of the politics of a region, that is, the process of conflict resolution and power monopoly and the patterns of cleavages and alliances in a particular state. By focusing on a detailed case study such as *coronelismo*, the most basic and localized form of Brazilian oligarchy, I seek to develop new regional perspectives of the politics of the First Republic.

Tocqueville once observed that during a period of transition, such as from aristocratic monarchy to democratic republic, a crisis of legitimacy and effectiveness of government often occurs. When this happens, informal, personalistic leaders such as Brazilian *coronéis* are often preferred to the formal, distant state authority. The First Republic constituted such a transitional phase in terms of regional diversity in social and economic development and in the political behavior of dominant classes. The incongruities inevitably led to an unstable political order, where power was tightly clenched by the traditional oligarchies of coronéis in municípios, by a congregation of personality- or class interest–oriented parties and bands in the state capitals, and by formal and informal alliances of state oligarchies in the federal capital. Viewed in this fashion, coronelismo was the bedrock of the politics of the transitional phase that allowed the traditional oligarchies to sustain themselves in power.

The State of Bahia in the First Republic offers a number of advantages as a case study of coronelismo. Its physical and demographic size, economic importance (sugar and cacao on the coast, cattle and mining in the interior), and a host of colorful political personalities (Rui Barbosa, José Joaquim Seabra, the Monizes, the Calmons, and the Mangabeiras) made Bahia an important secondary state in the hierarchy of federation politics of the First Republic. Bahia was the largest and most powerful state in northeast Brazil, often outdistancing its arch-rival, Pernambuco, in prestige and importance. Furthermore, the coronéis of Bahia during the First Republic represented a wide spectrum of subregional, social, and economic backgrounds, partisan activities, and even military campaigns in the service of a particular political group, the state, and the federation. Therefore, the study of Bahian coronelismo can be an important first step toward developing new interpretations of the history of the First Brazilian Republic and toward Latin American sociopolitical history as well. To this end, I chose to analyze and describe the complexities of the Bahian oligarchies and their role in local, state, regional, and federal politics for the period from the birth of the First Republic in 1889 to the Revolution of 1930 to the restructuring of the "old order" during the early years of Vargas' rule to 1934.

A final note on mechanical aspects of this book is in order. First, Brazilian orthography has changed many times in this century. The general practice among North American Brazilianists is to use the modern spelling in the text and preserve the original in the footnotes and bibliography. This has created nothing but confusion. Persons writing in the forties and fifties were not consistent with accent marks and double letters. Those writing in the second half of the last century capitalized the months, for instance, while in this century the lower case was adopted. In order to avoid confusion and maintain consistency, I have decided, at the publisher's request, to modernize names and titles in the text, footnotes, and bibliography. Thus, Ruy is converted to Rui, Arthur to Artur, Mattos to Matos, *archivo* to *arquivo*, *bahiano* to *baiano*, *monarchia* to *monarquia*, and so on. The only exceptions to the orthographic change that I have made are the names of foreign origin such Octavio Ianni (Italian), and such venerable names as Freyre, José Olympio, and Raymundo Faoro, and in direct quotations. Under a 1971 law, persons were permitted to retain old spellings of their names, if they wished.

Acknowledgments

THIS BOOK has a history. Before its form could be realized, I had to return to Brazil several times after the completion of the dissertation in 1970. In adding new materials, I have had to condense some of the original data; those interested in knowing the intimate details of Brazil's regional and Bahia's local politics should therefore turn to my dissertation.

In writing this book, I have become indebted to a number of institutions which have supported me financially. The Henry L. and Grace Doherty Foundation generously financed my first research trip to Brazil in 1967–68. Since then, I have had fellowships from the Social Science Research Council and American Council for Learned Societies (1972–73), the Center for Latin American Studies at Vanderbilt University (summer 1974), the American Philosophical Society (summer 1974), the Vanderbilt University Graduate Research Council (summer 1975), and the Exxon Corporation (summer 1975). These institutions supported my subsequent trips to Brazil and allowed me to gather further information that I have incorporated into this book, and to begin new projects as well.

There have also been countless people involved—Brazilians, Americans, Koreans, Lebanese, and Israelis—who have guided me in my search for data. In Rio de Janeiro, the following offered their kind assistance: Raul Lima, José Gabriel da Costa Pinto, Marita Iglesias, Arlindo Belém, and Margarida Diniz Câmara, all of the Arquivo Nacional; Pedro Calmon, Adelaide Alva, and Isabel Bulcão de Morais of the Instituto Histórico e Geográfico Brasileiro; Américo Jacobina Lacombe of the Fundação Casa de Rui Barbosa; Waldir da Cunha of the Biblioteca Nacional; Martha Maria Gonçalves of the Arquivo Histórico do Itamarati; Maria Amélia of the Museu Imperial in Petrópolis; and General Luís Serff Sellman, former director of the Biblioteca do Exército.

Also in Rio, I received valuable assistance from Dr. Euclides Aranha Neto, Dr. Ivo and Maria Helena Pinho Gama, and Fiel Fontes, all of whom placed personal archives of key politicians at my disposal. The late General Humberto de Sousa e Melo recounted for me his role in the Revolution of 1930 in Bahia; Colonel Newton Ourique de Oliveira, now retired, helped me secure permission to consult the archives of the Ministry of the Army. General Sun-Yup Paik, former Korean ambassador to Canada, Colonel Barry Ryan, U. S. Army, ret., and Minister-Counselor Bien Houhn and Consul Young Jae Hwang of the Korean Embassy in Brazil provided many valuable letters of introduction.

In Bahia, the late Professor Frederico Edelweiss not only offered his guidance but also allowed me to consult his personal library. Renato Berbert de Castro and Luís Henrique, director and former director, respectively, and Arlete Vieira of the Arquivo Público do Estado da Bahia graciously opened their doors; Professors Cid Teixeira, Thales de Azevedo, José Sena, José Calasans, Luís Monteiro, and other members of the Instituto Geográfico e Histórico da Bahia made me feel at home during my first and subsequent visits; Otto Seligsohn of the Instituto de Cacao, Carlos Torres of the Associação Comercial da Bahia, Nelson de Sousa Sampaio of the Law School of the Universidade Federal da Bahia, João Augusto Calmon of the Banco Econômico da Bahia, and Jorge Calmon of *A Tarde* all enthusiastically lent their support to my work.

The personal archives of *coronéis* and *bacharéis* in Bahian and Brazilian politics were indispensable sources for this book. I have been fortunate to have had access to them. In Bahia, the following people gave me their gracious permission to examine personal and family papers and assisted me in locating other private collections: Horacina de Matos Lima, Horácio de Matos Júnior, Tácio de Matos, Juty de Matos, Wilson Lins, Franklin Lins de Albuquerque Júnior, Morgan Duarte, the late Bolívar Santana Batista and Maria América de Sento Sé, Astor Pessoa, Laura Rodrigues da Costa Santos, Menandro and Nair Novais, Anísio and Bernardete Tanuri, Marieta Alves, José Andrade Filho, and Eurico Mata. In the interior of Bahia, Pedro Tomas Pedreira, José Joaquim Santana, the late Coronel Manuel Alcântara de Carvalho, and Sebastião Alves lent me much help. I have also greatly benefited from personal *amizade* with many *baianos* who refined my understanding of their society and culture, especially Consuelo Novais de Quadros, Kátia Matoso, Moema and Johannes Augel, and Leão and Sara Rozemberg. The late Rozembergs made our living in Bahia a constant pleasure and a fond memory.

In the United States, I am grateful to Professors Woodrow W. Borah, James F. King, Robert A. Scalapino, and Engel Sluiter, my teachers at the University of California, Berkeley, and Professor Rollie E. Poppino at the Davis campus, who served as my dissertation director and has become a steady source of guidance since its completion. At Vanderbilt University, my first and foremost appreciation goes to Professor William H. Nicholls, former director of the Center for Latin American Studies and a Brazilianist par excellence, for his constant encouragement; Professor Alexander Marchant read the entire manuscript and offered wise and constructive criticism; and Deans Jacque Voegeli and Ernest Q. Campbell have been generous with research grants that aided in the completion of this book. Laura Jarnagin, João Cabral, Chris Carbaugh, and Janice Pollok, my students at Vanderbilt, also read the manuscript and offered their comments. Laura deserves my warmest thanks for her unflagging support: she not only typed one draft in its entirety but also lent her expert editorial help on the final version and helped me organize the index of this book.

Professors Stanley Hilton of Louisiana State University and Ron L. Seckinger of the Universidade Federal Fluminense gave me much practical orientation in archival research during my first visit to Brazil. Stan Hilton has been especially helpful in locating private archives. Professors Richard M. Morse, Stuart Schwartz, John Wirth, Joseph Love, and Robert Levine read my dissertation and offered comments which I found to be of special value in completing this book. Professor Neill Macaulay of the University of Florida commented on an earlier draft of this book and offered many suggestions for improvement.

The maps in this book were prepared by Sônia Maria Gomes of Niterói, Brazil, and S. Dalonio of Hayward, California.

I wish to thank the following for use of photographs: the Arquivo Nacional; the Instituto Histórico e Geográfico Brasileiro; the Instituto Geográfico e Histórico da Bahia; Nertan Macedo, author of *Abílio Wolney, um coronel da Serra Geral* (Goiana: Legenda Editora, 1975); Fundação Casa de Rui Barbosa; Francisco Borges de Barros, *Memória sobre o município de Ilhéus* (Salvador, 1915); Américo Chagas, *O chefe Horácio de Matos* (São Paulo, 1961).

Finally, I am deeply grateful for the patience and understanding of my two families—Alex, Steve, and Linda, and Ki-Ok and mother—to whom I dedicate this book.

to

Alex, Steve, Linda, Ki-Ok, and mother

ABBREVIATIONS

AAAMP   Arquivo de Afonso Augusto Moreira Pena
ABC   Arquivo do Barão de Cotegipe
ABRB   Arquivo do Barão do Rio Branco
ACRB   Arquivo da Casa de Rui Barbosa
AEBa   Arquivo do Estado da Bahia
AESP   Arquivo de Epitácio da Silva Pessoa
AFAP   Arquivo da Família Araújo Pinho
AFLA   Arquivo de Franklin Lins de Albuquerque
AFMGC   Arquivo de Francisco Marques de Góis Calmon
AFP   Arquivo de Floriano Peixoto
AGM   Arquivo de Gonçalo Moniz
AHI   Arquivo Histórico do Itamarati
AHMI   Arquivo Histórico do Museu Imperial
AHQM   Arquivo de Horácio de Queiroz Matos
AIGHBa   Arquivo do Instituto Geográfico e Histórico da Bahia
AJAS   Arquivo de José Antônio de Saraiva
AME   Arquivo do Ministério do Exército
AMP Anais do Museu Paulista
AN   Arquivo Nacional
ANP   Arquivo de Nilo Peçanha
AOA   Arquivo de Oswaldo Aranha
AOM   Arquivo de Otávio Mangabeira
AQGPMEBa   Arquivo do Quartel General da Polícia Militar do Estado da
   Bahia
AQG6RM   Arquivo do Quartel General da 6ª Região Militar
ARCI   Arquivo Republicano "Convenção de Itu"
ASSV   Arquivo de Severino dos Santos Vieira
DOS/USNA   Records of the Department of State Relating to Internal Affairs
   of Brazil, 1910-29, United States National Archives
HAHR Hispanic American Historical Review
HGCB História geral da civilização brasileira
RBEP Revista Brasileira de Estudos Políticos
RH Revista de História
RIC Revista do Instituto do Ceará
RIGBa Revista do Instituto Genealógico da Bahia
RIHGB Revista do Instituto Histórico e Geográfico Brasileiro
RIGHBa Revista do Instituto Geográfico e Histórico da Bahia
RIHGSP Revista do Instituto Histórico e Geográfico de São Paulo
SDA/AEBa   Seção da Documentação Administrativa, Arquivo do Estado da
   Bahia
SH/AEBa   Seção Histórica, Arquivo do Estado da Bahia
SPE/AN   Seção do Poder Executivo, Arquivo Nacional

Contents

Maps appear on pages ii, 48, 50.

Picture section follows page 112.

1. Coronelismo: An Oligarchic Approach to Brazilian Politics

Tʜᴇ ɢᴇɴᴇꜱɪꜱ of Brazilian coronelismo is in colonial times, but the zenith of its influence was reached during the century 1850–1950. The term "coronel" literally means colonel, a military rank derived from the colonial militias of the late eighteenth century, although many historians believe that the title came from the National Guard.[1] "Coronel" in a generic sense

1. For conflicting views on the origin of the coronelismo as a form of political bossism, see the following. For the "colonial view," Victor Nunes Leal, *Coronelismo, enxada e voto (o município e o regime representativo no Brasil)*, p. 20, Basílio Magalhães' introductory footnote; John Norman Kennedy, "Bahian Elites, 1750–1822," pp. 427–31; Pernambuco, Secretaria do Interior e Justiça, Arquivo Público Estadual, *Documentos do Arquivo Público Estadual e da Biblioteca do Estado sobre a Comarca do São Francisco, selecionados, coordenados e publicados pelo Exmo. Snr. Barbosa Lima Sobrinho*, pp. 305–16. For the "National Guard view," see note 2. It will suffice to cite here one typical case: Maria Isaura Pereira de Queiroz, "O coronelismo numa interpretaçao sociológica," in *História geral da civilização brasileira III: O Brasil republicano 1: estrutura de poder e economia (1889–1930)*, vol. 8, ed. Boris Fausto (São Paulo, 1975), p. 155, hereafter cited as HGCB. The standard work on the National Guard is Manuel da Costa Leite, *Apontamentos históricos sobre o exército nacional de 2ª linha*; see also "A Guarda Nacional," *HGCB* 6:274–98; Brasil, Ministerio da Justiça e Negócios Interiores, *Notícia histórica dos serviços, instituições e estabelecimentos pertencentes a esta repartição, elaborada por ordem do respectivo ministro, Dr. Amaro Cavalcanti*, a section designated as "Guarda Nacional"; Nelson Werneck Sodré, *História militar do Brasil*, pp. 116–43.

was a military commander of a National Guard brigade or a regiment in a county (município). He was frequently a landowner (planter or rancher), the dominant component in the ruling class of agrarian Brazil, but members of auxiliary social classes such as merchants, lawyers, physicians, bureaucrats, teachers, industrialists, and even priests secured the rank of colonel from the guard.

However, the heart of coronelismo is not concerned with the role of the commanders of the National Guard but rather with those sociopolitical aspects of the power monopoly of the dominant and auxiliary classes under the monarchic and republican regimes in Brazil. In short, coronelismo is a monopolistic exercise of power by a coronel whose legitimacy and acceptance are based on and buttressed by his paramount status as the dominant element in social, economic, and political institutions such as prevailed during the transition period from a rural agrarian nation to an urban industrial one.[2] The demarcation of this era is the years 1850–1950. During this century of modernization, the nation experienced a series of fundamental structural changes in economy and polity. This was also a time of conflict between traditional and emerging forces of social

2. The standard work on coronelismo is Leal, *Coronelismo*, first published in 1948, an unrevised second edition in 1975. The unupdated English translation of Leal's work was published in 1977 by the Cambridge University Press. The standard recent works on coronelismo are: Montes Arraes, *Decadência e redenção no nordeste* (*a política dos grandes estados*), pp. 87–95; Leôncio Basbaum, *História sincera da república*, vol. 2, *de 1889 a 1930*, pp. 213–15; Jean Blondel, *As condições dá vida política no Estado da Paraíba*; Edgard Carone, *A primeira república (1889–1930)*, pp. 67–88, and *A república velha (instituições e classes sociais)*, pp. 249–67; Fernando Henrique Cardoso and Enzo Faletto, *Dependência e desenvolvimento na América latina: ensaio de interpretação sociológica*, pp. 63–67; Raymundo Faoro, *Os donos do poder*, 2:620–54; Octavio Ianni et al., *Política e revolução social no Brasil*, pp. 72–78; Zahidé Machado Neto, ed., *O coronelismo na Bahia*; Charles Morazé, *Les trois âges du Brésil*, chap. 6; Antônio Barroso Pontes, *Mundo dos coronéis*; Queiroz, *O mandonismo local na vida política brasileira (da colônia à primeira república)* (a reprint of six articles of the same title that first appeared in *Anhembi* [1956–57]) and "O coronelismo numa interpretação"; M. Auxiliadora Ferraz de Sá, *Dos velhos aos novos coronéis*; Celson José da Silva, *Marchas e contramarchas do mandonismo local*; Gláuco Ary Dillon Soares, *Sociedade e política no Brasil*, pp. 112–18; João Camilo de Oliveira Torres, *Estratificação social no Brasil*, pp. 82–140; Marcos Vilaça and Roberto C. de Albuquerque, *Coronel, coronéis*; Emílio Willems, *Uma vila brasileira: tradição e transição*, pp. 77–81; Abelardo F. Montenegro, "José Antônio do Fechado e o banditismo político"; Luís Viotti de Azevedo, "Evolução dos partidos políticos no município de São João Evangelista"; Levy Cruz, "Função do comportamento política numa comunidade do São Francisco."

and economic tensions and of a national political system that strove unsuccessfully to retain its stability. Coronelismo emerged precisely during this time of crisis and instability to command local and regional politics and not infrequently to function as a surrogate state in the backlands (sertão).[3] The maturation of coronelismo as a uniquely Brazilian institution took place under the First Republic (1889–1930), the critical four decades of transition from one socioeconomic phase to another.

THE RISE OF THE PRIVATE DOMAIN

The main function of coronelismo was the skillful use of private power amassed by a patriarch of a clan or an extended family.[4] The patriarchal social and economic base of coronelismo had its origins in the plantation (engenho de açúcar) and the ranch (fazenda de gado) of the sixteenth century. The plantation preceded the establishment of a formal colonial government in 1549, thus providing the first unchecked opportunity for the planter class to extend the power of the private domain to the public sector. The commanding position of the Brazilian planter class was further reinforced by the Portuguese monopoly of the overseas sugar trade in the second half of the sixteenth century; as a result, the politics of colonial Brazil came to be monopolized by this dominant class. The anthesis of the plantation society, especially in an export-oriented economy, fostered the rise of a multilayered class system.[5]

Structurally, the Portuguese planter presided over his domain as the absolute lord. This planter class, though small in number, dominated the dependent local population. Immediately below the planter's family was a hierarchy of workers:

3. "Sertão" will be translated as hinterlands, backlands, and/or interior throughout this book.

4. This view is typical of the works cited in note 2. For representative cases, see Queiroz, "O coronelismo numa interpretação," pp. 155–56; Dora Leal Rosa, "Coronelismo na Chapada Diamantina," in Machado Neto, ed., O coronelismo na Bahia, pp. 23–59, esp. p. 49.

5. For such a revisionist view, see Stuart B. Schwartz, Sovereignty and Society in Colonial Brazil, pp. 95–121, 171–90, and "Free Labor in Slave Economy: The Lavradores de Cana of Colonial Bahia," in Dauril Alden, ed., Colonial Roots of Modern Brazil, pp. 147–97; A. J. R. Russell-Wood, Fidalgos and Philanthropists: The Santa Casa da Misericórdia of Bahia, 1550–1755, pp. 116–45; Kennedy, "Bahian Elites."

the overseer (*feitor*), the mill-master (*mestre de açúcar*), and other minor functionaries who served the planter-patriarch, and below them a vast number of black slaves and their children who together provided the bedrock of the plantation as they toiled, planted, harvested, and ground the sugarcane.[6] Outside this immediate retinue, the planter often lent the use of milling facilities to free farmers (*lavradores*) and leased land to tenants (*agregados, arrendatários, parceiros*).[7] The planter also hired wage laborers (*jornaleiros*), both poor white and black, contracted artisans, and retained merchant-purveyors. The dependency of such a multilayered work force promoted the rise of the planter-patriarch to sociopolitical pre-eminence over his domain or region; a patron-client relationship based on a superior/inferior economic relationship arose between the rich and poor. This tie strengthened social paternalism, which the planter adroitly exploited for political purposes and routinely used to justify his exercise of power in the public domain. This system of the political supremacy of one man, whose power was based on privileged social and economic status, is the colonial antecedent to the coronelismo of the nineteenth and twentieth centuries.

Aside from creating socioeconomic dependency ties, the monoculture that flourished in colonial times discouraged the rise of nonagrarian classes to positions of equal power and prestige such as were held by the dominant planter class. The weak crown failed to curb the power of the planter elite since the king's laws and bureaucrats fell under the control of the latifundiary elite. Merchants, artisans, civil and military servants, and other minor social elements aspired to become landowners, thus further enhancing the prestige of the dominant class and denigrating the status of rival social classes. It was not until late in the eighteenth century that the landed class was challenged by the urban mercantile class. Until

6. Fernando de Azevedo, *Canaviais e engenhos na vida política do Brasil*, pp. 90–92; Luís dos Santos Vilhena, *Cartas de Vilhena: notícias soteropolitanas e brasílicas*, chap. 5. The new edition of the Vilhena's work appeared under the title *A Bahia no século XVIII*. A better known source for colonial plantation life is Gilberto Freyre, *The Masters and the Slaves (Casa Grande e Senzala) A Study in the Development of Brazilian Civilization*.

7. For various types of dependent agrarian population, see Manuel Diégues Júnior, *População e açucar no nordeste do Brasil*, chap. 6; Manuel Correia de Andrade, *A terra e o homem no nordeste*, pp. 65–95.

then, the planter class succeeded in excluding members of rival social classes from politics, and the town council (*senado da câmara*), which was the principal local administrative corporation, became the fount of public power for the planter elite.[8] Except in a few major colonial trade centers, local politics was closed to the merchant class. In time, the distinction between the private interest of the planter class and public concerns of the município became blurred, and in many interior towns they became synonymous. Under the monarchy and the republic, the município continued to serve as the bailiwick of the planter-coronel, who used and abused the area as his personal fief. The absence of a powerful centripetal state for the century 1850–1950 abetted the flowering of coronelismo as the only viable institution of power.

OLIGARCHIC CLAN FEUDS AND VIOLENCE

The Brazilian clan or extended family has always included consanguine and nonconsanguine members of its sphere of influence. In addition to both patrilineal and matrilineal in-laws, the clan extended its membership to incorporate socioeconomic dependents, especially for political purposes. As the colony grew in demographic and economic terms, armed conflicts between rival clans were inevitable. Each clan maintained a retinue of private armed soldiers, known as *jagunços, capangas,* and *cabras,* all meaning "ruffians" in the regional vernacular,[9] who were recruited from the ranks of the clan's dependent population. These feudal armies collided over land and water rights, in electoral disputes, and, not infrequently, in passion-inspired crimes. The more celebrated clan wars in Brazilian

8. Dauril Alden, *Royal Government in Colonial Brazil,* pp. 422–23; Caio Prado Júnior, *The Colonial Background of Modern Brazil,* pp. 365–67. For historical development of municípios, see João Martins de Carvalho Mourão, "Os municípios, sua importância política no Brasil-colônia e no Brasil-reino." An interesting comparative study on colonial municipal councils was written by C. R. Boxer, *Portuguese Society in the Tropics: The Municipal Councils of Goa, Macao, Bahia, and Luanda, 1510–1800.* Three other items are worthy of mention: Brasílio Machado Neto, *O município no Brasil;* Orlando M. Carvalho, *Política do município (ensaio histórico);* and Edmundo Zenha,*O município no Brasil (1532–1700).*

9. Freyre, *Nordeste: aspectos da influência da cana sobre a vida e a paisagem do nordeste do Brasil,* pp. 184–85; Luís Câmara Cascudo, *Dicionário do folclore brasileiro,* lists only cabra and jagunço, no capanga.

history were fought by the Pinheiros and the Ramalhos of São Paulo, the Filgueiras and the Arnauds of Ceará, the França Antuneses and the Guerreiros of Bahia, the Pereiras and the Carvalhos of Pernambuco. In the twentieth century, similar clan wars wracked the backlands of Brazil. In Bahia, the Matoses and the Sás of the Lavras Diamantinas and the Albuquerques and the França Antuneses of the Middle São Francisco Valley inherited the clan feuds of former years.[10] In Mato Grosso, where the federal government was also to exert its authority, such political clans as the Murtinhos and the Correia da Costa (Pedro Celestino) family routinely wiped out rival clans, while in Paraíba, the Pessoas who ruled the state during the First Republic were effectively challenged by the Pereiras of Princesa.[11] Although interclass feuds, such as those between the landowning and the mercantile classes, were rare, class interests did inspire one war in the early eighteenth century, the War of the Mascates in Pernambuco, from which the victorious merchants succeeded in obtaining administrative independence for Recife.[12] But such a war was not known in later centuries.

The legitimation of violence was often attained through the

10. The standard work on clan feuds in Brazil is L. A. Costa Pinto, *Lutas de famílias no Brasil (introdução ao seu estudo)*, esp. chaps. 4, 5. See Quieroz, *O mandonismo*, p. 18. On Pernambuco, see Ulisses Lins de Albuquerque, *A luta dos Pereiras e Carvalhos*, which was also published in *Um sertanejo e o sertão (memórias)*. On Bahia, see Brás do Amaral, *História da Bahia do império à república*, p. 153; Wilson Lins, *O médio São Francisco: uma sociedade de pastores e guerreiros*, pp. 47–66; *Fala dirigida à Assembléia Legislativa Provincial da Bahia, na abertura da sessão ordinária do ano de 1845, pelo presidente da província Francisco de Sousa Soares d'Andrea*, p. 4, hereafter cited as *Fala da Bahia*. On Ceará, see Nertan Macedo, *O bacamarte dos Mourões*.

11. On Mato Grosso, see General Malan no Comando da Circumscrição Militar Mato Grosso 1924–1926 (MS), in Cx II, no. 13—Revolução no Estado de Mato Grosso em diversos anos, Arquivo do Ministério do Exército, hereafter cited as AME; Carone, *A república velha*, p. 264. For details of politics in Mato Grosso in the earlier period, see M. Balbino de Carvalho, *A luta no Graças*; Generoso Ponce Filho, *Generoso Ponce, um chefe*; and Virgílio Correía Filho, *Pedro Celestino*. On Paraíba, see José Américo de Almeida, *Memórias de José Américo (o ano do Nêgo)*, pp. 44 ff.; Delmiro Pereira de Andrade, *Evolução histórica da Paraíba do Norte*, pp. 230–59; Apolônio Nóbrega, *História republicana da Paraíba*, pp. 183–84. A collection of documents dealing with the Princesa revolt is in *João Pessoa—Aliança Liberal—Princesa*, vol. 24 of *Obras Completas de Epitácio Pessoa*.

12. Charles R. Boxer, *The Golden Age of Brazil 1695–1750*, chap. 5; Gilberto Osório de Andrade, *Montebelo, os males e os mascates*, chaps. 2, 3.

exercise of public offices by clan members. The colonial and imperial armies were relatively small in size and were concentrated mostly in coastal towns. In many of the interior municípios, the state lacked the means to provide law enforcement and administration of justice; these voids were quickly filled by the Solomon-like patriarch and his private armies. As a practical matter, armed groups under the command of a planter remained beyond the control of royal or imperial authorities, who were eventually obliged to grant them legal or quasi-legal status as militia units. As the sanctioning of violence was thus institutionalized, the transformation of private power into public power was a short process. Toward the end of the eighteenth century, major planters and ranchers in the colony were granted militia ranks of coronel or *capitão-mor* to complement their social and economic prestige.[13] In some instances, confrontations between armed groups of the private and public domain occurred, and these became even more frequent as the state and local potentates often became entangled in electoral disputes in the nineteenth and twentieth centuries.

THE ORIGIN OF THE GUARDA NACIONAL

Some historians have attributed the titlemania among the Brazilian rich and poor to the introduction of a system of nobility and the establishment of the National Guard in the early nineteenth century. The title of coronel was overshadowed by five categories of nobility grades, *duque, marquês, conde, visconde,* and *barão,* in descending order; furthermore, the academic titles of *bacharel* for a lawyer and an engineer and *doutor* for a physician drew greater prestige than "coronel." The honorific commendations and academic degrees, however, remained beyond the reach of most Brazilians, making the paramilitary commissions more accessible and appealing. In the process, "coronel" became an inferior title, having a parvenue, if not pedestrian, connotation. Such a class distinction was even more accentuated in the late nineteenth century.

The proliferation, or vulgarization, of the title "coronel" owed much to the political changes that took place after 1831. The

13. Pernambuco, Secretaria do Interior e Justiça, *Documentos do Arquivo Público Estadual,* pp. 305–16.

imperious Pedro I, the first constitutional emperor, abdicated the throne to his five-year-old son, Pedro Alcântara Brasileiro, who was legally barred from governing the nation until he was eighteen. The Constitution of 1824 required a regency to rule in the name of the child emperor. The rising tide of Lusophobia after 1831 convinced the Triune Regency (1831–35) that the Portuguese-officered regular army should be reduced in size.[14] To maintain domestic law enforcement and national defense against external enemies, the regency established the National Guard, a citizens' army modeled after the well-known French institution. The officer corps of the guard was drawn from the landed gentry and their auxiliary classes. In each município, the guard unit assumed the responsibilities of local police under the supervision of the imperial minister of justice and the provincial authorities. Replacing the colonial militias, the National Guard emerged as the prestigious institution in the backlands and coastal municípios, drawing its members from the dependent population of a planter-patriarch.

The popularity of the guard titles spread quickly during the monarchic and republican periods. Leading families of agrarian and mercantile origins routinely decorated their heirs with titles. The Pinheiro Cangaçu family in Rio de Contas, Bahia, boasted three generations of titleholders from the grandfather Capitão-Mor Antônio of the colonial militia to the grandson Coronel Exupério of the National Guard. The military honors buttressed the existing social and economic supremacy of the Pinheiro Cangaçu clan as the major latifundiary elite of the Rio de Contas region. Capitão Antônio, the largest rancher, was Rio de Contas' economic lord and political chief in addition to being its militia commander. The grandson was the boss of the Liberal Party's local directorate, the keeper of justice, and the dispenser of welfare. For three generations the townspeople depended on the Pinheiro Cangaçu family for their livelihood and political orientation.[15] At mid-century, the clan's power remained unchallenged, although the partisanization of the backlands gradually helped the emergence of a rival power elite.

14. By May 1831, the regular army had been reduced from about 30,000 to a mere 14,000 (Sodré, *História militar do Brasil*, p. 130).

15. Lycurgo Santos Filho, *Uma comunidade rural do Brasil antigo*, pp. 136–43.

The demand for National Guard titles was not confined to the uneducated backland aristocracy. In the more traditional sugar plantations of the Recôncavo, the regional gentry also sought military ranks. Felipe Ferreira de Araújo Pinho, a Sorbonne-trained Bahian planter in Santo Amaro, was commissioned lieutenant colonel ten years after his *bachelier ès sciences mathematiques*.[16] Likewise, father and son of the Costa Pinto clan of Santo Amaro (the Conde de Sergimirim and the Visconde da Oliveira) were commanders of the local guard unit.[17] In Pernambuco, the Barão de Vila Bela of Pesqueira, the Barão de Atalia of Aguas Belas, and the Barão de Exu of Exu, to cite well-known cases, were colonels in the National Guard.[18] This planter elite commanded the largest private armies in their municípios, and with or without the titles, they were veritable lords of structured violence. Both the imperial and the republican regimes were quick to appreciate the armed preparedness and granted the indelible mark of recognition by appointing them guard commanders. The social prestige of the guard continued to rise through the 1850s and 1860s as the grateful empire valued its military services in the war against the Rosas regime in Argentina and in the Paraguayan War (1864–70).[19]

THE PARTISANIZATION OF THE GN

In colonial times, the concession of military honors was not partisanized. Crown agents, serving in office at the pleasure of the Portuguese ruling dynasty, did not need the voting power of the colonial town elite in order to hold office. Politics, particularly electoral politics, was confined to the câmara level, for

16. Patentes, December 20, 1852, June 5, 1867, Lata 546/Docs. 2–3 and Diploma, Université de France, December 30, 1842, Lata 546/Doc. 1, Arquivo da Família Araújo Pinho, hereafter cited as AFAP. This is a collection of two personal archives, the father's and the son's.
17. 1° Barão de Smith de Vasconcelos and 2° Barão de Smith de Vasconcelos, *Arquivo nobiliárquico brasileiro*, pp. 318, 474.
18. Albuquerque, *Um sertanejo*, pp. 283–84.
19. About 80 percent of the Brazilian fighting men came from the Guarda Nacional and the Voluntários da Pátria during the Paraguayan War. Bahia alone contributed 15,197 men, of whom 5,312 were men and officers of the GN, 9,164 voluntários, and 721 recruits and freed slaves. For more details, see Leite, *Apontamentos históricos*, pp. 38–40.

colonial Brazil did not possess a legislature, nor did it have the right to dispatch elected deputies to the metropolitan Cortes in Lisbon.

Under the empire a semblance of a democratic system was instituted in which certain offices were attained by electoral processes. This democratization of the political system after 1822 accounted for the partisanization of political and military honors. As the empire matured, the delineation of political interests along partisan lines (the Conservative and Liberal parties and the two minor Progressive and Republican parties) became sharper.[20] Not only did the concession of titles become a partisan concern, but the appointment of a command post became an important political consideration of a dominant party. At least on paper, the control of the local guard units assured the partisan use of policing power, a crucial factor in the elections of the empire and the republic.

Thus in 1870, Coronel Exupério of Rio de Contas was ousted from the guard service as the Conservative government in Rio sought to reward its followers in Bahia; Coronel José Luís de Almeida Couto, who became Bahia's last Liberal provincial president in 1889, was also stripped of his command.[21] In 1884, the local Conservative Party chiefs in the Middle São Francisco Valley hounded the Barão de Cotegipe to arrange a mass distribution of guard titles to build up a patronage army in an election year.[22] The Barão de Cambuí, a Conservative politician in Minas Gerais, demanded in 1888 the restoration of the guard commission that the Liberals had revoked.[23] Finally, the

20. The classic work on the politics of the empire was written by Joaquim Nabuco, *Um estadista do império*, part of the *Obras completas* of the author. One recent dissertation is worthy of mention: José Murilo de Carvalho, "Elite and State-Building in Imperial Brazil."

21. *Relatório apresentado a Assembléia Legislativa da Bahia pelo excelentíssimo senhor Barão de S. Lourenço, presidente da mesma provincia, em 6 de março de 1870*, pp. 10–11, hereafter cited as *Relatório da Bahia*.

22. A. J. Magalhães to Barão de Cotegipe, Xique-Xique, Bahia, October 12, 1880, Luís Viana to Cotegipe, Xique-Xique, November 6, 1885, and another letter dated October 28, 1885, Arquivo do Barão de Cotegipe, hereafter cited as ABC. These documents were consulted before the archive was catalogued; therefore, they have no "lata" number. Those documents consulted after the organization will have the catalogued lata number.

23. Cândido Melo e Sousa to Antônio Ferreira Viana, Fazenda da Barra de São Pedro (Minas Gerais), August 15, 1888, IJ6-453, Série Guarda Nacional 1878–79, Seção do Poder Executivo, Arquivo Nacional, hereafter cited as SPE/AN.

command of a local guard unit became the precipitating factor in a clan war between the Guerreiros and the França Antuneses of the Middle São Francisco Valley.[24]

The politicization of title concessions persisted under the republic. Marshal Floriano Peixoto routinely dispensed commissions to his supporters in the civil war in Santa Catarina and Paraná in the 1890s;[25] João Pandiá Calógeras, then a federal deputy from Minas, was asked by a local merchant to secure the rank of *general* in exchange for political support.[26] In brief, under both empire and republic, the duration of a coronel's command was often as unstable as his party's tenure in power.

GN Titles as Socioeconomic Barometers

It was not uncommon to find in a backland município that the most powerful rancher was a coronel, a town's chief merchant a *tenente-coronel*, a town clerk a *major*, a storeowner a capitão, and a town innkeeper a tenente. Until 1917, when the guard was finally retired as a reserve force (*exército da 2ª linha*), a title served as a good barometer of one's station in a community. Local potentates always succeeded in obtaining commissions, and many held multiple ranks as they rose in local politics. It was customary for a local politician to seek a higher rank when his status in the galaxy of the power elite moved upward. Socially, "coronel" became synonymous with the designation of a political chief; people preferred to be addressed as "coronel" rather than the more mundane "senhor." "Senhor coronel" and "senhor doutor" were used to exaggerate one's respect for a superior.

An official report of 1916 on the National Guard revealed that the proliferation of the title "coronel" had already reached ridiculous proportions. The administrative federalism of the First Republic created many more elective offices, some of which had been appointive under the empire. Politicians aspiring to state and federal offices needed electoral support from local political chiefs, and the concession of National Guard titles often served

24. Lins, *O médio São Francisco*, pp. 55–57.
25. Documentos de Administração Política 1892–93 (Santa Catarina), Caxeta 1,197, Arquivo de Floriano Peixoto, hereafter cited as AFP.
26. Joaquim de Sales, *Se não me falha a memória (políticos e jornalistas do meu tempo)*, p. 187.

as a convenient means of dispensing patronage. The minister of justice, under whose jurisdiction the National Guard remained until 1917, made routine distributions of commissions on the political recommendations of governors, federal deputies and senators, and others with political power. In 1916, Brazil had 231,044 officers in 8,778 brigades. Bahia alone had 420 brigades, of which 247 were listed as infantry, 114 as cavalry, 10 as artillery, and the rest reserve.[27] Between 1902 and 1914, the federal government granted 11,369 commissions to Bahians.[28] In many instances, a person went through a series of "promotions" from an inferior rank to a higher one, often buying the commission. In number of guard brigades, Minas Gerais led the country with 477.[29] Two years later, Minister of War Calógeras observed that Brazil had 44,242 National Guard officers on "active duty"; Rio Grande do Sul led with 5,908, São Paulo had 5,490, and Bahia 5,020.[30] Fortunately, these officers "served" gratis, causing no financial drain on the federal government.

THE MUNICÍPIO: ITS STRUCTURE AND FOUNDATION

The município was the political-administrative bastion of a coronel. In most states, it was the lowest administrative-legislative unit in the Brazilian federation. It was further divided into one or more districts, but the chief executive and the local legislature were situated in the seat of the município. It was here that a coronel battled his rivals to retain political domination of the administrative and legislative processes. As a rule, a coronel was a paramount chief of a município and occasionally rose to the offices of deputy and senator (state and federal) and state governor.

Under the First Republic, the chief executive of the Brazilian município was known by three different names: *intendente, prefeito,* and *superintendente.* Nine states, including Bahia, called their chief executive officers intendentes. Amazonas and Santa Catarina (after 1910) called the municipal chiefs superinten-

27. Leite, *Apontamentos históricos,* pp. 51–53; *A Tarde,* December 21, 1916.
28. Livros de Registro de Patentes de Oficiais 1868–1918, nos. 44, 58, 62, 69, Guarda Nacional-Estado da Bahia, AME; [João Pandiá Calógeras], *Relatório apresentado ao Presidente da República dos Estados Unidos do Brasil,* pp. 124–26.
29. *A Tarde,* December 21, 1916.
30. Calógeras, *Relatório,* pp. 124–26.

dentes. The term prefeito, which has become since 1930 the official designation for the chief officer of the município, was used in Pernambuco and Paraná. Seven states left undefined the office of the chief executive, and Rio Grande do Norte combined the legislative and administrative powers in the hands of the president of the municipal council. Minas Gerais made no mention of the subject of the chief of the município in the state constitution, but an amendment in 1891 assigned the administrative responsibilities to the president of the council.[31]

THE POLITICAL CONTROL OF MUNICÍPIOS

The most common tenure of office for the chief executive was two or three years, although the four-year term had been provided in state constitutions. The reduction of the tenure to a shorter term certainly was politically desirable for governors (who served a term of four years, except in Rio Grande do Sul) to control local politics.[32] Under various administrative reforms between 1891 and 1920, only five states retained the four-year term; seven chose three years, and four reduced the tenure to two years. Ceará resorted to an annual election of intendente by the municipal council (indirect election) until 1914; then the governor nominated the chief executives. The state of Rio de Janeiro instituted a cumbersome but politically astute balance of double executives—the governor appointed one and the municipal council elected another.[33]

The governor's control of the município, for reasons of electoral manipulation, was also attained by other stringent methods. No state instituted the appointive system under the first state constitutions, but as the politics of municípios became important in state politics, particularly on the future of the "in" party, administrative reforms were introduced by governors to prop

31. Castro Nunes, *As constituições estaduais do Brasil,* 1:162; 2:281 (Art. 9, Lei 845, February 14, 1916); 2:364 (Art. 36, Lei 108, July 28, 1898); 2:528 (Art. 32, Lei 2, September 14, 1891).

32. Ibid., 1:115–16. Eleven states (Maranhão, Ceará, Paraíba, Sergipe, Espírito Santo, Rio, São Paulo, Rio Grande do Sul, Minas Gerais, Goiás, and Mato Grosso) called their chief executives "presidents"; the remaining nine (Amazonas, Pará, Piauí, Pernambuco, Alagoas, Bahia, Paraná, Rio Grande do Norte, and Santa Catarina) used the term "governor." The president of Rio Grande do Sul served a term of five years.

33. Ibid., 2:350 (Art. 36, Lei 33, November 10, 1892); 2:462 (Art. 13, Lei 1620, November 11, 1919).

up their personal, partisan positions. Consequently, Paraíba (after 1915), Bahia (1915–20), Rio de Janeiro (after 1919), and Ceará (after 1914) allowed governors to appoint chief executives. These four states, coincidentally, were politically unstable. Stable states such as São Paulo (the municipal council elected the intendente), Minas Gerais (the president of the council doubled as the chief executive), and Rio Grande do Sul (the only state to use the four-year elective term, first defined in the state constitution of 1891) did not tamper with the administrative system of the município as a means of bolstering their dominant parties. By the mid-1890s, the political parties of these stable states had firmly established institutional control over the municípios. As a whole, the majority of states did not allow immediate re-election, that is, self-succession but did permit election every other term. Alagoas, for instance, unconditionally prohibited any re-election of an intendente, who served for two years (see Table 1).[34]

Political control of the município also depended on its size, population, and distance from the state capital. The variations that each state adopted to define the município reflected the economic geography *cum* political objectives of the ruling parties. The small state of Piauí sought to avoid the proliferation of *coronelista* municípios by requiring both minimum population (5,000) and minimum size (3,000 square meters). On the other hand, Minas probably had political reasons for limiting the number of districts to fourteen per município, which was too big for one coronel to dominate. More likely, a group of families clustered to form a ruling coalition for controlling municipal politics. São Paulo and Minas Gerais always boasted high literacy rates while Bahia and Pará suffered from low ones. Hence, the two northern states imposed a literacy requirement as a condition for municipal status. This requirement was the key factor in determining electoral eligibility for males over twenty-one years. Often backland municípios had an average number of voters on a statewide scale. Using 1912 as the base year, the state of Bahia had 108,463 voters; with 144 municípios, the average per município was 753 voters, closely conforming to the actual number of voters in the backlands (Table 2). Legislators in Bahia, and probably in other states, too, used the statewide

34. Ibid., 2:394 (Art. 14, Lei 8, May 13, 1892). Tables begin on p. 207.

literacy average as a legal criterion for município incorporation. In Bahia, 10 percent of the município's population, a minimum of 1,500 persons, had to be literate. Since women were not enfranchised under the First Republic, approximately one-half of the 1,500 literate citizens (Bahia's average being 753) were male voters.

ORGANIZING ELECTIONS

The elections of the First Republic were farcical, to say the least. The first battle for electoral victory began with a drive for voter registration. Under existing practice, each município or *comarca* (a judicial district comprised of two or more municípios) set up three boards to carry out elections: a registration board (*junta de alistamento*), an election execution board (*junta* or *mesa eleitoral*), and a tabulation board (*junta de apuração*).[35] Slight variations in name and organization existed in each state, but the three-step approach from registration through tabulation was the same throughout the country. All three boards consisted of a governor-appointed judge of the comarca (*juiz de direito*), a locally elected municipal judge (*juiz municipal*), and members drawn from the local electorate. As always, the councilmen and intendentes managed to get onto these boards and dictate procedure and outcome of the elections.

The dominant party used varying means, including violence, to prevent supporters of the rival candidate from registering; once registration was completed, the rival factions flooded the município with election enforcers—paid henchmen, generally well armed, whose express purpose was to intimidate voters. When the votes were cast, the tabulation board reviewed the results and issued certificates (*diplomas*) to all candidates with the specific number of votes received. Candidates for municipal and state offices had to submit the diplomas to the state senate, in the case of Bahia, for final scrutiny. The senate then set up a recognition committee (*comissão de reconhecimento*) which selected the final winner.

A number of extenuating circumstances and instances could, and did, mar the orderly conduct of an election. Often the juiz de direito found a convenient reason to leave the county seat; many

35. Eul-Soo Pang, "*Coronelismo* in Northeast Brazil," pp. 80–84; Albuquerque, *Um sertanejo*, pp. 46–47.

lived in the state capital. In their absence, the substitutes (*suplentes de juiz*) would take over the duty of supervising the election. The suplente was a governor's appointee, always selected from the local coronéis, and was likely an understudy of the dominant coronel. By order of the political chief, the suplente carried out elections. If a close election were anticipated, violence broke out well before voter registration could take place. Violent confrontations often canceled an election; at times, the dominant coronel held the registration at his home, open only to his supporters.[36] When these tactics failed to produce the desired results, the coronel resorted to other means: padding the roster with ineligible voters and buying votes became normal procedures. The literacy requirement was not vigorously enforced, if at all; hence, many illiterate friends, employees, and even paid imports from another município or state were put on the list. In Goiás, a missionary priest observed that one backlander named Clementino missed his turn to vote (the voting was done in alphabetical order), for he was taught to write his name with the letter Q.[37] A "Bastião" showed up when "B" was called, although his legal name should have fallen under "S" for "Sebastião." Not infrequently, a "José" insisted on voting under "Z" since he was generally called "Zé."

ELECTORAL FRAUDS

Paid voters and ghost voters also "participated" in the election. Buying votes was definitely a product of the capitalist system, wherein cash became the principal tool for exchange of goods and services. In the burgeoning export economies of São Paulo, Minas Gerais, Rio Grande, and even some coastal municípios in the north where commercial agriculture flourished, such as Ilhéus in Bahia, the political loyalty of a constantly mobile population could not be extracted by means of personalism alone. Planters and merchants had to rely on a contractual relationship for hiring workers, and this custom of buying services undoubtedly extended to electoral politics. Two decades after the demise of the First Republic, one United Nations official noted that many illiterate voters dropped their lunch tickets into the urn instead of the premarked ballots given them with

36. Pang, *"Coronelismo* in Northeast Brazil," p. 83.
37. Frei José M. Audrin, O.P., *Os sertanejos que eu conheci*, pp. 173–74.

the complimentary meal coupons by a political boss.[38] Distribution of new clothes, shoes, hats, and other essentials was common during election rallies.

More serious abuses involved enrollment of non-existent voters. Such a fraudulent electoral practice was known as a pen sketch (*bico de pena*). Names of the deceased came from country graveyards; phantom voters (*fantasmas*) or match sticks (*fósforos*),[39] as they were called in the electoral jargon of the day, were not only registered in the book by the dominant coronel but also "cast ballots." The false results were recorded in election books by ambidextrous men, and it was not uncommon for an eager coronel, weak in arithmetic, to produce more votes than there were registrants. Such discrepancies were subject to "correction" by state and federal legislatures. In short, the outcome of elections under the First Republic was a collaborative product of those who controlled the municípios (the coronéis) and those who controlled the legislatures (presidents and governors). In 1930, to cite an extreme case, President Washington Luís instructed the docile congress to reject the entire congressional delegation of Paraíba, whose state governor was the opposition vice-presidential candidate in the bitterly fought election of that year.[40] Governor Severino Vieira of Bahia ordered the mindless state senate to revoke the mandate of the intendente of Ilhéus, which the same body had granted two years earlier.[41] Such examples of executive peremptory rejection were abundant. The control of the coronéis, from the standpoint of governors and presidents, was a sine qua non for all electoral victories. In the central south, such control was secured through the creation of dominant parties. In the north and far west, so-called parties came and went, but the real

38. Leslie Lipson, "Government in Contemporary Brazil."
39. Albuquerque, *Um sertanejo*, p. 46; R. Magalhães Júnior, *Rui, o homem e o mito*, pp. 24–25.
40. João Neves da Fontoura, *Memórias*, 1:366–67; Epitácio Pessoa, *Revolução de outubro de 1930 e república nova*, vol. 25 of *Obras Completas de Epitácio Pessoa*, pp. 120–21 (similarly affected were fourteen deputies from Minas Gerais); Afonso Arinos de Melo Franco, *A alma do tempo*, p. 234; Virgílio de Melo Franco, *Outubro, 1930*, pp. 222–25; Aurino Moraes, *Minas na Aliança Liberal e na revolução*, pp. 254–55.
41. *Mensagem apresentada à Assembléia Geral Legislativa pelo Exm. Sr. Dr. Severino Vieira Governador do Estado em 11 de abril de 1901*, pp. 11–12. For the details of the politics of Ilhéus, see Eul-Soo Pang, "The Politics of Coronelismo in Brazil: The Case of Bahia, 1889–1930," pp. 81–85.

political bastion was the oligarchies, whether they were a tribal type as was Rosa e Silva of Pernambuco, a personalistic type as was Seabra of Bahia, or a collegial type as were the Calmons of Bahia.

PRs AND REGIONAL OLIGARCHIES

The foot soldiers of the Brazilian PRs, or *partidos republicanos*, and of the various oligarchies came from the ranks of the coronéis. Although the Republican party movement began in 1870, it did not gain a foothold until the mid-1890s.[42] The Partido Republicano Paulista (PRP) came into operation in 1873, but it was not until 1891 that it secured control of the state government. The Partido Republicano Mineiro (PRM), the occasional rival of the PRP, was founded in 1871, but the first decade of the First Republic was wasted on an internal power struggle among the major state regional oligarchies who finally came to a reconciliation as a ruling elite in 1897.[43] In Rio Grande do Sul, the Partido Republicano Riograndense (PRR) was organized in 1882, but ideological and personality differences ignited a civil war (1893–95) involving federalists and positivist-centralists. The latter emerged the victor, remaining in power for the entire three and a half decades of the First Republic, with Borges de Medeiros serving as the PRR governor for twenty-five years.[44] In these states, the PRs served as a durable and workable means of mediating disputes among the leading contenders for municipal power and of monopolizing their political loyalty.

In the north and far west, however, the Republican movement

42. The standard work on the PRs is George C. A. Boehrer, *Da monárquia à república: história do Partido Republicano do Brasil (1870–1889).* Oiliam José, *A propaganda republicana em Minas,* and José Maria dos Santos, *Os republicanos paulistas e a abolição,* treat the PR movements in those states. For the details of the first Paulista Republican movement, see Ata da reunião geral dos membros do Partido Republicano de Itu aos 10 dias de setembro de 1872, Livro de Atas das Reuniões Gerais do Partido Republicano deste cidade de Itu, Arquivo do Museu Republicano "Convenção de Itu." Célio Debes, *O partido republicano na propaganda (1872–1889),* updates the existing studies on the subject.

43. Carone, *A república velha,* pp. 272–74, 311.

44. The best work on the politics of Brazil's southernmost state is Joseph L. Love, *Rio Grande do Sul and Brazilian Regionalism, 1882–1930.*

was either of minor importance or non-existent. In Pernambuco and Bahia, Republican clubs were created before 1889 but failed to emerge as the dominant PRs.[45] When an oligarchic group did succeed in founding a party, it did not last long. It was replaced by an equally closed group. In Pernambuco, the alliance between Barbosa Lima and Conselheiro Rosa e Silva broke up in 1896, by which time the former Conservative minister of justice emerged as the undisputed leader of the Partido Republicano Pernambucano (PRPe).[46] When various factional chiefs of the former Liberal and Conservative parties reconciled, sugar interests in the Recôncavo organized the Partido Republicano da Bahia (PRB) in 1901.[47] But neither of these two pseudo-parties lasted long. In 1911, the Rosista clique fell, replaced by a group led by General Dantas Barreto, while a more urban-oriented party replaced the PRB as the state ruling group in Bahia in 1912.[48] Similarly, in Mato Grosso, the tribal oligarchy of Pedro Celestino and the Generoso Ponce coalition had secured a firm grip on state politics by 1906.[49] In Goiás, the Liberal political dynasty of the Bulhões continued to dominate the state after 1889, proliferating its political progenies for the oligarchy that soon absorbed the Caiados and the Jardims. The familiocratic rule of the Bulhões was terminated by 1912, succeeded by the oligarchy of the Caiados, who ruled until 1930.[50]

OLIGARCHIES REDEFINED

The term "oligarchy" has been much used and abused in Latin American history; Brazil, Peru, Argentina, Colombia, and Mexico provide well-established cases. But few academicians

45. Brás do Amaral, "Memória histórica sobre a proclamação da república na Bahia"; Antônio de Araújo de Aragão Bulcão Sobrinho, "O pregoeiro da república: Virgílio Clímaco Damasio," and "A proclamação da república na Bahia"; Boehrer, Da monarquia à república, pp. 150–54, 156–63.

46. Carone, A república velha, pp. 276–79; Albuquerque, Um sertanejo, pp. 40–41; João da Costa Porto, Os tempos de Rosa e Silva.

47. See chapter 2.

48. Carone, A república velha, pp. 278–79; Albuquerque, Um sertanejo, pp. 91, 150–52; João da Costa Porto, Os tempos de Dantas Barreto.

49. Carone, A república velha, p. 264; Carvalho, A luta no Graças; Correia Filho, Pedro Celestino; Ponce Filho, Generoso Ponce.

50. Maria Augusta Sant'Ana Moraes, História de uma oligarquia: os Bulhões, p. 208.

have agreed on its precise definition.[51] In simple terms, it is defined as rule by a few, but on a more complex level, the problem is the definition of a few. It is assumed that the foundation of Brazilian politics was in the family system: since colonial times, the *paterfamilias* of a clan has exercised influence on politics from the município to the state to the federation. This type of political rule was classified by Max Weber as "traditional rule" as well as "patrimonial rule."[52] For the purpose of building a simple, descriptive typology of oligarchies in Brazil, the term familiocracy is introduced here to mean the predominance of a family in local or municipal politics. Upon closer look, the oligarchies of Brazil during the First Republic can be divided into four basic groups: familiocratic, tribal, collegial, personalistic (Table 3). Since these terms have been devised for this study, they must be explained.

Familiocratic Oligarchy

The majority of Brazilian coronéis fall in this category. Typically organized by a chief of a single family or clan, the sphere of influence was found in and confined to a município. The membership of a familiocratic oligarchy (clan in this case) included the nuclear family, members of the same lineage, in-laws, ritual offspring (baptismal godchildren adopted at birth and marriage ceremonies), and, at times, the socioeconomic dependent populace. Unlike the clans of China and India, the

51. For a critical view on "oligarchy" in Latin American Studies, see James L. Payne, "The Oligarchy Muddle," first published in *World Politics* (April 1966). For definition(s) of oligarchy, see Gaetano Mosca, *The Ruling Class* (*Elementi di scienza politica*): "oligarchy [is] . . . a closed clique jealously barring from public offices all elements that were not of the clique, whatever their wealth or personal merit" (p. 354). Moraes' work on the Bulhões oligarchy in Goiás closely follows the concept of Gaetano Mosca. Camilo Torres, *Revolutionary Priest*, defines oligarchy as "this economic caste, the few families which own almost all of Colombia's riches" (p. 421), directly contradicting Payne's contention that Colombia has no oligarchy. Stanislav Andreski, *Parasitism and Subversion: The Case of Latin America*, classifies oligarchies as two subcategories of "forms of government" (pp. 132–45). Guerreiro Ramos, *A crise do poder no Brasil*, p. 73, routinely uses oligarchy to mean a ruling class. Finally, José Luís de Imaz, *Los que mandan* (*Those Who Rule*), seems deliberately to avoid the use of "oligarchy"; in pp. 121–25, he prefers "elite" in his discussion of the traditional landowning class; in pp. 207–10, he uses oligarchization to mean the entrenchment of a few top leaders of socialist and communist parties in power for a long time. From these random cases, it is clear that there is no standard definition of oligarchy other than its normal inference of the ruling, elitist, closed nature of a group in power.

52. Reinhard Bendix, *Max Weber: An Intellectual Portrait*, pp. 329–84.

Brazilian clan was not necessarily bound by such attributes as residential unity (fixed in this case), the same surname, and exogamous marriage habits. It has several unique characteristics: the successor to the chief need not be a direct heir of the clan headman; members could be geographically dispersed; both horizontal and vertical solidarity in external competition were allowed.[53] The desire to seek public power was motivated by the clan's need to defend its social and economic interests, such as redress for individual and collective honors and revenge and control over agropastoral landholdings. The legitimacy of this type of rule was obtained by a clan chief's ability to grant favors to its members. For instance, planters and ranchers exploited the socially and economically dependent people (the agrarian proletariat, tenants, the peasantry, and others who lived within the orbit of clan domination), turning them into an electoral herd. The vote-drawing power of the familiocratic oligarch rested, in turn, on his ability to extract social and political loyalty from his dependents. He tapped the clan purse to pay for expenses incurred by his retinue, arbitrated disputes among them, and intervened with the government to secure favors. In short, the coronel accumulated various roles at his own expense that were normally filled by the state. Such practices prevailed and even thrived in the absence of a strong state. The metamorphosis of the familiocratic oligarchy occurred when Brazil was able to forge a centralized state with sufficient authority to replace this system.

Tribal Oligarchy

This category was a confederation of segmentary family groups of the first type. A tribe is defined in anthropology as an organization of an unspecified number of multifamily groups with these characteristics: it exhibits autonomous tendencies by maintaining social and economic sustenance; it is a "congeries of equal kin group blocs"; it can unite against outside threat for tribal survival. Aside from the possession of a common territory, a tribe provides a democratic, decentralized form of government in which the legitimacy of the tribal leader is sustained at the risk of offending the autonomy of its segmentary groups.[54]

53. F. L. K. Hsu, *Clan, Caste, and Club*, p. 61; George P. Murdock, *Social Structure*, pp. 68–69; Queiroz, "O coronelismo numa interpretação," pp. 164–65.
54. Marshall D. Sahlins, "The Segmentary Lineage: An Organization of

Political anthropologists consider the tribe "a way-station between band and state in the evolution of political organization."[55]

In Brazil, such a type appeared in northern and far western states and interstate regions of the single-party-dominated states of São Paulo, Minas Gerais, and Rio Grande do Sul. The headman—a bacharel or a coronel—of a tribal oligarchy served as the surrogate ruler (*padrinho influente*) for a cluster of families and clans, respected the autonomy of its associate members, and promoted an equitable distribution of favors and rewards, in particular, the largess of the state and federal governments. Imposition of arbitrary, dictatorial demands by the tribal chief on its members often destroyed unity and cohesion. The afflicted clan chiefs either moved out of the sphere of tribal politics or transferred to a different group, either another wing of a PR or a rival party. The Néri brothers and the Monteiro clan in Amazonas, the latifundiary Lemos and Chermont families in Pará, the Benedito Leite and Urbano Santos group in Maranhão, the Aciolis in Ceará, the Medeiros in Rio Grande do Norte, the Maltas and Regos in Alagoas, the Rosa e Silvas in Pernambuco, and the Dórias and Lobos in Sergipe all constituted prime examples of tribal oligarchies.[56] Similarly, the Bulhões and Caiados in Goiás and the Murtinhos and the Correia da Costas in Mato Grosso built this type of rule.[57]

At the intrastate level, the Prestes family of Itapetininga politically dominated its region. The father (Coronel Fernando) and the son (Dr. Júlio) each served as governor of São Paulo; in 1930, Júlio Prestes was elected president of the republic.[58] The district of Batatais, also in São Paulo, was the fief of Washington Luís, constituting one of the ten electoral districts of the

Predatory Expansion," in Ronald Cohen and John Middleton, eds., *Comparative Political Systems: Studies in the Politics of Pre-Industrial Societies*, pp. 93, 95–96.

55. Carl J. Friedrich, *Man and His Government: An Empirical Theory of Politics*, pp. 533 ff.; Morton H. Fried, *The Evolution of Political Society: An Essay in Political Anthropology*, p. 169.

56. Carone, *A república velha*, pp. 271–84; Basbaum, *História sincera da república*, 2:214–15; Afonso Arinos de Melo Franco, *Um estadista da república (Afrânio de Melo Franco e seu tempo)*, vol. 2, *fase nacional*, p. 702; Ramos, *A crise do poder*, pp. 53–54.

57. Moraes, *História de uma oligarquia*; Correia Filho, *Pedro Celestino*; Ponce Filho, *Generoso Ponce*.

58. Carone, *A república velha*, p. 265.

state. Similarly, the tribal oligarch Rodrigues Alves, whom one sociologist called "um grande coronel nacional,"[59] rose to the presidency (the only man elected twice under the First Republic) from the município of Guaratinguetá. In Minas Gerais, the political leadership of the Zona da Mata was provided by Senator Carlos Vaz de Melo, one of the most powerful chiefs of the PRM, and his son-in-law Artur Bernardes.[60] João Pinheiro, another tribal oligarch of the PRM, staked out the município of Caeté, where his family owned a ceramics factory.[61] Other intrastate potentates were Bueno Brandão, governor of the state and the regional chieftain of Ouro Fino and its satellite municípios, and the Melo Franco family who dominated Paracatu. The power of these regional leaders, who incidentally comprised the various wings in the PRM, was clearly respected by all sitting governors. No change of command at the município level was initiated by a governor without first consulting the regional political chief.[62]

Collegial Oligarchy

This type of rule was a combination of the familiocratic and/or tribal types, urban economic interest groups, and even individual followers coming from all professions. Not surprisingly, it appeared most frequently in the better developed and PR-dominated states of São Paulo, Minas Gerais, and Rio Grande. As a rule, the collegial oligarchy organized itself into a party. The party served as a mouthpiece for collegial interests, and its leadership often rotated among chiefs of major factions, or segments, to borrow an anthropological term. The Comissão Diretora of the PRP had a proportionally well balanced distribution of seats among the principal tribal oligarchs—Bernardino de Campos, Campos Sales, Rodrigues Alves, Prudente de Morais, Jorge Tibiriçá, and others—who frequently rotated the governorship and the presidency among them. In Minas, a similar line-up of regional tribal chiefs can be noted in the Comissão Executiva of the PRM: Cesário Alvim, Bias Fortes, and Afonso Pena were replaced by the younger but similar oligarchic

59. Queiroz, "O coronelismo numa interpretação," p. 162.
60. Daniel de Carvalho, *Francisco Sales, um político de outros tempos,* pp. 81–82.
61. Silva, *Marchas e contramarchas,* pp. 28–35.
62. Carvalho, *Francisco Sales,* pp. 88–89.

groups of Francisco Sales, Artur Bernardes, Antônio Carlos, and João Pinheiro in the later years of the First Republic. The friction caused by personal rivalries and regional socioeconomic differences crippled the PRM, often harming its position in the federation. As a whole, the PRM executive committee was controlled by the Bias Fortes/Francisco Sales faction for the period 1891–1918 and by the Bernardes faction after 1918.[63]

The collegial oligarchies that began to appear only after 1910 in the northern states were also characterized by the leadership of key families and clans. The Calmons and the Mangabeiras of Bahia were the builders of the collegial PRB oligarchy in 1927. The Calmons were a prominent agrarian clan whose principal interests were sugar and banking; the Mangabeiras were a political family, founded upon the personal acumen of two brothers, who relied on the urban sectors of Salvador and Ilhéus for their major support. The motive for the unity between these two groups was to compete against a rival party in order to secure monopoly of state government for the benefit of clan members. As in a tribal oligarchy, decentralization was honored, but this system promoted collective leadership, allowing democratic centralization at the top. In the other northern states, the party of General Dantas Barreto of Pernambuco can be classified in this category after 1911, judging from the major sources of the general's support: urban merchants, sugar planters, and refiners. Dantas Barreto also drew considerable support from the military, the church, liberal professionals, urban workers, and even the peasantry.[64] These groups had constituted opposition of varying intensity to the tribal oligarchy of Rosa e Silva that dominated state politics between 1896 and 1911.

Personalistic Oligarchy

Of the four categories, this is the closest conceptually to Max Weber's charismatic rule. Characteristically traditional, personalistic oligarchy was a transitory type. It could evolve into either collegial or tribal oligarchy, or even cease to exist. The factor holding the clusters of families, clans, and at times indi-

63. Carone, *A república velha*, pp. 271–73.
64. Porto, *Os tempos de Dantas Barreto*; Griffith to Secretary of State, Pernambuco, November 26, 28, 29, 30, December 1, 1911, Records of the Department of State Relating to Internal Affairs of Brazil 1910–1929 (823.00/51–823.5067), United States National Archives, hereafter cited as Internal Affairs of Brazil, DOS/USNA, with the code number.

vidual followers together in the system was the personal charisma of the leaders.[65] The bond of allegiance was forged on a
personal basis between the leader and his followers. This system
appeared at a particular time, when the society had not yet
developed coherently formulated social and economic interest
groups. Once the class and regional interests were well defined,
the utility of the personalistic oligarchy disappeared. The objective of the group was to glorify the personal rule of the leader,
on one hand, and to maintain the status quo of the members, on
the other. Time forced it to degenerate from an anti-traditional
party into a conservative one or to impose personal and arbitrary rules that often threatened to destroy its membership. The
Seabra-controlled Partido Republicano Democrata (PRD),
which ruled Bahia from 1912 to 1924, was of this type. The
Dantas Barreto group began in this fashion but transformed
itself into the collegial type. Typically, the "out" parties of the
First Republic, such as the Partido Republicano Conservador,
the Civilista party, and the Partido Republicano Liberal, all
organized by Rui Barbosa, and the Reação Republicana forged
by Nilo Peçanha and Seabra, fall in this category.[66]

SOCIAL AND ECONOMIC BASES OF CORONELISMO

Despite the institutional aspects of oligarchic rule, a coronel was
foremost an individual politician, autonomous, rich, and at times
well insulated from outside interference. It has been traditionally asserted that a Brazilian coronel was a latifundiary landowner.[67] Consequently, the economic aspect of landholding has
been greatly stressed, as seen in the works of Victor Nunes Leal.
This generalization is derived from historical observations of
the agrarian elite since colonial times. The *senhor de engenho*
was the absolute chief of his own family or clan whose power
and influence were pervasive in his município. On his engenhos—
the rich had more than one—he had a regiment of slaves, car-

65. The concept of charisma is used herein in the classic Weberian sense,
one of intensely personalistic relationships between the ruler and the ruled.
See H. H. Gerth and C. Wright Mills, eds., *From Max Weber: Essays in Sociology*, pp. 245–52, esp. p. 249, and S. N. Eisenstadt, ed., *Max Weber on Charisma
and Institution Building*.
66. Ramos, *A crise do poder*, pp. 73–74; there were at least two PRCs, one in
Bahia in the 1890s and another in the 1910s. These parties were not related.
67. Ianni, *Política e revolução*, p. 72.

penters, artisans, and tenants, and a cordon of small-scale land-owners who produced for the internal consumption of the engenhos. In addition to these personnel, the lord enlarged his vassalage by acquiring a condottieri of private soldiers, whose chief function was to defend the plantation from outside threats. These dependents lived off the senhor's land and income. Sick slaves or tenants were cared for by the planter. At baptisms and weddings, the planter was asked to be the godfather (padrinho) whose responsibility was not merely ceremonial but called for extending his economic and social protection to the godchildren (*afilhados*); the Portuguese word *afilhadagem* means an act of protection.[68] When an independent farmer needed a loan, he turned to the planter-patriarch. The town priests habitually relied on generous handouts from the economic czar of the município. Merchants sold necessary provisions to the planter and bought produce from him for export. The planter was called on to serve in a parajudicial capacity, mediating disputes among his followers, speaking out for his flock in external affairs, and transforming his plantation into a mini-state—all in the absence of formal authority. These social and economic functions of a planter were the bases for his political rise under the empire and the First Republic, for his dependents served as his electorate.

Between 1850 and 1950, changes in Brazil placed a strain on the dysfunctional multi-layered class structure of the predominantly agrarian society. The once unchallenged supremacy of the latifundiary lord of the colonial period began to erode. As auxiliary social classes such as lawyers, physicians, urban merchants, military officers, civil servants, and even priests entered the political arena under enlarged electoral opportunities, the dominant class was forced to compete for its share of the dependent population against intruders. They, too, commanded private resources to attract voters, and, once they were in power, the wanton use of public funds and favors generally sufficed to fill the needs of the patronage army of political supporters. In short, the primary reliance on land—latifundiary or otherwise—as the source of power and prestige was grossly exaggerated. In fact, under the First Republic, landholding and distribution patterns, or land tenure, had little bearing on the flowering of

68. Aurélio Buarque de Holanda Ferreira, *Pequeno Dicionário Brasileiro da Lingua Portuguêsa*, 11th ed. (Rio, 1967).

coronelismo. It is tempting to reinforce the traditional hypothesis by adding that a state with a great number of medium and large farms such as Goiás (over 100 hectares as defined in the 1920 census) produced the most powerful coronéis in the country. Conversely, a state with small number of medium and large farms such as the Federal District should exhibit the least coronelista tendencies in politics. In this schema, Goiás, Pernambuco, and Ceará fall in the category of being the most coronelistic, while the Federal District, Bahia, and Rio Grande do Sul should be the least coronelistic (Table 4). In fact, this is erroneous. Land tenure tells us very little about the structure and operation of coronelismo during the First Republic.

AN OPEN AND CLOSED AGRARIAN SYSTEM

In fact, the success of a coronel as a local oligarch depended largely on his ability to exchange social, political, and economic favors for votes. First, he had to build a network of promises that represented the largest number of voters possible. Areas of *latifúndios* were generally characterized by an underutilization of land and thereby held fewer voters than the crowded coastal regions. The cattle-grazing sertão promoted an "open" and "democratic" nature of economic and social relationships between the *fazendeiro* and his *vaqueiros*. Cowboys were generally given a small plot of land, or *roçado*, were set free with the herd for days and even weeks without interference, and were contractually entitled to a fourth of all calves born under their supervision. On the coastal plantations, the workers were paid very little, even in the twentieth century, thus heightening their dependence on the landowners. Furthermore, in the northern part of the country, little opportunity existed in cities in the way of alternate means of livelihood that would attract backlanders to urban areas. It was in the coastal regions that a "closed" and "autocratic" social system emerged.[69] In theory and in practice, the democratic backlands allowed a great degree of political participation, yet it was here in the São Francisco Valley and the Lavras Diamantinas that the most autocratic coronéis emerged.

The texture of coronelismo was tempered by other social and

69. Th. Pompeu Sobrinho, "O homem do nordeste," and "Povoamento do nordeste brasileiro"; Sá, *Dos velhos aos novos coronéis*, pp. 40–43.

economic factors. In Rio Grande, Paraná, and certain parts of Santa Catarina, known as the *zona colonial* where immigrants built prosperous family farms, the traditional political elites had no influence whatever. The Konders of Santa Catarina, the Muellers of Paraná, and the Abbotts of Rio Grande were the few salient examples of the *colono* power elite. These ethnic politicians occupied a legitimate place within the ruling PRs in the veritable tradition of tribal oligarchs. The impact of the commercialization of agriculture and of urbanization was directly related to the rise of colonos to local, regional, and state power positions. Nearly five million immigrants entered Brazil between 1819 and 1947, and almost all of them settled in the states of the central south.[70] The expanding coffee economy linked the backlands and cities with railroads and roads while more virgin lands were open to accommodate commercial and subsistence agriculture. Internal migration from rural to urban areas resulted. With the revolutionary change in the economic geography in this region, the distribution of power among the traditional oligarchies also underwent alteration. After World War I, some of the most salient changes were the increasing dependence of local coronéis on the PRs, a steady flow of state aids to modernize and expand the principal branches of the economy, and the eventual rise and recognition of the state as a higher authority.

Brazilians have never been known, even today, for the Hegelian veneration of the state. Coronelismo represented the antithesis of the acceptance of a higher authority. In the northern half of the country, it was not until the ascent of Getúlio Vargas in 1930 that the state as such gained some acceptance. In the central south, the state emerged as the patron early in the twentieth century. In a parallel response, absolute loyalty to the familiocratic oligarchy of the PR-dominated states began to shift from local to state leaders. Various state and federal economic schemes to subsidize dominant sectors such as coffee turned masses of local coronéis of the central south into obedient political pawns of the PRs. Consequently, the southern coronel, more so than his northern counterpart, had access to public support—in this case, state and federal funds and patronage—in addition to his personal sources. Since the regional coffee econ-

70. J. Fernando Carneiro, *Imigração e colonização no Brasil*; see the foldout statistical table.

omy occupied a prominent position in the 1910s and the 1920s, control over the PR coronéis became easier. Hence, it was here that the institutionalization of coronelismo took place. The domineering PRs remolded the nature of oligarchic rule, often exercising a strangulation hold on local elites. In Rio Grande do Sul, an additional factor was at work: ideological considerations reinforced by the personalism of Borges de Medeiros (Table 5).

In the northern half of the country, the state did not figure prominently in the First Republic's history. Loyalty was channeled from the rural masses to the coronel, who in turn expressed his support to a particular party or clique (tribal, personalistic, or collegial) on a quid pro quo basis. The failure to develop organized parties in Bahia, Ceará, Goiás, and other less-developed states in the region is easily accounted for by the absence of dynamic economic activities that could spur the flow of capital and manpower from region to region, or from Europe to America. The dominant sugar sector, in decay in the 1830s, experienced brief cycles of small booms and sporadic modernization, as evidenced by the rise of *engenhos centrais* (refineries) in the 1880s and the 1890s, but it never fully recovered enough to influence other economic sectors. Cattlemen in Bahia and Pernambuco continued to compete against imported beef from Rio Grande and elsewhere. Without a booming economy, there was no need to expand railroads and roads beyond the confines of the localized sugar industry. This relative physical and economic underdevelopment of the backlands and the coastal region contributed substantially to the perpetuation of segmentary political groups, thus permanently crippling the rise of dominant PRs in the northern states. Without having the backland oligarchs economically dependent on the coast and on the state, no political party could emerge as a dominant force. In brief, a non-institutionalized form of coronelismo prevailed in the north, the northeast, and the far west.

Two Coronelismos

The economic characteristics of the "two Brazils" of Jacques Lambert's recently criticized but still useful dichotomy helped gel the coronéis' political behavior.[71] In the PRP and the PRM of the south, for instance, there was a vertical relationship between

71. André Gunder Frank, *Capitalism and Underdevelopment in Latin America*, pp. 145–46; Lambert, *Os dois brasís*.

the coronéis and the party hierarchy in the state capitals. No southern coronéis organized horizontally into intermunicipal alliances in an effort to trounce a tribal chief. In the north, however, coronéis not only rebelled against the state and its dominant tribal, collegial, and personalistic parties but also formed interstate alliances with neighboring coronéis. When the southern coronéis engaged in perfidious behavior, they were at most either bolting one political tribe to join another or flouting the party (PR) directives. To illustrate, the ruling coronel of Ribeirão Preto (São Paulo) decided to prevent the election of the PR candidate named by the statewide directorate. Fearful of reaction from above (at both tribal and collegial levels), he meekly instructed his electoral herd to divide votes while his family voted for the party choice to stress their personal loyalty.[72] A similar incident was reported in one election in the early 1950s in Jeremoabo, Bahia.[73] Such action could be initiated by the PR directorate, too: with due respect to the authority of one tribal chief of the Paraíba Valley (São Paulo), the PRP once ordered the defeat of the ruling coronel's candidate by quietly mobilizing support for a local rival, and the coronel was humiliated but not overthrown.[74] In the PRM, a faction-ridden confederation of regional political tribes, the governor and the directorate always respected the authority of such chiefs as João Pinheiro and Bernardes. When tribal alliances were successful in imposing a compromise candidate for governor, such as Olegário Maciel in 1930, the victor lacked the power to control municipal coronéis, except when they exhibited gross incompetence and/or malfeasance. As the only state that escaped federal intervention during the First Republic, Minas Gerais boasted a band of loyal coronéis who truly believed that "there is no salvation outside the PRM."[75]

Elsewhere, the familiocratic coronéis often challenged the state with private armies. When in conflict, they did not hesitate to mobilize the jagunços and to overthrow the government. Thus, in Ceará in 1914, the personal armies of Padre Cícero and

72. Queiroz, *O mandonismo*, p. 94. For a similar case of the PRP and município rivalry (Lorena, São Paulo), see Aroldo de Azevedo, *Arnolfo Azevedo, parlamentar da primeira república*, pp. 50–51.

73. Maria Isaura Pereira de Queiroz, *O campesinato brasileiro*, pp. 108–16.

74. Queiroz, *O mandonismo*, p. 94.

75. João Camilo de Oliveira Torres, *História de Minas Gerais*, 5:1,265. The title of the fifth chapter is "Fora do P.R.M. não há salvação. . . ."

his coronéis of the Carirí Valley descended upon Fortaleza and overthrew the Franco Rabelo government; in its place, Cícero restored the Acioli-led state oligarchy. In Mato Grosso in 1906 Governor Antônio Paes de Barros of the ruling family of Itacici was forced to leave office following an armed assault by the personal armies of Generoso Ponce and Pedro Celestino.[76] In one of the elections of the 1890s, the ruling coronel of Triunfo (Pernambuco) disagreed with Governor Barbosa Lima on the electoral outcome and mobilized his army in a vain attempt to unseat the governor. In Goiás in 1919, Governor José Alves de Castro of the Caiado oligarchy attempted but failed to annihilate the Wolney clan in the north, even with the aid of federal intervention. In 1919 and 1920, coronéis of the Bahian backlands rebelled to end the tyranny of coronéis of the Seabrista party, to be stopped short of overthrowing the state government only by federal intervention.[77] These were the well-known cases of coronelista rebellions against the rulers of the coastal region during the First Republic.

INTERSTATE CORONELISMO AND REGIONAL COMPACTS

The rise of northern interstate trading centers, whose effect was to pull a number of neighboring states into one bloc, was largely responsible for encouraging the martial adventures of the non-

76. For brevity, only major works on Ceará are cited here: Ralph della Cava, *Miracle at Joaseiro*, pp. 151–56; Rui Facó, *Cangaceiros e fanáticos*, pt. 3; Edmar Morel, *Padre Cícero: o santo do Juàzeiro*; Lourenço Filho, *Juàzeiro do Padre Cícero*; Irineu Pinheiro, *O Juàzeiro do Padre Cícero e a revolução de 1914*; Floro Bartolomeu, *Juàzeiro e o Padre Cícero (depoimento para a história)*; Simoens da Silva, *O Padre Cícero e a população do nordeste*; Francisco Fernandes do Nascimento, *Milagre na terra violenta: Padre Cícero, o santo rebelde*; Rodolfo Teofilo, *Libertação do Ceará*; Octacílio Anselmo, *Padre Cícero: mito e realidade*. In *RIC* the following articles are of special importance: Pe. Azarias Sobreira, "Floro Bartolomeu—o caudilho baiano"; Livio Sobral, "Padre Cícero Romão" (three articles); Fernandes Távora, "O Padre Cícero." On Mato Grosso, see "Revolução no Estado de Mato Grosso em diversos anos," Cx II, no. 13, AME.

77. On Pernambuco, see Ulisses Lins de Albuquerque, *Moxotó brabo*, pp. 46–47. For the details of the Castro-Wolney confrontation in 1919, see Pang, "The Politics of *Coronelismo*," pp. 165–69. According to Moraes, *História de uma oligarquia*, p. 173, the Wolneys controlled the northern part of Goiás, Douro-Conceição region. The clan controlled at least 2,000 electoral votes. On Bahia, see Pang, "The Politics of *Coronelismo*," chap. 4; an earlier version of this chapter was published as "The Revolt of the Bahian *Coronéis* and the Federal Intervention of 1920."

institutionalized coronéis. The most important economic center was the São Francisco Valley. Economic, social, and political ties existed among the coronéis of six states: Bahia, Minas, Goiás, Pernambuco, Piauí, and Maranhão. Geographically closer to the valley, cattlemen, planters, and merchants in the sertão of these states were drawn into the trade of the São Francisco zone; the legacy of the gold boom of the eighteenth century and the brief diamond-mining activities in the Lavras Diamantinas and Goiás stimulated the use of Brazil's Nile to carry people and goods into this region. Many of Bahia's leading coronelista families married into families of their business partners in southern Piauí, eastern Goiás, southern Maranhão, western Pernambuco, and northern Minas. Economic ties and a kinship network reinforced the political alliances of these coronéis as mutual aid groups. The Wolneys drew heavily from Bahian coronéis in their fight against the Caiados in Goiás, while Coronel João Duque of Carinhanha was almost a dual citizen of Bahia and Minas. Wolney ran for the federal chamber of deputies from Goiás, but the Bulhõeses opposed his election. Once transplanted to Bahia, however, the coronel was immensely successful in the regional politics of the Middle São Francisco Valley.[78]

The political consequences of interstate coronelismo cannot be discounted. The alliances that emerged from the major trading center, whether formal or informal, always constituted a threat against the coastal oligarchies. The importance of the interstate or intrastate compact was duly recognized by many governors who frequently witnessed its significance. An illiterate coronel of southern Ceará was elected vice governor in spite of constitutional restrictions. In the same region, a political priest was elected vice governor and federal deputy because of his command of a large bloc of votes.[79] An unschooled merchant-turned-warlord in the Lavras Diamantinas of Bahia was recognized by the federal government in 1920 as the titular lord of a region, comprising twelve municípios, with the full right to keep his personal armed forces and the privilege of naming his own deputies to the state and federal legislatures.[80] Abílio Wolney, João Duque, and José Honório Granja all successfully

78. Pang, "The Politics of *Coronelismo*," p. 256.
79. della Cava, *Miracle at Joaseiro*, p. 145.
80. Pang, "The Revolt of the Bahian *Coronéis*," pp. 22–23.

aspired to local political offices in Bahia, although their economic and social ties were in Goiás, Minas, and Piauí, respectively.[81] Autonomous "nations of coronéis" blossomed in the São Francisco Valley and the Cariri Valley of Ceará, willfully ignoring existing state boundaries and building interstate compacts of coronelista oligarchies.

The same phenomenon was also noted in the Cariri Valley, originally a sugar-growing region in the sertão of Ceará, becoming a national center of folk Catholicism under the First Republic. As such, it constituted an important interstate coronelista enclave for Ceará, Pernambuco, Piauí, and Paraíba. In the São Francisco Valley, economic ties and clan linkages forced coronelista alliances, but in Cariri, religious fanaticism provided an incentive for unifying the devout from all parts of northern Brazil. Padre Cícero Romão Batista, now a lay saint, began to attract a throng of displaced backlanders in the early 1880s. A native of the Cariri Valley, Cícero returned home an ordained priest in the 1870s. His work, in addition to routine parish duties, expanded to include the missionary activity of caring for the hungry and jobless peasants roaming the backlands of Brazil in the wake of the Drought of 1877–79. By the early 1890s, Cícero's work had proliferated, but the real expansion of his work took place after the incident of the so-called miracle of Juàzeiro. National attention was directed to reports of communion bread having turned into blood at the mouth of one *beata* Maria.[82] Medical and theological examinations of the controversy eventually resulted in Padre Cícero Romão's excommunication from the official church, while his fame as a miracle maker spread far and wide among backland denizens. The population of his community grew, providing cheap labor to the local economy, and Cícero soon became the successful entrepreneur of various ventures in the Cariri Valley. Local coronéis rallied around him because he attracted labor and provided a market for the dominant economic activities. In 1911, the priest was instrumental in forging the Pact of Coronéis, a tribal compact of the oligarchs in southern Ceará formally tying them to the Acioli machine as an indispensable political ally. From

81. On Coronel Granja, see "Activities of Rebel Troops in the State of Bahia," Howard Donavan (American consul), Bahia, June 1, 1926, Internal Affairs of Brazil, Reel 7, 823.00/568–652, DOS/USNA.

82. della Cava, *Miracle at Joaseiro*, p. 31.

then until his death in 1934, the Patriarch of Juàzeiro reigned as one of the few truly powerful coronéis of the northeastern sertão. As in the São Francisco Valley, the economic activities of the surrounding states gravitated toward Juàzeiro do Norte, Cícero's redoubt. Exports from that region to the outside world were channeled through Pernambuco's capital, not Ceará's. Such autonomous tribal nations of coronéis were not obliterated until the late 1930s.

THE POLÍTICA DOS GOVERNADORES, THE PRP, AND THE PRM

Coronelismo as a form of oligarchic rule was further strengthened by the political developments of the First Republic, especially with respect to the role of the federal president and that of the two rival state parties, the PRP and the PRM. Brazil, unlike the rest of Latin America, failed to develop a working national party system. An effort was made in this direction when the Partido Republicano Federal (PRF) was set up by the chieftains of the PRP. The PRF was to have been a means of imposing the regional supremacy of the coffee-producing states on the federation, but it soon became a victim of internecine squabbles. With the ascendancy of the PRP oligarch President Manuel Ferraz de Campos Sales in 1898, the PRF was doomed to fail. A thoroughgoing federalist and a historic republican, Campos Sales sought to practice the credo that "the Union thinks what the States think" in his relations with the various state ruling parties and cliques.[83] To this end, the president allowed state groups a greater direct voice in federal politics by pre-empting the need for a national party and assured official state parties of representation in the federal congress. In 1900, the celebrated doctrine of the "politics of governors" was thus clearly enunciated.

That year was a turning point in Brazilian political history. Up to that time, the federalism practiced in Brazil under the Constitution of 1891 did not guarantee the full representation of dominant state parties in the federal congress. As the Bahian case so well demonstrated before 1900, the composition of state congressional delegations was not a political expression of the

83. José Maria Belo, *A History of Modern Brazil 1889–1964*, pp. 140–48; Campos Sales, *Da propaganda à presidência*, p. 252. On the scion of the PRF, see Edgard Carone, *A república velha II (evolução política)*, pp. 159–63.

governor. Often, such eloquent deputies as César Zama and Artur Rios were not the governor's men; instead they often cultivated independent ties with the prestigious national politicians of the PRP, PRM, and PRR. The selection of presidential cabinet ministers was often determined by the personal preference of the chief executive, who disregarded the geopolitical representation of state ruling parties. By changing the rules of congressional seating arrangements, Campos Sales assured proper representation of the political views of the dominant state parties in the federation.

CONGRESSIONAL REJECTION

The chairmanship of the congressional verification committee that was empowered to review the credentials of elected deputies was transferred from the oldest member to the former speaker of the chamber. The speaker of the last legislature in 1901 was able to reflect the presidential views in the organization of the verification committee. Those who were acceptable to the president were seated; those who were not presidential supporters were rejected, regardless of the votes they had accumulated in state elections. Executive exercise of this peremptory power of rejection (*degola*, literally meaning throat-cutting) at once guaranteed the supremacy of the president and the recognition of the tribal, personalistic, and collegial oligarchies as the legitimate state parties. The PRP, PRM, and PRR were able to harness their control over municípios as a result of the power of degola, as the ephemeral parties in the north and the far west were made and unmade at the whim of a particular president. Predictably, the negative aspect of the "politics of governors" was to provide the executive branch (and, by extension, the president-producing parties of southern PRs) with secure control of the legislature and to reduce the northern parties to the status of junior partners. This trend continued to the end of the First Republic in 1930, fortifying the control of the federal presidency by the southern PRs.

Along with the ability to develop parties, or inability to do so in the case of the northern states, the expanding role of the federal president also contributed to refining the traits of the two coronelismos. Coronéis in the PRP, PRM, and PRR became pawns, obedient and docile instruments of the party, while those in the northern states sought to develop a Darwinian instinct of survival. Any permanent association with one particular faction or party could be fatal; hence, the coronéis of the north became more individualistic and selective in their participation in state politics, this tendency being accentuated as the economies of municípios failed to tie into national and international markets. The semi-autarkic nature of the backland economies, such as those in the São Francisco, northern Goiás, and even the diamond-producing Lavras Diamantinas, contributed to the rise of independent-minded coronéis, who were the last to join and the first to rebel against the rotating state oligarchies. It is important to remember that northern coronelismo was built upon the particularistic qualities of individual coronéis. Therefore, the prestige and influence of a coronel were to be judged in terms of his personal ability, not his relative standing in the statewide partisan structure.

TYPES OF CORONÉIS

The preceding discussion clearly demonstrates that all Brazilian coronéis do not fit a common mold as coronel-fazendeiro. The assumption that all coronéis were landowners is simply false. The rise of coronel depended on many external factors peculiar to his profession, domain, and personal resources. It is possible, therefore, to devise seven types of coronéis which can be divided into two major categories, occupational and functional.

Occupational

Coronel-landowner.—Although this was the Brazilian archtype, geographical distinctions should be made. The chief differences between a coronel-landowner on the coast and one in the sertão were their use of violence and their degree of dependency on the state government. Coastal municípios such as Ilhéus and Santo Amaro in Bahia were firmly linked to the national and international economies. As a consequence, the coronéis of such a region were more susceptible to control by the state. The converse was true of the backland coronel for whom violence—not state arbitration—became the key instrument of conflict resolution.

Coronel-merchant.—The Luso-Brazilian custom of crowning

one's economic success by becoming a landowner was still prevalent in the First Republic, but in the cities and the coastal and interior towns, the political power of the merchants began to surpass that of the landowning class. In state capitals as well as in such interior cities as Juàzeiro and Feira de Santana in Bahia, Petrolina in Pernambuco, and Campina Grande in Paraíba, merchants, not landowners, dominated politics. Violence was not a determining factor in their political games.

Coronel-industrialist.—This type was rare in the northeast where industrialization was always subordinate to export agriculture, but in a few industrial enclaves, such as Paulista in **Pernambuco (the Lundgrens), Água Branca in Alagoas (Delmiro Gouveia), and the lower city of Salvador (Luís Tarquínio), captains of industry dominated local politics.**[84] **Factory workers, not the agrarian proletariat and dependent population, served as their electoral herd.**

Coronel-priest.—The single most important factor in the success of a priest in politics was the proclivity of the backlanders to accept the church and the man of the cloth as sources of moral guidance and material favor. Priests of both the official church and of "folk Catholicism" emerged as political elites. Monsenhor Hermelino Leão of the Lavras Diamantinas (Bahia) and Monsenhor Walfrido Leal of Areia (Paraíba), classic examples, were veritable coronéis who rose to become state senator (Leão) and governor and federal senator (Leal).[85] Padre Cícero, the finest of the religious leaders of folk Catholicism, was a recognized coronel of coronéis. Both types manipulated the popular trust and the willingness of the flock to follow. The personal desire to answer the political "call" of the people as an extension of priestly duties helped men of God rise to elite status in secular politics. Moral and religious justifications notwithstanding, the coronel-priest often indulged in violence as well as electoral frauds to maintain himself in power.

84. Raul de Góis, *Um sueco emigra para o nordeste*; F. Magalhães, *Delmiro Gouveia: pioneiro e nacionalista*; J. C. Alencar Araripe, *A glória de um pioneiro: a vida de Delmiro Gouveia*; Felix Lima Júnior, *Delmiro Gouveia—o Mauá do sertão alagoano*; three works of Pericles Madureira de Pinho: *Luís Tarqüínio: pioneiro da justiça social no Brasil*; *São assim os baianos*, pp. 37–115; "Luís Tarqüínio."

85. On Monsenhor Hermelino Leão, see chap. 2; for Monsenhor Walfrido Leal, see Nóbrega, *História republicana da Paraíba,* pp. 65–75, 107–8, 117–19, 125–28. On the political role of priests, see Eul-Soo Pang, "The Changing Roles of Priests in the Politics of Northeast Brazil, 1889–1964," esp. pp. 354–56.

Functional

Coronel-warlord.—As he was the highest form of a neo-feudal ruler, the territorial imperative of a warload was legally recognized by state and federation. Most frequently found in the sertão, such as in the São Francisco Valley and the Lavras Diamantinas, the coronel-warlord came from the ranks of landowner (cattle rancher, generally), merchant, and priest. The crux of his legitimacy as a warlord did not rest on his socioeconomic prestige in a given occupation but rather on his ability to act as tribal leader for a congregation of regional oligarchs. Violence and personal charisma were the factors on which balanced the life and death of a warlord in politics.

Coronel–party cadre.—This type was a standard fixture of southern PRs. As a professional politician and craftsman, a coronel of this type revolved around a key regional or wing leader within the PRP, PRM, or PRR. A party bureaucrat par excellence, this coronel served as a *cabo eleitoral* (election enforcer), a procurer of patronage, and even an officeholder. This readily identifiable type was frequently a kinsman of a political chief, such as Silvério Néri, Pinheiro Machado, Afonso Pena, or Rodrigues Alves.[86] The party cadre remained in power at the pleasure of the ruling faction and ingloriously fell with a change of command within the PRs.

Coronel–ward boss.—Most frequently appearing in cities where a coronel or a bacharel could not exercise control alone, ward bosses came from all professional categories, usually a merchant, a lawyer, or a physician from whom voters of a district received favors. Unlike the party bureaucrat, his survival in politics did not depend on the fortunes of one faction of the party, but on his own skill in transferring favors into votes and garnering votes with a promise of future favors. In the PR-dominated states of São Paulo, Minas, and Rio Grande, the ward boss was likely a free-lance political operator. The adept

86. Coronel Virgílio Rodrigues Alves (São Paulo), Coronel Antônio Pessoa (Paraíba), and Coronel Salvador Pinheiro Machado (Rio Grande do Sul) were vice governors and governor of their states. Constantino Néri (Amazonas) and José Marcelino da Rosa e Silva (Pernambuco) were federal senators. See "Relação dos cidadãos que têm governado o Estado de São Paulo desde 1889 até 1938"; [João] Dunshee de Abranches, *Governos e congressos da República dos Estados Unidos do Brasil 1889–1917,* 1:613–14 (Rosa e Silva), 2:3–4 (Constantino Néri); Nóbrega, *História republicana da Paraíba,* pp. 131, 134 (Antônio Pessoa).

use of city hall and state government—not violence—was his hallmark. His timely interventions secured licenses for merchants, facilitated relations with the police, and guaranteed bank loans for shopkeepers, all services frequently performed by ward bosses.[87]

Old and New Coronéis

The political fortunes of coronelismo as a dominant institution of the First Brazilian Republic did not even dissipate with the advent of Getúlio Vargas in 1930. More precisely, a modification—not a decline—of coronelismo took place as shown by recently concluded studies on Minas Gerais and Pernambuco.[88] Their findings are substantially like those for Bahia, with a few regional variations among the three. The economic ramifications of regional integration into international and national markets exerted a strong influence in molding the nature of coronelismo in the Zona da Mata, Pernambuco's sugar-producing region, and in Bahia's Recôncavo. Coronéis in these regions were closely identified with the state government and the ruling party. Harmonious relations with the state government were indispensable for profitable economic activities. Although proven correct in Pernambuco, the hypothesis that the capitalistic form of export economy on the coast, built upon national and international linkages, facilitated the rise of large-scale fazendeiros to political power does not apply to the southern Bahian case. In Ilhéus and Itabuna, the largest (and most capitalistic) landowners such as Misael Tavares and Oscar Falcão did not emerge as the most powerful political elite. The most plausible explanation for this can be found in demographic and geographic factors. Unlike the municípios in the Zona da Mata of Pernambuco, the populations of Ilhéus and Itabuna were too mobile and too diverse to be controlled by a single agrarian coronel. Here the local political influence of

87. Originally, I classified the "ward boss" type under the "party cadre" category. Upon further research, I came to recognize fundamental differences between the two in their origins and functions and thus decided to create separate types. For the earlier view, see Pang, "The Politics of *Coronelismo*," pp. 54–55.

88. Silva, *Marchas e contramarchas* (on Minas); Sá, *Dos velhos aos novos coronéis* (on Pernambuco); Vilaça and Albuquerque, *Coronel, coronéis* (on Pernambuco).

merchants, lawyers, and physicians proved pervasive and divergent as they often competed against each other. Far removed from the capital, Ilhéus and Itabuna also witnessed the rise of multifarious coronelista rule.

Another important regional variation between Pernambuco and Bahia is the stability of the familiocratic oligarchy. If a generalization can be derived from the case study of two families in Serra de Estralada of the São Francisco Valley of Pernambuco, then it is clear that the monarchic elite (the Quixabeiras of the Liberal Party and the Braúnas of the Conservative Party) continue to rule to this day.[89] Conversely, in the valley municípios on the Bahian side, elite circulation—not monopolization of power—was the rule. Again the most plausible explanation is found in geographic and economic variables. The valley consisted of semiautarkic municípios, only loosely connected to Salvador; within this context, the valley developed its own style of internalized elite circulation, especially after 1920, when commercial ties between the region and Salvador became more intense.

The Bahian case contrasts more sharply with that of Minas. The role of the PRM became an important factor in understanding the function of coronelismo in landlocked Minas, while the role of a party was less evident in the Bahian case. A more significant contrast was found in that only after 1933 did Bahia begin to experience the making of partisan-bureaucratic coronéis under the centripetal leadership of Juraci Magalhães. In Minas, such a type dominated before 1930. In both states, coronelismo continued to serve as the backbone of partisan activities after 1933. As shown in other earlier works, the case study of Minas Gerais confirms that coronelismo did not decline but evolved into another new form of oligarchic rule. The survival of coronéis in Bahia was as astounding as it was in Minas, thus calling into question the Leal hypothesis that coronelismo declined after 1930.[90] The alternative hypothesis is that as long as the Brazilian political system revolved around familiocratic components, coronelismo thrived. One recent study confirms that coronelismo in the 1960s simply retreated to the local level by confining to the município the

89. Sá, *Dos velhos aos novos coronéis*, pp. 77–108.
90. Leal, *Coronelismo*, pp. 251–58; Silva, *Marchas e contramarchas*, p. 55; Queiroz, *O mandonismo*, p. 127; Pang, "The Politics of *Coronelismo*," pp. 322–25.

traditional exercise of personal power by one man and by avoiding a confrontation between local autonomy and the expanding powers of the central government.[91]

Therefore, the modification, not the decline, of coronelismo should be the theme of post-1930 political history. The impact of the demographic explosion, the import-substituting industrialization and its accompanying urbanization, the rise of a multi-party system in 1945, and the increasing centripetal tendencies of the federal presidency all contributed to the modification of coronelismo. Coronéis became the power brokers of the various parties of the 1960s and the 1970s, thus re-emerging as a "new" modified partisan elite.[92] The financial backing of a party and even of the state and federal governments, rather than personal coffers, became the mainstay of building a partisan following. Modern federal and state armies deprived the coronel of his martial prowess by making meaningless the confrontation between the state and the private domain. The effects of uneven industrialization and urbanization have left certain backwaters untouched by the centralizing state, where coronéis of the old types still rule. But as a whole, Brazilian coronelismo has entered its twilight in the 1970s as family-based politics is being replaced by socioeconomic class- and interests-oriented groups vying for power.

91. Soares, *Sociedade e política*, pp. 117–21.

92. Queiroz, *O campesinato*, pp. 112–21. For an interesting case of the coronéis of the 1970s, see "Vale do Jequitinhonha: os coronéis contra o progresso," *Opinião* 182 (April 30, 1976):5 for an analysis of the pervasive influence of the coronelista families in Minas and Bahia. The prefeito of Salto da Divisa predicted the election of his twenty-four-year-old cousin ("He has just earned a law degree, has only twenty-four years of age, [and] is visiting the United States and the neighboring countries") with 90 percent of the votes.

2. The Quest for "Order and Progress" in Bahian Politics, 1889–1904

THE QUEST for "Order and Progress" in Bahian politics during the early years of the First Republic resulted in chaos, characterized by the emergence of multifarious political "parties" and cliques on the coast and the consolidation of the traditional ruling class in the backlands. The infusion of republicanism, the influence of the burgeoning urban classes, and fundamental changes in the labor structure of the central south stimulated political change but made little impact in the northeast. In spite of the longevity of the Martin and Haring Three-Pillar thesis, it is now clear that the fall of the Braganza monarchy was brought about by the modernizing forces of the newly emerging rural-urban interests of the export economy, on one hand, and by the civil-military alliance of Republicans and Positivists in the central south, on the other.[1] The north

1. Nícia Vilela Luz, "O papel das classes médias brasileiras no movimento republicano"; "A fronda pretoriana," in *HGCB II: O Brasil monárquico 5: do império à república*, ed. Sérgio Buarque de Holanda (São Paulo, 1972), pp. 344–60; Hélio Silva, *1889—a república não esperou o amanhecer* (Rio, 1972), pp. 103–6, 111–27, 131–36; Emília Viotti da Costa, *Da monarquia à república: momentos decisivos*, "A proclamação da república," and "Sobre as origins da república." The influence of urban middle sectors and "liberals" on the politics

and northeast had no role in this drama. The republic was born in the central south and was to die there four decades later. Perhaps such a change was in the offing by the 1870s, when the central south emerged as the locus of power, replacing the northeast which was stagnating in the atrophying sugar economy. When the empire was overthrown on November 15, 1889, there was no socioeconomic group in Bahia to rise to direct the new government.

In the first fifteen years of the First Republic, Bahian politics acquired several characteristics that persisted to its end in 1930: a political division between the littoral and the sertão; a strong personality-dominated, multiple-clique system; and a high degree of Pavlovian reflex politics dictated at the whim of the Rio government. The interaction of these political traits produced an unstable system of government, which in turn consolidated the power of the ruling classes in the sertão. In brief, it is important to place the formative years of Bahian politics in perspective in order to render a meaningful analysis.

The first symptoms of instability in the party and government systems appeared in the 1880s when Bahia failed to develop a strong indigenous Republican party while the two traditional monarchic parties suffered a leadership crisis. None of Bahia's star politicians came from the ranks of the feeble Republican Club, led by a medical professor, Virgílio Damásio. The roster of the club's leaders in the 1880s reveals no important political names.[2] Rui Barbosa and Jose Joaquim Seabra, two doyens of Bahian politics under the First Republic, remained in the traditional parties, even though they harbored anti-monarchic, liberal political sentiments. The Liberal Party, which dominated imperial politics from 1878 to 1885 and again briefly in 1889, was led by two politicians of similar rural backgrounds but different philosophical persuasions. José

of the 1870s and the 1880s was studied by Richard Graham, *Britain and the Onset of Modernization in Brazil 1850–1914*, pp. 252–76, esp. pp. 255–58; see also Décio Saes, *Classe média e política na primeira república brasileira (1889–1930)*, pp. 31–43, esp. pp. 33–34. The Three-Pillar thesis holds that the fall of the monarchy was caused by the withdrawal of support by the three pillars of Brazilian society—the slavocracy, the Church, and the military—as a result of a series of events in the 1870s and 1880s, the Church-State conflict, the military question, and abolition.

2. "República ou monarquia?" in *Diário de Notícias*, July 10, 1889; Oliveira Viana, *O ocaso do império*, pp. 106–9, reports that Bahia had three Republican clubs and one newspaper, Pernambuco six clubs and three Republican papers.

Antônio Saraiva was the first chief of the Bahian Liberal Party and served as prime minister twice, in 1880–83 and 1885. Countering his faction was Manuel Pinto de Sousa Dantas, another prime minister (1884–85). While Saraiva was closely tied to the slavocratic sugar interests in the Recôncavo of Bahia, Sousa Dantas was an abolitionist politician of the reformist wing of the party. Although the Dantas clan as a whole was firmly rooted in agrarian interests, the power base of the prime minister was in the urban sectors of Salvador. His two sons began their political careers in the capital, as did his protégé, Rui Barbosa. The senatorial election of 1889 was the first major open contest fought by the candidates of the two venerable chiefs; Antônio Carneiro da Rocha of the Dantas urban wing was the victor.[3]

On the Conservative side, the unchallenged ruler of the Bahian party was the Barão de Cotegipe. Enjoying a prestige comparable to that of Saraiva, the mulatto sugar planter was a staunch defender of slavocratic interests.[4] A member in good standing of the principal landholding clans of the Recôncavo, Cotegipe became prime minister (1885–88), only to resign after having attempted to prolong slavery against mounting abolitionist pressure. Cotegipe's party in Bahia was solidly united until the death of the barão in February 1889.

The principal subalterns of these two traditional parties came to dominate Bahian politics for the next three decades and to foster many of the factional struggles among the more than seventeen political parties and groups that existed during the First Republic. In one of the two major wings of the Liberal Party, João Ferreira de Moura, a scion of the sugar interests of Santo Amaro and one-time minister of agriculture in the 1880s, became the key deputy of Saraiva's rural wing and perhaps its political heir. In the other, Rui Barbosa and the two young Dantases were apprenticed as political craftsmen under Prime Minister Sousa Dantas. Rui often served as a mouthpiece for the Dantas urban wing in the imperial chamber of deputies; he was even offered a cabinet post by Prime

3. *Diário da Bahia*, December 4, 1887; Wanderley Pinho, "Uma escolha senatorial no fim da monarquia: a questão Moura-Carneiro da Rocha na correspondência do Conselheiro Saraiva."
4. Bahia's "indemnist" Conservatives were solidly united behind Cotegipe before and even after his death in February 1889: *Diário da Bahia*, November 13, 1888, August 28, 1889.

Minister Visconde de Ouro Preto, but he refused it.[5] The Liberal deputy from Salvador publicly espoused abolitionism and republicanism in the late 1880s. By June 1889, when the last cabinet of the empire was organized by Liberal Ouro Preto, Rui had established himself solidly with the new emerging military class that was already tinted by Republican and Positivist ideas. As the editor of one of the Rio's major dailies, Rui stoutly defended the military cause. His services were well compensated for when Deodoro da Fonseca named the Bahian Liberal deputy his de facto prime minister and the minister of finance in November 1889.[6] Rui thus became the first Bahian to serve in the federal cabinet under the First Republic.

When the empire was overthrown, Bahia was devoid of leaders. Cotegipe had died the previous February, leaving the top spot vacant; Sousa Dantas was forced to retire from active politics, as were the young Dantases.[7] Saraiva was elected to represent Bahia in the federal Senate but had retired from active politics by 1891 due to failing health as well as to his disenchantment with the raging anarchy in Bahia.[8] The ambitious Rui Barbosa was not interested in leading the Bahian Liberals on the state level. Therefore, both the Conservative and the Liberal parties were dominated by lesser weights—João Ferreira de Moura, César Zama, and José Luís de Almeida Couto (the last Liberal provincial president of Bahia)—who

5. Consuelo Novais Soares de Quadros, "Os partidos políticos da Bahia na primeira república." Conselheiro Moura of the slavocratic wing of the Bahian Liberal Party was a grandson of Antônio da Costa Pinto, founder-patriarch of the sugar aristocracy of Santo Amaro. Like his Conservative cousins, Moura was an agribusinessman and a defender of slavery. For his kinship to the Costa Pintos, see João da Costa Pinto Victoria, "Família Costa Pinto." For the full text of Rui's *parecer* on Dantas' abolitionist bill, see *Diário da Bahia*, September 19, 1884. The following year, the much-watered-down version of this draft became the Saraiva-Cotegipe-Dantas Law that freed sexagenarian slaves.

6. For the role of Rui in the early years of the First Republic, see R. Magalhães Júnior, *Rui, o homem e o mito*, pp. 47–91, and *Deodoro: a espada contra o império*, vol. 2, *O galo na torres (do desterro em Mato Grosso à fundação da república)*, pp. 142–66.

7. Rodolfo Dantas passed his time in Paris, taking care of family and personal business, in the 1890s. During that period, he also wrote many intimate letters to the Barão do Rio Branco on Brazilian politics. See 34.6—Maço no. 42 Daltro-Dawson (Pasta 1/16), Arquivo Particular do Barão do Rio Branco in Arquivo Histórico do Itamarati, hereafter cited as ABRB/AHI.

8. Saraiva to Paranaguá, Bahia (?), February 3, 1892, I-DPP, 1.1. (892), Sar. c-1-6, Arquivo Histórico do Museu Imperial, hereafter cited as AHMI; Paranaguá to Saraiva, Rio, August 1890, Lata 272/Pasta 17, and Luís Viana to Saraiva, Bahia, October 2, 1891, Lata 272/Pasta 34, Arquivo de José Antônio Saraiva, hereafter cited as AJAS.

sought to fill the void left by Saraiva and Sousa Dantas. On the Conservative side, Luís Viana, José Gonçalves da Silva, Severino Vieira, and a host of others fought for the top position. Such luminaries as José Marcelino de Sousa, João Ferreira de Araújo Pinho (the son-in-law of Cotegipe), and the Barão de Jeremoabo temporarily retired from the faction-ridden politics of Salvador to their plantations, only to re-enter state politics after 1900.

SPLINTER PARTIES AND FAMILIOCRATIC OLIGARCHIES

For the first eighteen months of the First Republic, five governors attempted to bring order to state politics, and nine political parties and clubs cluttered the scene.[9] The frequent change of governors was forced on Bahia by the political chaos in Rio. In 1892, Saraiva deplored the near-anarchy then raging in Bahian politics.[10] Living up to the image of the "Bay of All Saints" and its pious dedication to religion, the first political "party" to appear in Bahia was the Catholic Party, organized by the Archbishop of Bahia and the Primate of the Brazilian Church. It was soon disbanded by papal order.[11] Subsequently, other parties—the National Party (Partido Nacional) of José Antônio Saraiva, the National Democratic Party (Partido Nacional Democrático) of Almeida Couto, and the Republican Federalist Party (Partido Republicano Federalista) of José Gonçalves—all headed for oblivion, as the political situation in Rio proved untenable during the years of Deodoro da Fonseca and his successor, Floriano Peixoto. The Bahian parties fell victim to the power struggle in Rio, throwing the state into further political confusion.

The first major crisis of the new republic took place when

9. Between December 1889 and May 1892, nine political parties or clubs were formed and disbanded: Clube Popular Republicano, December 1889 (César Zama); Centro Republicano Democrata, January 1890 (Virgílio Damásio); Clube Popular Rui Barbosa, February 1890 (?); Clube Popular Virgílio Damásio, February 1890 (Virgílio Damásio); Partido Católico, May 1890 (Dom Antônio de Macedo Costa); Partido Operário, June 1890 (Gonçalo Espinheira); Partido Nacional, July 1890 (José Antônio Saraiva); Partido Nacional Democrata, April 1892 (Almeida Couto); Partido Republicano Federalista, May 1892 (José Gonçalves).

10. Saraiva to Paranaguá, Bahia(?), February 3, 1892, AHMI; Moura to Saraiva, Jacú, Bahia, May 2, 1892, 274/33, AJAS.

11. *Diário da Bahia*, July 4, 1890; *Jornal de Notícias*, August 7, 8, 1890.

Deodoro dissolved the federal congress in early November 1891, setting off a constitutional crisis. Three weeks later, the marshal resigned from the presidency, passing the office to Vice-President Floriano Peixoto.[12] Overnight, state politicians divided into pro-Deodoro and pro-Floriano groups, with Governor José Gonçalves leading the Deodoro wing and Federal Deputy César Zama the Floriano camp. There was pressure on José Gonçalves to resign from office after Zama and the federal army garrison in Bahia blatantly seized the state government. The constitutional heirs, Luís Viana and Sátiro Dias, president of the senate and speaker of the chamber of deputies, respectively, refused to inherit José Gonçalves' political troubles. Bahia was ruled by two rival governments for the time being: the governor and the military commander of the federal garrison.[13]

A civil war was averted only by a timely compromise among the major political factions, with the approval of Floriano Peixoto. Bahia elected a new state senate president to make the political transition possible. Joaquim Ferreira Leal, a former imperial admiral, became the fifth governor since November 1889 when he assumed that office in May 1892.[14] But Bahia was a long way from being politically settled. The Floriano government was besieged by a naval revolt that soon spread to the southern states, compounded by a civil war in Rio Grande do Sul. Such a chaotic state of affairs in the nation's capital was hardly conducive to the orderly transformation of Bahian politics.

While the politicians on the coast struggled to establish order, the backlands of the state proceeded to clean house. Under the First Republic, Bahia had four principal geoeconomic zones. Each of these represented an autonomous political sphere,

12. Magalhães Júnior, *Deodoro*, 2:359–75; Belo, *A History of Modern Brazil*, pp. 84–88.

13. The standard work on this crisis is João Gonçalves Tourinho, *História da sedição na Bahia em 24 de novembro de 1891*, esp. pp. 388 ff.; Almeida Couto to Saraiva, Bahia, November 27, 1891, 275/13, AJAS; Antônio Ferrão Moniz de Aragão, *A Bahia e os seus governadores na república*, p. 64; Brás do Amaral, *A História da Bahia do império à república*, p. 363; José Calasans, *Lulu Parola e os acontecimentos políticos de 1891* is a collection of Aloísio de Carvalho's (pseud. Lulu Parola) poems satirizing the political events.

14. Tourinho, *História da sedição*, pp. 397–98, 461–62; César Zama to Floriano Peixoto, March 8, April 4, 18, 1892, Bahia, Caxeta 1198, AFP. Zama recommended that Floriano allow (political) freedom to Bahian landowners ("Cesars" of the state), so that the Iron Marshal could count on them for support.

generally controlled by the major economic interests in each area.[15] First, the capital and its adjacent area—the Recôncavo and the northeast—continued to be ruled by the traditional families of sugar interests, commercial and financial houses, and ranchers. The Costa Pinto clan, headed by the Visconde da

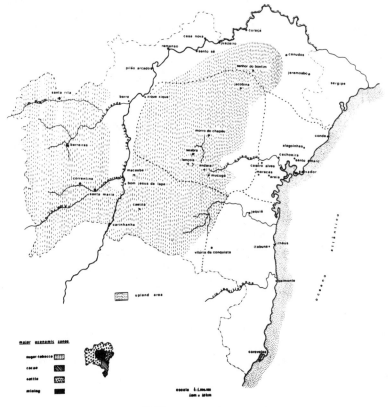

Bahian economic zones

Oliveira, and the Araújo Pinho clan dominated the politics of Santo Amaro. The Barão de Assu da Tôrre, a Liberal chief, ruled Mata de São João and its vicinity until 1920. The third Barão de São Francisco, one-time Liberal president of Bahia

15. Francisco da Conceição Menezes, "Geofísica baiana: superfície, limites e aspectos físicos do Estado da Bahia"; for the definition of the Recôncavo, see L. A. Costa Pinto, *Recôncavo, laboratório de uma experiência humana*, esp. pp. 15–20.

and defender of the sugar interests, became the first Republican intendente of the clan's redoubt, São Francisco do Conde. The barão was eventually to become state senate president in the early 1910s. In other municípios with commercial agriculture, the major landholding families of the monarchy continued to rule: Nazaré remained the fief of the José Marcelino family while Cachoeira became the political home of the Prisco Paraíso clan. Across the Paraguacu River from Cachoeira, the Tosta clan ruled São Felix. All in all, the important names in Bahian politics under the First Republic and to a degree even since 1930 have come from the capital and the Recôncavo municípios, the oldest economic hub of Brazil. The Araújo Pinhos, the Calmons, the Mangabeiras, the Prisco Paraísos, the Costa Pintos, the Tostas, the Monizes, the Aragãos, and the Vilas Boases represented the traditional economic clans of the capital and its adjacent region.[16]

In the northeastern corner of the state, the Dantases of Alagoinhas (Dantas Bião), Jeremoabo of Itapicuru, and José Gonçalves of Bomfim (formerly Vila Nova da Rainha) were the regional chiefs. The Barão de Jeremoabo and José Gonçalves were political allies since their days in the Conservative Party and in the imperial chamber of deputies. Although Jeremoabo was a member of the Dantas clan in northeast Bahia, he came from the wrong side of the political fence. A nephew of former Prime Minister Sousa Dantas, Jeremoabo found himself on the Conservative side; he was linked by marriage to the Conservative aristocracy of the Costa Pintos. He was one of the principal stockholders of Bahia's first sugar refinery (the fifth founded under the empire), opened in 1880.[17] Overshadowed by his powerful Liberal cousins, Jeremoabo was able to become the unchallenged political boss only in the northeastern part of the state when Liberal Sousa Dantas abandoned politics after 1889.

16. Afonso Costa, "Genealogia baiana"; Miranda Azevedo, "Baianos ilustres"; Pinho, *São assim os baianos;* Antônio de Araújo de Aragão Bulcão Sobrinho, *Famílias baianas;* Victoria, "Família Costa Pinto."

17. J. C. Pinto Dantas Júnior, *O Barão de Jeremoabo (Dr. Cícero Dantas Martins) 1838-1938,* is a short biography of "Geremoabo" (now spelled Jeremoabo) by his grandson. The contract for the Engenho Central do Bom Jardim is found in Pasta 14/Doc. 27, Arquivo do Instituto Geográfico e Histórico da Bahia, hereafter cited as AIGHBa; it was signed on October 22, 1877, and the mill was completed for operation in January 1880.

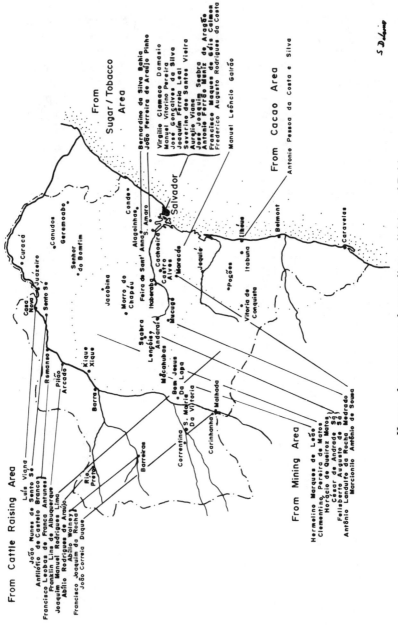

From Cattle Raising Area

Luís Viana
João Nunes de Sento Sé
Anfilófio de Castelo Branco
Francisco Leobas de França Antunes
Franklin Lins de Albuquerque
Joaquim Manuel Rodrigues Lima
Abílio Rodrigues de Araújo
Abílio Wolney
Francisco Joaquim da Rocha
João Correia Duque

From Sugar / Tobacco Area

Bernardino de Silva Bahia
João Ferreira de Araújo Pinho
Virgílio Clemaco Damásio
Manuel Vitorino Pereira
José Gonçalves da Silva
Joaquim Ferreira Leal
Severino dos Santos Vieira
Aurélio Viana
José Joaquim Seabra de Aragão
Antônio Ferrão Muniz
Francisco Marques de Góis Calmon
Frederico Augusto Rodrigues da Costa
Manuel Leôncio Gairão

From Cacao Area

Antonio Pessoa da Costa e Silva

From Mining Area

Hermelino Marques de Leão
Clementino Pereira de Matos
Horácio de Queiroz Matos
César de Andrade Sá
Felisberto Augusto de Sá
Antônio Landulfo da Rocha Medrado
Marcionilo Antônio de Sousa

S DeLong

Homes of governors and coronelista politicians of Bahia

The second most important region in politics was the São Francisco Valley, the Balkans of Bahia, where the pre-1889 oligarchies outlived the empire. The major shakeup of the elite would not take place until 1920. Juàzeiro, the most important city of the valley and the emporium of the riverine trade, was ruled by a succession of mercantile coronéis such as José Alves Pereira and João Evangelista Pereira e Melo. By the 1910s, coronéis such as Aprígio Duarte Filho and Leonidas Torres dominated city politics unrivaled.[18] Farther up the river, the município of Casa Nova was controlled by the Viana clan. Two Luís Vianas—father and son—became governors of Bahia with père in office from 1896 to 1900 and fils from 1967 to 1971. In 1974, Luís Viana Filho was elected an ARENA federal senator from Bahia.[19] Equally prestigious was the Castro clan, which produced Antônio Viana de Castro, the speaker of the Bahian state legislature in the late 1960s, another ARENA heavyweight, whose coronel-father served in various local posts under the First Republic.

In Sento Sé, the Sento Sés (Janjão and Tonhá) and the Sousas (Raul Alves) ruled the little fief. In Pilão Arcado and Remanso, both entrepôts for cattle and cotton from Piauí and Maranhão, the familiocratic oligarchies were the Castelo Brancos, the Franca Antuneses, and the Albuquerques, the latter an expatriate family from Rio Grande do Norte which was well connected with local clans through marriage. Originally, the two municípios were one, but, with the growth of commerce in the nineteenth century, Remanso acquired autonomy from Pilão Arcado.[20] Coronéis Anfilófio de Castelo Branco and Francisco Leobas de França Antunes, both of Remanso, and Franklin Lins de Albuquerque of Pilão Arcado were the most colorful backland chiefs in Bahian history. Together they directed

18. Edson Ribeiro, *Juàzeiro na estreira do tempo*, and Romualdo Leal Vieira, *Sento-Sé rico e ignoto*; interview with Bolívar Sant'Ana Batista, Salvador, July 4–7, 1971, and his *Discurso de despedida*; interview with Morgan Duarte, Salvador, July 8–9, 1971. The late Bolívar Sant'Ana was a state deputy from Juàzeiro and Sento-Sé, and Morgan Duarte is a son of Coronel Aprígio.

19. Bulcão Sobrinho, "O homem do norte—Luis Viana." Viana Filho was born in Paris but has identified politically with the traditional forces in Bahia.

20. Vieira, *Sento-Sé*; interview with Bolívar Sant'Ana, Salvador, July 4–7, 1971; Durval Vieira de Aguiar, *Descriçoes práticas da Província da Bahia com declaração de todas as distâncias intermediárias das cidades, vilas e povoações*, pp. 52–55. These two municípios were known as Remanso de Pilão Arcado.

regional politics as well as commerce between Bahia and other states.

Barra is located at the mouth of the Rio Grande, a tributary of the São Francisco River about halfway between Juàzeiro in the north and Carinhanha in the south. Founded in 1752, Barra had been a trading post during the gold rush and had become an educational center for the valley in the nineteenth and twentieth centuries. Cotegipe was born here, and the Wanderley and Mariani families were the traditional oligarchies.

The sparsely populated and sprawling western part of the São Francisco Valley was the home of neofeudalistic coronéis. In Barreiras, Antônio Balbino de Carvalho, Abílio Wolney, and Francisco and Geraldo Rocha were the governing elite. During the First Republic, the politics of Rio Preto was dominated by Abílio Rodrigues de Araújo, in Santa Ana de Brejos by Francisco Joaquim Flores, in Santa Maria da Vitória by Clemente de Araújo Castro, in Correntina by Felix Joaquim de Araújo, and in Bom Jesus da Lapa by two Moacir brothers, Francisco and Antônio.[21]

Still farther up the river, Carinhanha, located on the left bank of the São Francisco at the Bahia-Minas border, owed its prominence to its strategic location, developing as an interior commercial emporium for various parts of Bahia, Goiás, and Minas. No one family emerged as the ruling elite here. Politics in Carinhanha was unique in the sense that both Bahia and Minas, the stronger states of the three, were able to exert their influence on local families. The Duques and the Alkmims were among the major local oligarchies with connections in both Bahia and Minas.

The home of Brazilian cacao constituted the third economic zone, defined as the southern part of Bahia on the coast bordering Espírito Santo and Minas. In the 1530s, it was established as a separate hereditary captaincy. Its principal town, São Jorge dos Ilhéus, was founded in 1535 or 1536 as colonists began to arrive to cultivate sugarcane. Far removed from the major ports of Salvador and Rio, the captaincy was never an economic success. In 1761, the crown repossessed the colony from the heirs of the debt-ridden donatory. The region continued as a separate

21. Municípios sob a responsabilidade de Homero Pires (MS) and Pereira Moacir and Homero Pires to Góis Calmon, Rio, July 12, 1924, Arquivo de Francisco Marques de Góis Calmon, hereafter cited as AFMGC.

administrative unit until the early nineteenth century, when Ilhéus was incorporated into Bahia.[22]

The economy of Ilhéus was based on sugar and other subsistence farming until cacao was introduced in the eighteenth century. By 1870, Ilhéus became Brazil's chief producer of "God's drink," *theobroma*, turning out 1.2 million kilos that brought in 1.4 percent of the provincial revenue. Twenty years later in 1890, production had increased to 3.5 million kilos, and 21 percent of the state revenues came from the cacao export taxes. Since 1900, the cacao region has supplied an average of one-third to over one-half of the state revenues.[23]

The colonial families of the cacao zone, such as the Marquês de Barbacena (originally from Minas) and the Conde de Pedra Branca, did not remain in power when the Republic was born. The booming cacao economy attracted hordes of migrants from many parts of Brazil, creating a new socioeconomic elite. The *novos ricos*, the parvenue aristocracy, of Ilhéus and later of Itabuna came into being during the 1890s. Coronéis Antônio Pessoa da Costa e Silva, Domingos Adami de Sá, Manuel Misael da Silva Tavares, and many other planters dominated local politics. The world-renown Jorge Amado, a native of Ilhéus, put the region on the map through his colorful, humane treatment of its local history in numerous novels.[24] Standing above all other coronéis was Antônio Pessoa, who represented the cacao interests as the tribal oligarch throughout the forty-one years of the First Republic.

The fourth area, as important politically as the capital and its adjacent region, was the Lavras Diamantinas. In the 1840s, diamonds were discovered in the central-western part of Bahia that was thus christened the Lavras Diamantinas, "Diamond

22. The standard history of Ilhéus is [João da] Silva Campos, *Crônica da Capitania de São Jorge dos Ilhéus*; a more documented history is Francisco Borges de Barros, *Memória sobre o município de Ilhéus*.

23. The export figure on cacao from 1897 to 1923 is found in Mário Ferreira Barbosa, *Anuário estatístico da Bahia—1923*, p. 26; the figures from 1925 to 1930 are in Barbosa, *Economia e finanças: cifras e notas do Estado da Bahia*, pp. 3–10; on p. 49, the amounts of state revenues assessed and collected from 1889 to 1930 are given.

24. Coronel Misael Tavares appears as "Mané Miserável Saqueia Tudo" in *Cacau*, one of the first novels by Jorge Amado: see Jorge Amado, *O país do carnaval, cacau, suor*. Of some twenty novels that Amado has written, six are set in Ilhéus and the cacao country. The two best known that are available in English are *Terra do Sem Fim* (1943, *The Violent Land*) and *Gabriela, Cravo e Canela* (1958, *Gabriela, Clove and Cinnamon*).

Hills." The city of Lençóis became the capital of the Lavras, and at one time Bahia's new capital was to be located here.[25] Plans for constructing a railroad from the coast to Lençóis were never carried out; hence communication between the capital and the mining area remained difficult.

The Sá family dominated the politics of Lençóis until 1920. This clan, whose chief was Coronel Felisberto Augusto de Sá, was a transplant from Minas, as were many other local families. The Sá clan of Minas was powerful in at least three states, Bahia, Minas, and Ceará. Felisberto's brother, Francisco, was married to a daughter of Ceará's political patriarch, Acioli, and was to serve in the Artur Bernardes administration (1922–26) as the minister of transportation.[26] When the grand old man of the Bahian branch of the Sá clan died in 1897, his sons—Aureliano, César de Andrade, and two others—inherited the command of Lençóis. Lili (Aureliano) and César were political leaders in their own right: both served as intendentes of the city, and César eventually became a state senator.[27]

In Campestre (now Seabra), Coronel Manuel Fabrício de Oliveira, the political and personal enemy of Felisberto, easily retained control over the local populace until 1920 and became a major ally to the second generation Sás. In Mucugê, the dynasty of Rocha Medrado (Coronel "Douca") ruled the município without challenge. In Andaraí, the gateway to the mining area, Coronel Aureliano Brito de Gondim and his clansmen dominated town politics. In Chapada Velha, another Mineiro migrant

25. The following sources provide a brief history of Lençóis and the Lavras: Orville A. Derby, "Os primeiros descobrimentos de diamantes no Estado da Bahia"; Gonçalo de Ataíde Pereira, *Memória histórica e descritiva do município dos Lençóis*; Teodoro Sampaio, *O Rio de São Francisco . . . e a Chapada Diamantina.*

26. Brett to Department of State, Bahia, February 13, 1925, Internal Affairs of Brazil, No. 17 "Happenings of Importance in Local Government Areas—Political Occurrences in Bahia," ff. 556–60, Internal Affairs of Brazil, Reel 6, 823.00/400–567, DOS/USNA.

27. Américo Chagas, *O chefe Horácio de Matos,* pp. 13–15; Walfrido Moraes, *Jagunços e heróis,* pp. 39–45; Carone, *A república velha,* p. 260. Carone confuses Francisco Sá ("Major Chiquinho, one of the four sons of Felisberto") with another Francisco Sá of Minas and later of Ceará, when he states, "Francisco Sá, mais tarde senador pela Bahia." By inference, Carone thinks Chiquinho was the federal senator. It was not the case. Minister Sá (of Minas and Ceará) became federal senator in 1925 from his adopted state. However, the senator's son, Francisco Sá Filho, was elected to the federal Chamber of Deputies from the Lavras Diamantinas by Horácio de Matos in the 1920s. In short, there were three Franciscos with the same last name.

family, the Matoses, established control in the 1840s. Coronel Clementino was the patriarch of the clan, standing out as a Conservative in a land overrun by Liberals of Mineiro origin. In the other minor towns of Morro do Chapeu (Coronel Francisco Dias Coelho), Brotas (Militão Rodrigues Coelho), and Macaúbas (Monsenhor Hermelino Marques de Leão and his brothers), the pre-1889 traditional oligarchies continued to stay in power for another two decades (Appendix 4).[28]

Thus the regionalization of familiocratic and tribal oligarchies proceeded in the first decade of the First Republic with the absence of organized party rule. The leading political clans carved out their spheres of influence along geoeconomic boundaries, and, within each zone, one or more families emerged as the municipal oligarchy. Such was the state of oligarchic domination of Bahian politics in the four principal regions.

The Vianistas vs. the Gonçalvistas

By the mid-1890s, it became clear that the two contending power enclaves—the coast and the sertão—were heading for a confrontation. In 1893, the first national political party (Partido Republicano Federal) was organized in Rio under the tutelage of the Paulista politicians. The PRF secured Floriano Peixoto's support of the nomination of Paulista Prudente de Morais as the president for 1894–98 and the successor of the Iron Marshal. When the Paulista planter became the declared candidate of the PRF, he picked the former governor of Bahia Manuel Vitorino de Pereira as the vice-presidential candidate. A monarchic Liberal and one-time protégé of Rui Barbosa, Manuel Vitorino was Bahia's federal senator and a later convert to the Vianista camp.[29] With his entry into the federal government, the PRF-

28. Moraes, *Jagunços e heróis*, and Chagas, *O chefe Horácio*, are the two best sources for regional politics. For a brief description of Coronel Francisco Dias Coelho of Morro do Chapeu, see Frank Robert Jackle, "John Casper Branner and Brazil," p. 106. Branner, a geologist and later president of Stanford University, wrote extensively about Brazil's northeast, including the Lavras of Bahia. He was a founder of the Imperial Geological Commission in the 1870s, having worked with Orville Derby.

29. Manuel Vitorino later, perhaps for political reasons, stated that it was not Rui who named him governor of Bahia but Aristides Lobo and Quintino Bocauiva (*Manifesto político: o Dr. Manuel Vitorino, Vice Presidente da República à nação*, p. 19); however, the documentary evidence contradicts this assertion. Soon after

Bahia should have been assured of stability and an eventual rise to the status of an official party, but the contrary was the case.

As the tenth political party to form since December 1889, the PRF-Bahia, or the state branch of the national party, was essentially a congregation of professional politicians in Salvador. It replaced the Federalist Republican Party of Bahia which José Gonçalves had founded in May 1892. The rapid turnover of parties in the first three or four years of the new republic and the similar changes in the state governorship discouraged the Darwinian-minded chieftains of the familiocratic oligarchies of Bahia from becoming ardent supporters of any one particular group. But the PRF-Bahia was different. It was the presidential party, not a state party, and as such it exhibited all the qualities of becoming a stable political organization. Luís Viana and Vice-President Manuel Vitorino were going to serve as the state's major spokesmen, while the PRF-Bahia was to recruit local clans and regional chiefs beyond the confines of the capital and the Recôncavo.

No sooner had the elaborate work of shoring up the party base begun in the outlying regions than the off-year senatorial election (to replace Manuel Vitorino) confronted the party with its first major test of unity. The two rival factions, the Luís Viana group and the José Gonçalves wing of the PRF-Bahia, decided to use the election as a contest to determine their positions in the party. Luís Viana considered the victory for a Vianista candidate the first step in his bid for a higher office, the state governorship, while José Gonçalves regarded his election to the federal senate as a means of checking the power of the Vianistas in Rio and Salvador. Thus the senatorial election evolved into a factional fight, accentuating the fragmented geopolitics of Bahia. José Gonçalves became the declared candidate of his wing; Federal Deputy Severino Vieira was picked by Viana to lead the Vianista faction. The fiercely fought election resulted in the victory of the Vianista candidate. The Gon-

---

the fall of the monarchy, Rui sent the following telegram to Virgílio Damásio: "Governo provisorio nomea—o governador interino e pede lhe tomar conta da administração emquanto Dr. Manoel Victorino não a occupar. Governo appella para seu patriotismo e firmeza. Republica consolida—se. Conversa Victorino. Ruy Barbosa." This telegram is found in Arquivo de Virgílio Damásio, Pasta 32/Doc. 4, November 17, 1889, Rio. The only existing biography on Manuel Vitorino is by Ordival Cassiano Gomes, *Manuel Vitorino Pereira: médico e cirurgião.*

çalvistas bolted the PRF-Bahia in fury and founded a separate party, the PRC (Partido Republicano Constitucional), whose principal leadership came from the familiocratic oligarchies of José Gonçalves and the Barão de Jeremoabo of northeastern Bahia.[30]

With the election of Severino Vieira as federal senator, Luís Viana emerged as the unchallenged ruler of the fractured PRF-Bahia. In early 1895, the politics of dissent over the selection of a candidate for governorship further obstructed the unity of the dominant party, encouraging the exodus of some key regional coronéis to the PRC. Clearly, the advent of the two cliques in the mid-1890s attested to the absence of a viable state economy that would link the littoral and the backlands, forge alliances between the rural and urban sectors. Instead, Bahia in 1895 witnessed the tribalization of leadership in state politics, the ossification of regionalized oligarchies, and the weakening of its position in federation politics. In this sad state of partisan politics, Luís Viana was the sole gubernatorial candidate and was elected governor for the term of 1896–1900.

LUÍS VIANA AND THE POLITICS OF POLICE EXPEDITIONS

Luís Viana was born in 1846 in Casa Nova, a Middle São Francisco town. His father, Coronel José Manuel Viana, was a local political chieftain of the Conservative Party. After graduating from the Faculty of Law in Recife in 1869, Viana became a public prosecutor in the valley. His early mastery of the intricacy of valley politics drew the attention of Conservative chiefs; he had become a protégé of the Barão de Cotegipe by the 1870s. Luís Viana was every inch a coronel in his approach to politics, often leading a band of jagunços into various municípios to assure Conservative victories in elections.[31] Viana

30. Campos, *Crônica de Ilhéus*, pp. 316–26; *Diário da Bahia*, August 21, 1894; José Gonçalves and Luís Viana were among the founders of the PRF-Bahia, constituting two major "currents" of state politics. For this analysis, see *Jornal de Notícias*, June 23, 1893; Ralph della Cava, "Brazilian Messianism and National Institutions: A Reappraisal of Canudos and Joaseiro"; for a good analysis of the multi-party era, see Quadros, "Os partidos políticos da Bahia," pp. 11–24, 27–28.

31. A glimpse of Luís Viana as a de facto coronel in his early political career can be seen in his letters to Cotegipe. Between 1885 and 1888, Viana made several reports to the Conservative chief on the politics of the São Francisco Valley: see Viana to Cotegipe, December 17, 1885 (Barra); February 5, 1886 (Bahia); January 7, 1887 (Bahia); October 25, November 13, 18, 1887, January 6, 9, 1888

became one of the fastest-rising stars of the Conservative party hierarchy, and, on the eve of the fall of the empire, was rewarded with a judicial post in the Recôncavo. After the death of Cotegipe in February 1889 and the fall of the monarchy in November of that year, Viana became one of the key decision makers of the Conservative branch of state politics, surviving the turbulent formative years as the president of the state senate to become the second popularly elected chief executive of Bahia in 1896.

The initiation of the active use of police expeditions, or the politics of confrontation, came with the ascendancy of Luís Viana to the governorship. His political ambitions were not confined to the state level. Keeping one eye on the federal government, Luís Viana began to expand his personal power base throughout the state. To this end, he was not hesitant to use violence. The state police, or the Força Pública da Bahia, became personal jagunços of the governor.[32] In realistic terms, Viana had no other option. The PRF-Bahia lacked an organizational base or linkage with key regional oligarchies. Coronéis of the sertão and bacharéis in the capital still remained cautious in associating with a party, and those who did soon became the target of Viana's confrontation politics. In Ilhéus, the Lavras, and the northeastern part of the state, Viana's enemies, both PRC supporters and anti-Vianista PRF members, forcibly seized power. In the Lavras, Coronel Clementino de Matos, who opposed the governor, was condemned as a "bandit." In Belmonte and Canavieiras (two municípios in the cacao-producing part of southern Bahia), violence flared up between the contending parties. The zealous governor dispatched state

---

(Barra), ABC. These letters do not carry code numbers because I consulted them before formal cataloguing of the archive. The documents consulted afterwards will be cited with code numbers. In 1885, Luís Viana (presumably immediately after the December 1884 election) led some fifty "capangas" to Barra to influence the outcome of the election. See *Fala com que o Ilm. e Exm. Sr. Dez. Esperidião Eloi de Barros Pimentel abriu a 2ª sessão da 25ª legislatura da Assembléia Provincial da Bahia em 1 de maio de 1885*, pp. 17–18; a series of articles on his administration and political career to 1910 were published in *Diário de Notícias*, March 7–8, 10–12, 15, 17, 1910.

32. In 1894, the legislature authorized the establishment of a 2,000-man state police force, but the force (*regimento policial*) had only 1,812 men (*Mensagem da Bahia de 1894*, p. 75); the role of the Força Pública da Bahia still awaits a good study. The similar institution in São Paulo was studied by Heloísa Rodrigues Fernandes, *Política e segurança: Força Pública do Estado de São Paulo: fundamentos histórico-sociais*.

police to both areas to aid his supporters in the name of maintaining law and order. To the governor's surprise, the anti-Vianista coronéis of these regions succeeded in trouncing the badly led state police expeditionary units.[33] But further humiliation to the governor was to come from the northeastern part of the state.

CANUDOS: A DORMANT POLITICAL KINGDOM

The War of Canudos (1896–97) was one of the worst backland-littoral confrontations in Brazilian history. In view of recent scholarship that stresses the important political role of messianic movements, a brief analysis of that dimension of the war is in order. Canudos was located in Belo Monte, a sphere of influence claimed by the Barão de Jeremoabo, an anti-Vianista politician and a founder of the PRC in 1894. Formerly an abandoned ranch, Canudos began to prosper as a religious colony in the early 1880s under the leadership of a thaumaturge, popularly known as Antônio Conselheiro. The archbishop of Bahia began to receive complaints from local priests about strange rituals taking place in Canudos. The police chief of Itapicuru, the bailiwick of Jeremoabo, alerted the provincial president about the congregation of criminals and their suspicious activities; he in turn sought to place the Conselheiro in a mental hospital in Rio in 1887, but the minister of the empire rejected the plan.[34]

In spite of vigorous objections and allegations raised against socioreligious activities by the church and state, "the Kingdom of Belo Monte" was rapidly evolving into a political tribe under the command of Antônio Conselheiro. The membership of the fanatically devout swelled as the news of the paradise on earth spread. Local cattle barons began to lose their laborers to the colony; local merchants were concerned with the decline of

33. *Relatório da Secretaria de Polícia*, in *Mensagem da Bahia de 1892*, pp. 5–6; *Mensagem da Bahia de 1894*, pp. 6–7; *Relatório da Secretaria de Polícia*, in *Relatório da Bahia de 1895*, p. 2; *Relatório da Secretaria de Polícia*, in *Relatório da Bahia de 1896*, p. 5; *Mensagem da Bahia de 1897*, pp. 3–4; *Relatório da Secretaria de Polícia*, ibid., pp. 5–6.
34. The provincial president of Bahia, arguing that Antônio Conselheiro was an evil influence on the region and state, petitioned the imperial government to intern the fanatic at the Hospital de Alienados of the Santa Casa de Misericórdia in Rio: Melo to Mamoré, Bahia, June 15, 1887, Ofício do Governo da Bahia, 1887, SPE/AN; Ataliba Nogueira, *Antônio Conselheiro e Canudos: revisão histórica*, p. 9.

commerce and envied the economic progress in Canudos. Soon after the fall of the empire, local chiefs and state and church authorities described the Canudos community alternately as a nest of religious fanatics and as outright criminals. Rumor had it that Juàzeiro would soon be attacked, that Canudos was a hotbed for monarchism, and that it refused to pay taxes to the Republic. Worse yet, it was said that the Conselheiro was importing Austrian soldiers in an attempt to restore the Braganzas to Brazil and that Viana was a secret political ally.[35]

The anti-Vianista propaganda was deadly effective in arousing suspicion and hatred of Canudos in all quarters. To the federal army and the radical Republicans, Antônio Conselheiro presented a threat to the infant republic; to the Church, Conselheiro was a pervert and heresiarch; to local politicians, he exhibited every sign of being a new political elite. In this vein, the PRC chiefs suspected that Viana and Severino Vieira would use Conselheiro to undermine their power; such a fear was especially credible in view of the deteriorating political atmosphere. Pressure mounted on Governor Viana to eradicate Canudos, and he could no longer ignore these charges, however absurd they may have seemed. The rest of the story is well told by Euclides da Cunha in his eyewitness epic novel Os Sertões.[36]

One important consideration often neglected in analysis of this backland war is the political magnitude of the confrontation

35. The standard work on Canudos is Os sertões (Rebellion in the Backlands) by Euclides da Cunha, a reporter for O Estado de São Paulo. For the official view of the war which Cunha did not incorporate in his work, see Mensagem da Bahia de 1897, pp. 6–9; Relatório da Secretaria de Polícia de 1897, pp. 17–27. In Bahia, José Calasans is considered as the reigning expert on Canudos; see his No tempo de Antônio Conselheiro. More recently, two new works have appeared on the subject. Nogueira, Antônio Conselheiro, and Walnice Nogueira Galvão, No calor da hora: a Guerra de Canudos nos jornais—4ª expedição. See also della Cava, "Brazilian Messianism"; Maria Isaura Pereira de Queiroz, O messianismo no Brasil e no mundo, 1st ed., pp. 203–19, esp. notes 80, 81; Facó, Cangaceiros e fanáticos, pp. 77–122. Queiroz also stresses (pp. 303–4) that the Conselheiro "protected" the Vianista coronéis-fanzendeiros in the region and in turn received political support from various state legislators. For the Conselheiro's purported attack on Juàzeiro and monarchist conspiracy, see Moniz de Aragao, A Bahia e os seus governadores, p. 121; Mensagem da Bahia de 1897, pp. 5–9; Relatório da Secretaria de Polícia de 1897, p. 6.

36. The first Brazilian edition came out in 1901; the first North American edition (University of Chicago Press) appeared in 1944. Contrary to popular belief, the first book on Canudos in any language was not that of Euclides da Cunha. Manuel Benício, a Rio newspaper reporter, wrote O rei dos jagunços in 1899; its title could have given Cunha ideas about the organization of his future book. For instance, see Os sertões, pp. 88–92.

between the coastal government and the backland rulers. Aside from all the salient religious, socioracial, and even ideological ramifications, Canudos was not an isolated religious colony, divorced from the real world of politics; on the contrary, it seriously threatened to undermine the stability of coronelismo in that part of Bahia. It could have been another Juàzeiro do Norte, and, like Padre Cícero, Antônio Conselheiro could have turned into a political coronel. The local chiefs, cattle barons, merchants, and priests were steadily losing their dependent population to the fanatic leader. Politicians dreaded the spectre of losing supporters in the ever escalating electoral disputes of the early Republican era. The senatorial contest of 1893 had involved a prominent native son of the region (José Gonçalves), and when he lost the election, the coronéis in northeastern Bahia needed a scapegoat. No less important in this intraregional power struggle between the oligarchic forces of the coronéis and the newly emerging challenger (the outsider Antônio Conselheiro) was the expanding economic power of the colony. It is clear that the charge of the Conselheiro's monarchism was exploited to the hilt. Local merchants saw Conselheiro's anti-republicanism as an excuse for not paying taxes; priests imagined the worst ritualist orgies in the name of Christ; Lombrosian racists foresaw the humilating defeat of the white civilization by a group of racially mixed degenerates. Thus, the early republic found a cause célèbre for political unity in its campaign to demolish Canudos. After the eleven-month war that required four military expeditions, the worst massacre in Brazilian history unfolded in Bahia. Five thousand people died; Conselheiro's head was removed and brought to the medical school in Salvador for examination. The illustrious professor Nina Rodrigues declared that he found no abnormalities in the cranium, certifying the fanatic a normal being.[37]

The socioracial attitude toward the backlanders and especially toward coronéis in later years continued to prevail in the minds of the coastal bacharéis who dominated the state government. Often, racial slurs were hurled against rebellious backland coronéis: they were inferior, barbaric panjandrums who refused to accept rule by civilized persons. "Bandits" and "criminals" were terms most frequently applied to back-

37. Nina Rodrigues, "A loucura das multidões," *As coletividades anormais* (Rio, 1939), pp. 131–33, cited in Nogueira, *Antônio Conselheiro*, p. 33.

land political opponents, and in the heyday of Nina Rodrigues
and the kind of medical anthropology that influenced the
intellectual life of Brazil, political wars often degenerated into
struggles between the most fit and the most unfit.[38]

Although the battles were won by the military, Viana lost the
war against his enemies. The dominant party was viable
throughout the political storms only to be dissolved in 1898,
making the future of the PRF-Bahia uncertain. The new
president from São Paulo, Campos Sales, picked Severino
Vieira as his cabinet minister which added further political
clout to the Severinista faction of the PRF-Bahia. Salvador's
municipal election of 1899 was reduced to a small civil war
between the state police and the commercial community. One
hundred and twenty commercial and banking houses protested
the governor's complicity, and Viana's prestige plummeted.[39]

By December 1899, barely a month after the police violence in
Salvador, Governor Viana, with a tarnished image and diminished power, faced the question of his successor. Coronéis in
the backlands harbored deep suspicions about Viana as a
political leader, and on the coast the powerful mercantile colony
in Salvador's lower city turned against the governor with the
full blessings of the Bahian Commercial Association.[40] The
federal deputies of the PRF-Bahia in Rio quickly began to
initiate the nomination of Minister Severino Vieira as the next
governor. The PRF-Bahia Executive Committee, meeting in
early January 1900, made him their unanimous choice, as the
Speaker of the Chamber of Deputies Artur Rios announced it.
Governor Viana was later so informed.[41] In the press, there was
no indication that the governor ever formally endorsed the

38. At the turn of this century, Bahian physician Raimundo Nina Rodrigues
pioneered an anthropological theory, patterned after the theories of Cesare
Lombroso of Italy, that man's behavior was influenced by his eugenic and racial
makeup. According to this antiquated school of anthropology, race mixing was
responsible for all social deviance such as banditry, religious heresy, and the
like.

39. *Jornal de Notícias*, October 21–26, December 5, 1899; Moniz de Aragão, *A
Bahia e os seus governadores*, pp. 125–26; *Relatório da Junta Diretora da
Associação Comercial da Bahia de 1899* (Bahia, 1899), pp. 113–31, Anexo no. 13
(the mercantile protest manifesto).

40. *Jornal de Notícias*, December 5, 1899; the entire episode is recounted based
on newspaper articles and other sources in *O treze de novembre de 1899 da capital
da Bahia (subsídios para a história)*.

41. *Jornal de Notícias*, January 2, 1900.

Vieira candidacy. Thus the PRF-Bahia nominee became the third uncontested candidate to become governor and the eighth man to occupy that office since 1889.

THE VICTORY OF THE SEVERINISTAS

Governor Severino dos Santos Vieira was born in 1849 in Vila de São Francisco do Conde, a sugar-producing Recôncavo município. The famous Jesuit-owned plantation that the eighteenth century chronicler João Antonil described is located here. It was also the home of the first agronomy school of Bahia, founded on a Benedictine-owned plantation, and of Bahia's major noble families: the Barão de Cajaíba, the second Barão de Pirajá, the Visconde da Tôrre de Garcia d'Ávila, the first two Barões de Rio das Contas, the Condessa de Barral, the three Barões de São Francisco, among others, were born and lived here.[42] A graduate of the Faculty of Law in São Paulo in 1874, Severino began his career as a prosecutor. By the 1880s, he was elected to the provincial legislature by the Conservative Party. After 1889, he allied himself with another rising star of the former monarchic party, Luís Viana. A diminutive, goateed Severino was named a cabinet minister by Campos Sales; this placed him among the top contenders for the state leadership of the PRF-Bahia, which had been helped by the rapidly sagging political fortunes of Luís Viana after the War of Canudos.

Although vindictive and even brutal in his dealings with his political enemies, Governor Vieira was an efficient administrator. His education programs, electoral reforms, state aid to the construction of sugar refineries, and other public works projects were universally applauded.[43] Vieira was also responsible for revamping the system of granting state contracts, one of the major sources of patronage. Viana's often heralded but low-productive public works projects, such as construction of dams and encouragement of immigration, were riddled with political favoritism and nepotism. Viana routinely named backland chieftains to public works commissions to curry

42. The list of leading landowning families of São Francisco do Conde was published in *Diário de Notícias*, January 31, February 2, 1889; Wanderley Pinho wrote a superbly documented history of one engenho in that município, *História de um engenho do Recôncavo*.
43. *Mensagem da Bahia de 1901*, pp. 14–16.

political favors. Anxious to become his own man and to build up his reputation as an administrator, Vieira summarily dismissed Viana appointees from the state payroll. The appointment of Miguel Calmon du Pin e Almeida as the state secretary of agriculture was his single most important merit-based decision in modernizing the state economy.[44]

However, Severino Vieira's contribution to Bahia was found not in the administration of the government but in the forging of a new tribal oligarchic party. Having eliminated the Vianistas from the state government, the governor moved to shore up his position in the Recôncavo and the interior; the recruiting of the Calmons of Santo Amaro, the Sousa clan (José Marcelino) of Nazaré, and similar scions of oligarchies was the first step. As proven by his predecessors, the business of securing support from backland coronéis was tricky. The governor was convinced that Bahia could rise high in the federation once a strong party structure was laid. He therefore chose to build a new party as he was well aware of the political crisis that ripped the state apart in the 1890s. The bastion of this new party, the Partido Republicano da Bahia (PRB) was drawn from the latifundiary clans of the Recôncavo.

THE PRB AND OLIGARCHIES

The plenary meeting of the Bahian Republican Party was held on March 1, 1901. Attending the meeting were some of the major political leaders of Bahia, representing all factions and persuasions. At the outset, the meeting bogged down over the problem of membership, but it finally resolved to include *all* political currents of the state; the entire Bahian federal and

44. It seemed routine for Luís Viana to name coronéis for public works commissions on the município level: in Caetité (Cleofano Meireles and Deocleciano Pires Teixeira), July 24, 1897, Pasta 21; Bom Conselho (Francisco Sales e Silva, João Quintiliano dos Santos, and Manuel Longuinho do Nascimento), July 29, 1898, Pasta 22; and Sento-Sé (Leopoldo Nunes de Sento-Sé, Tomás Lins de Albuquerque, and João Nunes de Sousa [Sento-Sé?]), August 8, 1898, Pasta 22. Furthermore, the governor also named coronéis on statewide commissions: Coronel Leonidas Gonçalves Torres, a well-known merchant in Juàzeiro, was named to manage the Linha Fluvial do São Francisco, June 18, 1898, Pasta 22, and Coronel Alexandre Portela Passos, a merchant in Santo Amaro, was named director of the Santo Amaro Railroads Co., April 20, 1898, Pasta 22, Atos e Decretos/1898/ Secretaria da Agricultura, Seção da Documentação Administrativa, Arquivo do Estado da Bahia, hereafter cited as SDA/AEBa. See also *Mensagem da Bahia de 1903*, pp. 34–35.

state legislators, two delegates from each município, the councilmen of Salvador, and the district ward bosses of the capital were invited. At the mid-April party convention, two hundred delegates organized the first statewide political party. With the sugar interest group in charge, José Marcelino de Sousa was easily elected president of the Executive Committee. The election of the sugar planter–refinery owner of Nazaré was no surprise; he was a legitimate representative of the agrarian and commercial sectors and, furthermore, carried greater prestige than the governor. The party leadership was to be shared by the two men, and to keynote the new spirit of tribal collaboration in politics, the composition of the PRB General Council, to which the Executive Committee reported, reflected wider geographic representation than had any other previous Bahian political parties. At least three well-heeled backland chiefs were elected to the council: Coronel Abraham Cohim of Mundo Novo, representing the zonal chiefs of northern Bahia; Coronel Francisco Joaquim Flores of Santa Ana dos Brejos, acting as the delegate of the São Francisco Valley; and Coronel Temistocles da Rocha Passos, speaking for the backwater municípios of the Recôncavo.[45] By inviting leaders of the familiocratic oligarchies to have a voice in the council, the PRB sought to broaden its regional base but still remain a predominantly agrarian-based party—a tribal confederation of sugar-producing clans. As such, the PRB limited its options as a truly statewide party.

Some problems influenced the molding of the party: personality differences, the governor's dislike of certain coronéis and bacharéis, and strained relations between the federal president and Bahia's leading politicians. José Joaquim Seabra, a federal deputy and a personal foe of the governor, and Rui Barbosa, Bahia's federal senator but no enthusiastic supporter of Severino Vieira, were declared ex officio members of the party but played no visible role in party deliberations. César Zama, a talented physician and a frustrated politician, was invited to join the official party but declined to do so. Luís Viana, self-exiled to Europe, was not even mentioned in the party roster. In 1902, the third planter president from São Paulo, Rodrigues Alves, picked Federal Deputy Seabra as his minister of justice, a ges-

45. *Jornal de Notícias*, March 2, April 16–17, 1901.

ture that contemporary politicians interpreted as presidential expression of personal dislike of Governor Vieira.[46] The PRB's failure to garner a federal ministerial portfolio, or rather the governor's inability to place his own man in the presidential cabinet, seriously weakened Severino Vieira's power, while the oligarchs of the sugar clans (Miguel Calmon, José Marcelino, and Araújo Pinho, among others) quietly strove to expand their tribal power base.

On another front, while attempting to heal the political scars of the 1890s and to become the official party, PRB trepidations were raised when Governor Vieira carried out personal vendettas against some of the most powerful coronéis. Such action discouraged cautious backland chiefs from joining the dominant party. In Ilhéus, Coronel Antônio Pessoa of the opposition PRC won the election in 1899 for the intendency; in Lençóis, the reaction to Luís Viana's police expedition was felt in an election, when a group of anti-Vianista coronéis were sent to the municipal council. Elsewhere, local coronéis seized power with the help of padded electoral rosters. In the name of electoral reforms, the governor ordered the state senate to revoke selectively the mandates of opposition coronéis such as Antônio Pessoa.[47] In 1902 and 1903, the backland coronéis of Bahia did not scramble to join the PRB.

It is ironic that Severino Vieira could have become the political unifier of Bahia, seeking alliance with the coronelista oligarchies instead of breaking up the status quo. But his indulgence in vendettas that were personally motivated and his intoxication with power were dangerous to the future of any party. This self-destructive trait of personal abuse of power at the expense of partisan unity was inherent in Bahian politics and was a constantly looming threat to the dominant group. In 1903, the PRB fathers gathered to consider the successor to Governor Vieira; their first concern was to find a political moderate who could bring the party together. No other man was better qualified than José Marcelino de Sousa.

46. Afonso Arinos de Melo Franco, *Rodrigues Alves: apogeu e declínio do presidencialismo*, 2:493. When Seabra was appointed to the federal cabinet, he was forty-seven years old with a solid reputation of being "anti-Florianista and Republican."

47. *Mensagem da Bahia de 1903*, pp. 8–9, 17–18.

3. The Coronelista Oligarchy in the Sertão and the Fall of the PRB, 1904–1912

The NOMINATION of José Marcelino de Sousa as the successor to the governor seemed fitting. The owner of the Usina de Conceição in Nazaré and the president of the Nazaré Tramroad (the railroad that linked Cachoeira to Nazaré), "Zé" was a perfect political spokesman for the planter class in Bahia. Born in 1848, he was the son of a Conservative politician and planter. José Marcelino was to follow the familiar path of many monarchic politicians: legal training at the Faculty of Law in Recife, internship as county prosecutor and judge, service in the provincial and imperial legislatures, in short, one step removed from mandarindom. José Marcelino soft-pedaled his Republican political career; he was elected to the state senate in 1891 and was one of the key drafters of the state constitution. Always preferring to remain behind the scenes, Zé Marcelino stayed out of state politics during the troubled 1890s, devoting himself to such entrepreneurial ventures as the construction of a railroad and a sugar refinery. As a successful businessman, he commanded respect among planters and merchants alike. He was untainted by the bitter political factionalism of the PRF-Bahia and the PRC. In 1901, Governor Severino invited Sousa back to politics. His election to the governorship was uncontested and carried a hint of the restoration of power to the coastal sugar interests after a fifteen-year rule by urban-oriented governors.[1]

During his first two years as governor, José Marcelino devoted himself to the economic development of Bahia, especially its agriculture, transportation, and commerce. In his accomplishments as governor, he easily outdid all other governors during the First Republic. With his patriarch's mane and white mustache and beard, the governor inspired public confidence. His first important decision was to retain Miguel Calmon as his secretary of agriculture and dispatch him to Ceylon to study advances in cane sugar cultivation. The state government contracted a German agronomist to study improvements in cacao farming, now the first source of state revenues, as well as cotton cultivation in the arid backlands.[2] New money and interest were injected into the moribund state agricultural school to revive its research efforts. Several riverine and oceangoing vessels were ordered from England to refurbish navigation and commerce. As the governor often said, there could be no commercial prosperity without cheap, efficient transportation. The riverboats were sent to the São Francisco River; seagoing vessels were put into use for coastal transportation of sugar from the Recôncavo and cacao from southern Bahia.[3]

The governor's plan to build up Bahia's agriculture did not end with public works and research. The Bahian Agricultural Credit Bank (the Banco de Crédito da Lavoura da Bahia) was set up to provide cheap capital, generated from agricultural export taxes.[4] The problem of capital formation had been a major cause

1. On the concept of mandarins as it applies to Brazilian history, see Eul-Soo Pang and Ron L. Seckinger, "The Mandarins of Imperial Brazil." There are two biographies on José Marcelino, both written by his daughter, Maria Mercedes Lopes de Sousa: *José Marcelino de Sousa e sua obra administrativa no São Francisco* and *Um estadista quase desconhecido*. See also Antônio de Araújo de Aragão Bulcão Sobrinho, "Relembrando o velho senado baiano," pp. 168–70.

2. Calmon to Rio Branco, Bahia, May 28, 1905, Pasta Miguel Calmon, Sousa to Rio Branco, Bahia, September 18, 1906, 307/4/2, Pasta Bahia: Telegramas Recebidos 1888–1926, ABRB/AHI.

3. Sousa, *José Marcelino de Sousa*; see also Pang, "The Politics of *Coronelismo* in Brazil," pp. 101–2.

4. *Relatório apresentado ao Exmo. Sr. Dr. José Marcelino de Sousa Governador do Estado da Bahia pelo Dr. João Pedro dos Santos Secretário do Tesouro*

of the atrophying of commercial agriculture in the 1870s and 1880s, when the modernization of sugar was a most urgent need. The governor appointed a renowned planter and a former Conservative politician, João Ferreira de Araújo Pinho, as first president of the bank. Recognizing the important role of the landholding coronéis in state politics, Henrique Teixeira was named director and Viriato Ferreira Maia Bitencourt secretary; both were influential coronéis in the Recôncavo.[5] The operation of the bank was wisely entrusted to the powerful sugar interests. The Maia Bitencourt family intermarried with the Calmons,[6] and the astute Teixeira wielded much influence among the leading export merchants.

The economic interests of the backland coronéis were equally pampered. The São Francisco Transportation Company was state owned and operated. The navigation firm had been organized under the provincial presidency of Manuel Pinto de Sousa Dantas, when the Liberal politician ruled Bahia in the 1860s. Financial troubles delayed immediate operation; it was not until 1872 that official traffic opened. In the late 1880s, the provincial government granted monopoly rights to a private navigation firm, which was forced into bankruptcy as a result of mismanagement. In 1893, the state took over the firm, extending traffic to the tributaries of the São Francisco, thus bringing Goiás and Maranhão closer to Bahia. Ships ran monthly between Juàzeiro and the interior towns of Minas and western Bahia. This newly acquired, easy access to Minas and Goiás fostered the growth not only of commerce and agriculture but also of numerous interstate political alliances of coronéis.[7] With these impressive accomplishments, Governor José Marcelino and the PRB sought to establish themselves as the state's dominant party. As the new benefactor to Bahian commerce, agriculture, and, above all, the interior coronéis, the governor restored Pax Bahiana.

---

e Fazenda, pp. 157–74; *Mensagem apresentada à Assembléia Geral Legislativa do Estado da Bahia na abertura da 2ª sessão ordinária da 9ª legislatura pelo Dr. José Marcelino de Sousa Governador do Estado*, p. 9.

5. Sousa, *Um estadista*, pp. 65–68.
6. Afrânio Peixoto et al., *Góis Calmon in memoriam*, p. 107.
7. Sousa, *Um estadista*, pp. 123–43, *José Marcelino de Sousa*, pp. 54–60; Jean Tricart et al., *Estudos de geografia da Bahia*, pp. 30–34; Pang, "The Politics of *Coronelismo*," pp. 86–91; Donald Pierson, *O homem no vale do São Francisco*, 3:29–66.

The presidential election of 1906 further enhanced the PRB's prestige in the state and its relations with the federal government. In 1906, former governor of Minas Gerais and then Vice-President Afonso Augusto Moreira Pena became the official candidate for president, with the support of São Paulo. In Bahia, the Young Turks of the PRB organized a political group, "the Kindergarten" (Jardim da Infância), for the Pena candidacy.[8] The PRB officially endorsed this candidacy, and the election of Pena was readily assured by the "in" parties elsewhere in the country. The victorious Pena named young Miguel Calmon, the leader of the "Kindergarten" group, as minister of agriculture. Calmon was the youngest federal minister in the history of the First Republic, if not in the twentieth century, at twenty-eight years of age. Calmon's entry into the new administration assured the PRB of national acceptance and minimized considerably the trepidations that Rodrigues Alves had caused with the nomination of Seabra. The official visit of President Pena to Bahia cemented a good relationship between the PRB and the PRM, to which the Calmons in Bahia would adhere politically for the next thirty years as the principal spokesmen for the Mineiro faction in Bahian state politics.

THE PRB'S TWO CHIEFS

By 1907, the tradition of the incumbent governor naming his own successor had yet to be firmly established in Bahia. For one thing, the PRB had two chiefs, Governor José Marcelino and Federal Senator Severino Vieira. The political clout of the governor was greatly enhanced by the induction of Miguel Calmon into the Pena administration and the subsequent growth of a working relationship with the presidential faction of the PRM. Senator Severino Vieira was the titular leader of the federal deputies from Bahia in the national capital and was said to have higher ambitions in federal politics. In short, both considered the ability to name the next governor the key test of their future leadership.

Another factor inhibiting the naming of one's successor was that Bahian politics was complicated by the entry of a new breed of politicians. These young politicians, the majority of

8. Afonso Arinos de Melo Franco, *Um estadista da república* (*Afrânio de Melo Franco e seu tempo*), 2:482–83.

whom practiced politics for the first time after 1889, directed their loyalty to a strong personality rather than to the PRB. Thus, brothers Miguel and Antônio Calmon and Ernesto Simões Filho (the future founder of *A Tarde*, the major daily newspaper of Salvador) belonged to the governor's faction, while Pedro Lago and João Mangabeira followed Severino Vieira. Outside the two major currents of the PRB, Seabra led an opposition group, which also attracted such talented young politicians as Antônio Moniz and Moniz Sodré—the first served as governor of Bahia (1916-20), the other was elected federal senator (1920-27). This new generation of politicians represented a maze of class and regional interests, further complicating the workings of state politics.

Thus, when Severino Vieira openly sought to strengthen his hand within the party, the power struggle between him and José Marcelino threatened the Pax Bahiana as well as the stability of the PRB. There was a personality conflict between the two politicians. At first glance, the division of labor appeared to be a sound arrangement, Severino speaking for the party in Rio and José Marcelino minding the party in Bahia. Federal Senator Pinheiro Machado of Rio Grande do Sul and Governor Borges de Medeiros of the PRR had a similar modus vivendi, fortifying the Gaúcho position in the council of federation politics. Due to the superficial resemblance, Bahian politicians perhaps had not noticed the underlying problem in the leadership of the PRB, hoping that Bahia, too, would become another Rio Grande. By April 1907, such a dream indeed remained unrealizable. It was rumored in Salvador that "Severino and Zé are going to have it out in the open."[9]

Unlike Borges de Medeiros, Governor Zé Marcelino had aspirations for national office. He was determined to defend his position in the PRB and was well aware that he had to demonstrate his ability to check Severino Vieira. In mid-April, the governor unveiled his candidate with the full endorsement of his faction: Araújo Pinho, the Conservative planter and first president of the Bahian Agricultural Credit Bank. In the forty-two-member state chamber of deputies, ten came forth to support the governor's candidate, ten remained uncommitted, and twenty-two chose to stay with the "party chief," Severino.[10]

9. *Diário de Notícias*, April 11, 1907.
10. Ibid., April 13, 15-16, 1907.

THE SCHISM OF 1907

The so-called schism of 1907 was to have a far-reaching impact on the future of one-party rule in state politics and, not incidentally, on the development of coronelismo. On the whole, the majority of backland coronéis seemed to favor the governor's wing of the PRB. In 1907, the governor served as an intermediary in matters of federal patronage, electoral arrangements, and even contacts with the southern PRs. The coronéis took up their business with the governor or with state deputies or senators. For this reason, the José Marcelino faction had advantages in corralling support from coronéis for its candidate. From Morro do Chapeu, Coronel Francisco Dias Coelho, the prestigious black coronel, announced his support of Araújo Pinho; many backland chieftains in the Lavras and the Middle São Francisco Valley soon began to fall in with his lead.[11]

However, the coronéis of the coastal municípios were a bit more discriminating in their choice of candidate. Some were under pressure from the state government, and others for reasons of personality differences, divided their loyalty. Coronel Antônio Pessoa, who had been "overthrown" from the intendency of Ilhéus by Severino Vieira, supported the candidacy of Araújo Pinho. The incumbent intendente of Ilhéus, João Mangabeira, fell in behind his chief, Coronel Antônio. Coronéis Firmino Alves and Henrique Alves, both adversaries of Antônio Pessoa, naturally swung to Severino's camp. While Ubaldino Assis of Cachoeira backed his neighbor Araújo Pinho, the Barão de Assu da Tôrre, chief of Mata de São João, declared for Severino. In Monte Alto, Cardoso father and son announced their endorsement of the governor's candidate. The political priest Cônego Manuel Leôncio Galrão, state senator from Areia, also supported the governor.[12] The divisiveness among the coastal coronéis was easily understandable, for their principal economic activities (sugar, cacao, tobacco, and other commercial agriculture) required them to cull favors from politicians of the incumbent party. Many planters relied on their state deputies and senators for bank loans, land acquisitions, and even tax tampering. Unlike the interior coronéis, the coastal chiefs had a strong working re-

11. Ibid., April 15–16, 1907.
12. Ibid.

lationship with prominent politicians, and in 1907 the delineation of their electoral loyalty simply followed the lines of business politics.

The "party chief" Severino Vieira convened the PRB state meeting, where he revealed his choice for governor: Joaquim Inácio Tosta, a federal deputy and an equally prestigious planter-dynast in São Felix. Tosta, like Araújo Pinho, backed the modernization of agriculture, especially tobacco, which was the mainstay of São Felix and its adjacent municípios. As a federal deputy, Tosta was no less a genuine spokesman for the traditional interests in Bahia. Coming from the same clan that produced two noblemen (the marquês and visconde de Muritiba), Joaquim Inácio was a big name in the monarchic Liberal party, as was Araújo Pinho in the Conservative Party. In full approval of Severino's choice, the state convention proceeded to formalize Tosta's candidacy. One hundred and seventy delegates attended the meeting, representing only fifty-seven municípios, less than one-half the state's total. Judging from the list of delegates, the majority came from the capital and the coastal municípios and represented the interests of the counterelite who hoped to profit by supporting Severino's candidate. Ten of Salvador's districts were represented by aspiring ward bosses; the three most populous districts, Sé, Brotas, and Vitória, were conspicuously missing.[13]

For the first time in Bahian history—but certainly not the last —there was open endorsement of gubernatorial candidates by high-level federal politicians. In Rio, President Pena, the Gaúcho Senator Pinheiro Machado, and Rui Barbosa led others in supporting Araújo Pinho's candidacy.[14] The direct involvement of the federal president in pressuring state legislators to support the governor's candidate was unprecedented in Bahian politics. Minister Calmon was successful in extracting public endorsement for Araújo Pinho from other high officials in the Pena administration and was probably working under the orders of Governor José Marcelino in so doing.

The first hotly contested election since 1895 destroyed the ruling party. In Castro Alves, a Recôncavo município, a Marcelinista coronel armed four hundred men to assure the

---

13. Joaquim Inácio Tosta, *Renúncia de mandato: discurso proferido na Câmara dos Deputados na sessão de 29 de dezembro de 1907*, pp. 35–37, 57–61.
14. Lemos Brito, *A cisão: páginas de crítica*, pp. 98–99.

organization of a pro-government electoral board. In Ilhéus, where the expansion of cacao plantations created a boom-town atmosphere, political fights among the two PRB factions took a nasty turn, involving the deaths of state policemen and many agricultural laborers. In the Lavras, Coronel Aureliano Gondim of Andaraí fought the pro-government coronéis to retain control of Ituaçu for the Severino camp.[15] Furthermore, the clumsily concocted assassination attempt against the governor in mid-October further widened the schism of the PRB and added vigor to the contest. The police forced a confession from José Circumcisão da Silva, one-time servant to former Governor Luís Viana, who was thought to be in sympathy with the Severino camp.[16] More violence in other interior municípios ensued, marring the election day.

THE RECOGNITION BATTLE

The election results were in dispute. By one account, the governor's candidate won victories in eighty municípios compared to thirty for Tosta. This preliminary tally gave 49,000 votes to Araújo Pinho, 14,000 to Tosta.[17] Since each side claimed victory for its candidate, the final canvassing of the votes was to be done in the state legislature. The emergence of two victors, or a *duplicata*, was a common occurrence in the First Republic in federal and state elections; by law, the legislative branch had the right to resolve the dispute. In Bahia, major electoral laws of 1891 and of 1902 assigned the onerous duty to the state senate in the case of municipal elections and to the both houses in the case of the governorship.[18] As of January 1908, the governor could

15. *Diário de Notícias*, October 11, November 16, December 31, 1907, January 2, 1908.

16. Pedro Viana to Rio Branco, Bahia, October 18, 1907, 307/4/1, Pasta Bahia: Diversas Autoridades—Recebidos e Expedido 1903–1930, AHI; the newspaper reports in 1907 were either very confusing in pinpointing the culprit(s) of the crime or were wholly biased. Years later, one newspaper reported that Luís Viana was behind the attempt: *A Bahia*, November 7, 1911; interview with Dona Marieta de Sousa (also known as Maria Mercedes Lopes de Sousa), Salvador, October 15, 1973. Marieta, the daughter-biographer of José Marcelino, did not confirm the involvement of Luís Viana in the attempt on her father's life but stated, "Many people are still living and I do not wish to discuss the matter." She did not categorically deny his involvement, however.

17. Brito, *A cisão*, pp. 113, 128.

18. *Diário de Notícias*, January 18, 1908.

count on the firm commitment of seven senators and an unspecified number of deputies, while Severino Vieira claimed the support of twelve of twenty-one senators and twenty of forty-two deputies, or exactly the legally required minimum to win.[19] Various techniques for coaxing legislative support developed: federal politicians applied pressure, back-room brokering was common practice, the state police resorted to intimidation by violence, and private armies counteracted likewise. Similar scenes would be re-enacted during later gubernatorial elections of the First Republic. On this particular occasion, Governor José Marcelino ordered the city and state police to the legislative assembly in a show of force. The opposition brought in their own jagunços to counter the police. Eleven senators of the Severino camp led a charge against the police, resulting in many injuries.[20] The government's strategy was to keep the legislature open until a quorum was formed and Araújo Pinho was verified the winner—all under police supervision.

In sharp contrast to previous years, both sides now actively sought the federal president's intervention on behalf of their candidates. Rui Barbosa, who had earlier supported the Araújo Pinho candidacy, prudently stayed out of the verification fight. President Afonso Pena was under intense pressure from Miguel Calmon to reaffirm publicly his endorsement of the official candidate. The partisan involvement of the president had an effect on lower level federal officials. Eager employees at the post office voluntarily censored the opposition's telegrams and passed relevant information to the pro-government faction.[21]

On March 28, 1908, the government side managed to form a quorum with the help of the state police, who then simply locked the legislators in until they rendered a verdict: Araújo Pinho was formally declared the winner with 49,371 votes to Joaquim Inácio Tosta's 12,102. By all accounts, Salvador remained calm after the formal announcement of the Araújo Pinho victory. When all was over, the Severino wing still counted thirty-two legislators in its corner. The federal president accepted the

19. Augusto Araújo Santos et al. to Afonso Pena, Bahia, March 30, 1908, Severino Vieira et al. to Afonso Pena, Bahia, March 21, 1908, Arquivo de Afonso Augusto Moreira Pena, hereafter cited as AAAMP.
20. Miguel Calmon to Afonso Pena, Rio, March 23, 1908, ibid.
21. Pedro Lago et al. to Afonso Pena, Bahia, March 24, 1908, ibid.

verification, and the state legislature prudently recessed for the remainder of 1908 to cool its temper.[22]

THE BEGINNING OF THE END OF PRB RULE

Governor João Ferreira de Araújo Pinho, the fifth "popularly" elected chief executive of Bahia, was born in 1851 in Santo Amaro. As the Conservative politician, he amassed an impeccable record as a typical mandarin. His father, a Sorbonne graduate, was a planter and local politician. João studied law at the Recife academy and graduated in 1871. He began his political career as a prosecutor and served as a Conservative provincial and imperial deputy. In the mid-1870s, he was appointed provincial president of Sergipe. A son-in-law of the Barão de Cotegipe, Araújo Pinho was likewise a defender of slavocracy and an adroit spokesman for the sugar interests. After the fall of the empire in 1889, he remained one of the heirs of former Conservative politics but chose to maintain a low profile, thereby minimizing his close tie with the ancien régime. During a brief term in the state senate, Araújo Pinho allied himself with the PRC, along with José Gonçalves and the Barão de Jeremoabo in 1893. Three years later, he ran for the federal senate against Rui Barbosa. His defeat by the former Liberal temporarily halted his political career, until 1902 when he was elected to the state senate as a PRB candidate.[23] His subsequent service as president of the Bahian Agricultural Credit Bank and his background as a planter later made him a perfect choice for the state's top job when the revival of commercial sugar agriculture became the goal of the two PRB administrations of Vieira and José Marcelino.

When Araújo Pinho took office for the term 1908–12, he was

22. Manuel Duarte de Oliveira to Afonso Pena, Bahia, March 28, 1908, Rui Barbosa to Afonso Pena, Petrópolis, March 23, 1908, ibid.; Antônio Ferrão Moniz de Aragão, *A Bahia e os seus governadores*, p. 235. Moniz' version of the election and its aftermath is biased (pp. 195–237), giving especially favorable impressions of those politicians who supported Seabra in 1910.

23. Bulcão Sobrinho, "Relembrando o velho senado baiano," pp. 159–64. There is no biography of Araújo Pinho. João Maurício, one of his grandsons, is in the process of organizing personal papers for a biography (parts of this collection are already in various research institutions in Rio and Bahia). An unknown quantity of the personal papers (political and family-related) is in the hands of João Maurício, unavailable for consultation by "outsiders."

to become the second governor in Bahian history since José Gonçalves to renounce the office amid a political crisis. Politics became the primary concern of the administration. No outstanding contributions to public works, agriculture, or commerce were made during his disappointing performance as governor. The attempt by the cacao sector to seek federal valorization support (as the coffee industry in the central south had done with the Convênio de Taubaté in 1906) received the governor's endorsement, but with the diminished prestige of the divided official party, Araújo Pinho was unable to win federal support.[24] Party dissension alone was not entirely to blame for the failure, but Bahia's declining political clout certainly accounted for the lack of interest among the state's major economic groups.

In spite of a low-key, humdrum approach to administration, the governor was unable to restrain political factionalism among the PRB chieftains. In 1909, Bahia's leading Republican, Virgílio Damásio, stepped down from the federal senate, and former Governor José Marcelino was elected in his place. In that year, Severino Vieira was still a PRB senator but could no longer claim to be boss of Bahian politics. The governor sought to dominate state politics, while two PRB senators carried on their 1907 disputes in the federal senate. In fact, when the presidential election of 1910 was under way, the PRB had two major irreconcilable factions.

THE POLITICS OF CAFÉ CONTRA LEITE

The presidential election of 1910 was one of the most bitterly contested campaigns in Brazil's political history, expressing both class conflict and regional economic rivalry. No less devastating was its post-election impact on the PRB and other "in" parties throughout the northern half of the country. The year 1910 also marked a new era in state and local affairs: partisan presidential intervention in regional politics. Federal

---

24. Associação Comercial da Bahia, *Relatório da Diretoria da Associação Comercial da Bahia apresentado e lido em reunião de Assembléia Geral Ordinária de 15 de fevereiro de 1912* (Bahia, 1912), pp. 235–47. The international conference on the Convênio do Cacau, attended by Portugal, Ecuador, and Brazil, was held in Bahia in October 1911. The purpose was similar to that of the Convênio de Taubaté, also known as the Convenção de Taubaté.

presidents after 1910 frequently used federal armed forces to resolve state and local political disputes in favor of their supporters. The interventionist trend expanded through the 1920s, effectively undermining the harmony built into the system of the "politics of governors" by Campos Sales.

Contrary to existing interpretations, the "coffee with cream" (café com leite) alliance between São Paulo and Minas was not a working political marriage. It should more properly be called café contra leite. Adversaries since the mining days of the eighteenth century, São Paulo and Minas began to emerge as political rivals and continued so through the nineteenth and twentieth centuries. More important and wealthier São Paulo, the leading coffee producer, found reasons to oppose Minas (the most populous state during the First Republic) in an effort to control the federal government. Coffee was not the principal economic activity of Minas, but agriculture was, especially pastoral activity. Southern Minas was a rich coffee-growing area that has been tied traditionally to the economic interests of São Paulo. Political trends of this area (the Zona da Mata) were pro-Paulista. As coffee production in the 1890s resulted in several super-harvests, beyond the world market's demand, São Paulo began to institute a number of measures to protect its economy by restricting the planting of coffee trees and artificially fixing the price of coffee by buying up the surplus. In 1906, the coffee-producing states of São Paulo, Minas, and Rio joined forces to set up a national defense plan for coffee interests, known as the Convênio de Taubaté, under which the federal government was committed to aid this dominant economic group. Bahia, for once, vigorously protested what seemed to be a blatant attempt to peculate the federal treasury in order to subsidize regional economic interests.[25]

When President Afonso Pena died in 1909 without solving the question of his successor, the main concern of the planter interests of São Paulo was to find a means of continuing the valorization program that had begun in 1906 and had proved so

25. For Bahia's opposition to the Convênio de Taubaté, see Associação Comercial da Bahia, *Representação dirigida ao congresso legislativo federal contra a aprovação do Convênio de Taubaté sobre valorização do café e fixação do valor da moeda* (Bahia, 1912), pp. 5–6, 24–25; see also Felix Flugel, "Coffee Valorization in Brazil"; Thomas H. Holloway, *The Brazilian Coffee Valorization of 1906: Regional Politics and Economic Dependence*; Carone, *A primeira república*, pp. 125–28, and *A república velha*, pp. 38–45.

vital to state interests. Pena's probable successor was his minister of finance, David Campista, a Mineiro politician.[26] After the death of the president, Vice President Nilo Peçanha, a native of sugar-producing Campos (Rio), showed little sympathy for the Campista candidacy. Gaúcho Senator Pinheiro Machado, uncrowned king of federal politics who had been at odds with the deceased president, found a sympathetic ear in President Nilo Peçanha. With the full support of his state party of the PRR and the principal tribal oligarchies of the northern half of the country, Pinheiro Machado clenched the presidential nomination for a fellow Gaúcho and the former minister of war in the Pena administration, Marshal Hermes Rodrigues da Fonseca. The dominant group of the PRM, with the exception of the Campista supporters, found the choice palatable and committed itself to the PRR/Army candidate. Support from the PRM was firmly assured when Minas Governor Wenceslau Brás was designated the vice presidential candidate.

The Paulista politicians expected the worst for the coffee sector from the Hermes–Wenceslau Brás candidacy. Economic considerations about federal aid to the coffee sector were among the major reasons that the PRP resolved to oppose the PRR/Army/PRM alliance. Rui Barbosa was chosen as the standard-bearer of the opposition, with Governor Albuquerque Lins of São Paulo as his vice-presidential candidate. For the second time since 1894, São Paulo and Bahia were thrown into a political alliance. The PRB found a new cause for the badly needed unity, temporarily bringing the two factions together for the Barbosa candidacy.

SEABRA AND THE ELECTION OF 1910

The political kingmakers of the PRR/Army/PRM group took full advantage of the shaky PRB position in Bahia. To manage the pro-Hermes campaign, they picked J. J. Seabra, an enfant terrible of Bahian politics, who had been on the losing side during much of his political career, since 1889. After opposing Floriano Peixoto, Seabra was exiled to Uruguay; upon his return in 1894, he was elected to the federal congress and soon moved up to the federal ministry of justice under President

26. Franco, *Um estadista da república*, 2:586–94; Carone, *A república velha II*, pp. 231–41; Belo, *A History of Modern Brazil*, pp. 203–7.

Rodrigues Alves. After Afonso Pena and José Marcelino blocked the election of Seabra sympathizers for the federal and state legislatures, Seabra was once again forced into exile, this time to Europe. Upon his return in 1909, he found a political home with the Hermes forces. Thus, in late July 1909, Seabra set up the Bahian Republican Committee for Hermes and Wenceslau, actively recruiting anti-PRB Young Turks such as Otávio Mangabeira and Antônio Moniz, among others. Luís Viana, still an outsider to the two factions of the PRB, accepted Seabra's invitation to join the committee.[27] Discontent with the PRB began to spread rapidly in Salvador. Always a spell-binding orator, Seabra aroused the emotions of the poor masses of the capital who were to serve as his means of seizing control of the state government two years later.

The confident Seabra cabled President Nilo Peçanha in early March 1910 that there would be no need for the federal president to intervene in Bahia to influence the outcome of the election.[28] Salvador was traditionally a bastion of political opposition, and Seabra felt the need to carry Hermes' campaign to the interior. But it was in the Recôncavo that Seabra and his party ran into stiff resistance among the PRB jagunços and state police. Upon their arrival in Cachoeira, the first interior campaign stop, Seabra and his entourage were viciously attacked by state police, who were joined by a group of terrorists allegedly hired by Severino Vieira. Together, they assaulted the crowd that had gathered to hear Seabra speak; five persons were seriously injured, forcing the Hermes campaign manager to abandon his tour.[29]

Seabra's lackluster campaign in Bahia was to have little effect on the election, however. According to one source, eleven northern states, minus Bahia, returned 147,277 votes to Hermes; only 5,599 went to Rui. In Espírito Santo, Sergipe, Alagoas, Pernambuco, and Paraíba, the official candidate "won" by a fifty-four-to-one margin. In the states north of the "hump"—Rio Grande do Norte, Ceará, Piauí, Maranhão, Pará, and Amazonas—Hermes received 86,659 votes compared to Rui's 4,470,

27. *Diário de Notícias*, January 24, February 2, 1910; Francisco Borges de Barros, *Dr. J. J. Seabra: sua vida, sua obra na república*, pp. 31–33.

28. Seabra to Nilo, Cachoeira, February 21, 1910, Pasta–February 1910, Arquivo de Nilo Peçanha, hereafter cited as ANP.

29. Ubaldino Assis to Nilo, Cachoeira, February 23, 1910, Seabra to Nilo, Bahia, February 24, 1910, ibid.

winning by a nineteen-to-one margin. In Rio, the stronghold of the opposition candidate, forty-nine of the fifty-three polling places were not opened.[30] Violence, backroom maneuvering, and false ballot counting were used by both parties. In the final count, the Brazilian congress declared Hermes and Wenceslau the winners.

THE FOUNDING OF THE PRD

The ascent of Marshal Hermes da Fonseca to the federal presidency proved to be fatal to the PRB sooner than anyone had anticipated. J. J. Seabra, though unsuccessful in winning Bahia for the president, was rewarded for his effort with a cabinet post, thus becoming one of two Bahian politicians of the First Republic to hold a federal portfolio twice. Under Seabra's direction, the Republican Democratic Party (Partido Republicano Democrata) was formed out of the old campaign committee and became the principal opposition to the PRB in Bahia. Luís Viana, profiting from his political support of Hermes in the 1910 election, was made chief of the Bahian branch of the Conservative Republican Party, led by Pinheiro Machado; this was no relation to Bahia's anti-Vianista PRC of the 1890s. Together the PRD and the PRC-Bahia opposed the PRB, the party of agrarian interests.[31]

State and federal legislative elections always served to strengthen or weaken the power base of a party in Brazil. The 1911 state legislative and municipal elections were hotly contested by four groups: the two traditional wings of the PRB and the two new parties. When the dominant factions of the PRB conspired for complete control of the nomination, Minister Seabra and his PRD were only too eager to involve the federal president in the election. To the federal minister, victory in these elections could serve as a first step in his rise to the state governorship. Keeping this perspective in mind, Seabra was determined to gain a foothold in the PRB-dominated state legislature, even at the price of federal intervention.

When the PRD chief made known his intent to trounce the

---

30. Dudley to Secretary of State, Petrópolis, March 4, July 30, 1910, No. 500, fls. 6-9, No. 566, fls. 45-47, Internal Affairs of Brazil, Reel 4, 823.00/51-225, DOS/USNA.

31. *Diário de Notícias*, October 5, December 23, 1910.

PRB from the state house, many of the deputies and senators of the "in" party were moved to put their own elections before the party interests. Three deputies, representing the two main PRB currents and the PRD, approached their party chieftains to propose a pre-electoral paring of legislative seats among the three groups. Federal Judge Paulo Martins Fontes was selected as arbiter, and he divided the entire forty-two seats of the lower chamber and seven senate seats (one-third of the total who were renewing their mandates) into three equal portions. This would give each faction fourteen deputies and at least two senators. The compromise was accepted by the federal minister, the governor (speaking for the Marcelino wing), and Severino Vieira. One group left out of this compromise was the PRC-Bahia, whose chief, Luís Viana, denounced the PRD-PRB deal.[32]

When the electoral results were reviewed, the Seabra party had acquired fourteen new deputies and one senator in the state legislature. These PRD solons were to serve as the advance guard in planning Seabra's rise to power over the next two years. Some of them became lifelong supporters of Seabra: Antônio Moniz, Moniz Sodré (Antônio's cousin and brother-in-law), Raul Alves, Coronel Frederico Costa, and Coronel Antônio Pessoa.[33] In 1930, Costa, as Bahia's state senate president, became the last governor of the First Republic, while Antônio Pessoa remained as the regional power broker and state senator for cacao-producing southern Bahia.

The compromise of 1911 which led to the initial victory of the PRD and the partisan erosion of the PRB in the state capitol was the first of a series of attempts by the "house party" of the Hermes administration to dislodge the traditional oligarchs from power in the country. Between 1911 and 1913, Minister of Transportation Seabra and Minister of War Dantas Barreto, supported by the president's son and aide-de-camp, Lieutenant Mário da Fonseca, were power-seekers opposing the Pinheiro Machado–dominated PRC. The election of Hermes in 1910 had been skillfully engineered by Pinheiro Machado, who wove a series of alliances with the ruling oligarchs in the northern part of the country. The victory, though gratifying to the president's

32. Fontes to Seabra, Bahia, March 20, 1911 (telegram), in Moniz de Aragão, *A Bahia e os seus governadores*, pp. 334, 336–38; Nelson de Sousa Sampaio, "Meio século de política baiana," p. 113.
33. Moniz de Aragão, p. 335.

supporters, further inflated the power of the Gaúcho senator. It was well known at the beginning of the Hermes presidency that the real power in the regime was Pinheiro, not the marshal. Fearing the prospective presidential candidacy of Senator Machado in 1914, Seabra, Dantas Barreto, and Mário Hermes led a group of anti-Pinheiro army and civilian politicians who together organized a movement later known as the "politics of rescue" (*política da salvação*). The objective of this group was to "rescue" northern politics from the hands of the ruling tribal oligarchies that the Gaúcho senator controlled.[34] In this battle, Seabra and Dantas Barreto became the main leaders of the movement.

THE PRB STILL DIVIDED

In June and July 1911, both the PRD and PRB were gearing up for the nomination of their candidates for governor. The opposition party held its convention first and unanimously named J. J. Seabra its candidate. To highlight the dissension in the official party, federal deputies Miguel and Antônio Calmon of the PRB endorsed the Seabra candidacy.[35] Badly shaken by the defection of the Calmons, the PRB met in late July to nominate its candidate. Once the meeting was underway, it was clear that each faction sought to impose its candidate on the party. Rui Barbosa picked José Pinho; Severino chose Domingos Guimarães, a federal deputy and an old crony of Marshal Deodoro da Fonseca.[36] José Marcelino, unwilling to support Severino's man, put up his candidate, a political priest and the state senate president, Cônego Manuel Leôncio Galrão. The incumbent governor seemed to be leaning toward Guimarães. The convention was deadlocked until José Marcelino withdrew his nominee and gave his support to Guimarães,[37] but the intramural fight over the official candidate had not ended.

Domingos Rodrigues Guimarães, if elected, would have been the first governor from Ilhéus, representing Bahia's most

34. Belo, *A History of Modern Brazil*, pp. 219–22; Fernando Setembrino de Carvalho, *Memórias: dados para a história do Brasil*, pp. 106–11.
35. Moniz de Aragão, *A Bahia e os seus governadores*, pp. 351–52, 355–56.
36. *A Bahia*, September 20, 1911; contradiction of this theory (appeasing the federal president) is advanced by Bulcão Sobrinho, "A Bahia não se dá e não se vende."
37. Moniz de Aragão, *A Bahia e os seus governadores*, p. 376.

powerful economic region. As soon as the convention closed, some die-hard PRB politicians accused the Guimarães group of making a deal with the opposition. The candidate's son, a staff member in the governor's office, was flirting with the Seabristas. The governor was automatically implicated with wrong-doing by those PRB regulars who wanted to see Guimarães resign his candidacy,[38] and they succeeded. The PRB's only hope to stop Seabra rested with the state legislature, which was badly bruised by internecine party squabbles. Two-thirds of the legislators were still "controlled" by the PRB, and they could turn down Seabra's bid for the governorship if they remained unified.

RESCUE POLITICS IN PERNAMBUCO

From September 1911 to January 1912, the whole country carefully watched political developments unfolding in Pernambuco, which was to become one of the first victims of the "politics of rescue." In September 1911, Federal Senator Rosa e Silva, who had been living in Europe for two years, and Dantas Barreto, who resigned from the ministry of war, put their campaign for governor in high gear. As the campaign picked up momentum, Governor Estácio Coimbra, unable to maintain law and order in Recife and its adjacent municípios, simply quit the office, throwing the state into anarchy.[39] By early November, when the election was over, both Rosistas and Dantistas claimed victory for their candidate.[40] The federal army in Recife supported General Dantas while the state police remained loyal to Senator Rosa. Violence broke out everywhere in the capital and in nearby municípios, causing many deaths on both sides. In Bom Conselho, for instance, a Rosista bomb killed twenty Dantas supporters, while in the capital two battalions of the state police became prisoners of the federal army. The entire

38. José de Sá, *O bombardeio da Bahia e seus efeitos*, p. 80; Pang, "The Politics of *Coronelismo*," p. 114.

39. Griffith to Secretary of State, Recife (Pernambuco), n.d. (telegram), fl. 97, Internal Affairs of Brazil, Reel 4, 823.00/51–225, DOS/USNA; the date of receipt of this telegram in Washington was September 12, 1911. See also Carvalho, *Memórias*, pp. 105–6; Albuquerque, *Um sertanejo*, pp. 91, 150–51.

40. Griffith to Secretary of State, Recife: November 6, 1911, no. 122, fl. 113; November 28, 1911, no. 134, fls. 132–33; November 29, 1911, no. 135, fls. 134–35; November 30, 1911, no. 136, fls. 136–37; December 7, 1911, no. 139, fls. 146–47, Internal Affairs of Brazil, Reel 4, 823.00/51–225, DOS/USNA.

month of November was rocked by violence between the contending parties. Finally, Dantas was declared the winner by the state legislature, and he took office on December 19, 1911.[41]

ARAÚJO PINHO'S RESIGNATION

The lesson of Pernambuco was hardly lost on the PRB hierarchy in Bahia. Although Hermes did not directly involve himself by declaring federal intervention, the Dantas forces had unyielding support from the federal garrison. The strongest support for Seabra in Bahia came from the federal army and the federal employees of the state.[42] The PRB was hopelessly divided over replacing the fallen Guimarães candidacy. As a result of this political impasse, the exhausted governor decided to quit the government and politics altogether. Only three days after Dantas Barreto took office in Pernambuco, Governor Araújo Pinho resigned in Bahia. The senate president, therefore the constitutional heir, Cônego Galrão, pleaded ill health as an excuse for passing the governorship to the speaker of the chamber of deputies. The speaker, Aurélio Rodrigues Viana, accepted the office the day that Araújo Pinho resigned.[43]

The election had been set for January 28, 1912. The resignation of the governor, as in the case of Estácio Coimbra in Pernambuco, set the PRB into disarray. The interim governor, acting under pressure from the bicephalous party, proclaimed that the state legislature would meet in Jequié, about a hundred miles south of Salvador. The manifest motive for the transfer of the legislature, in the interim governor's words, was "to resolve the resignation of Dr. João Ferreira de Araújo Pinho, to set the date for the election for his successor, and to prepare for measures required of the situation."[44] But the real reason seemed to be the desire of the Marcelinistas to deprive the Seabra faction, especially its deputies and senators, of an opportunity to form a quorum. In Jequié, the legislature could

41. Griffith to Secretary of State, Recife, December 21, 1911, no. 144, fls. 150–51, ibid. Consul Griffith reported that General Dantas Barreto had been the victor.
42. Rives to Secretary of State, Petrópolis, February 10, 1912, no. 801, fls. 158–64, ibid.
43. Mueller to Secretary of State, Bahia, February 27, 1912, no dispatch no., fls. 165–73, ibid.; Moniz de Aragão, *A Bahia e os seus governadores*, pp. 398–99.
44. Moniz de Aragão, p. 407.

act without interference from the federal army. The governor immediately ordered the state police to occupy the state capitol in an effort to keep the Seabrista deputies and senators out.[45]

The municipal election in Salvador on December 28, 1911, resulted in duplicata, both sides deadlocked.[46] This was a bad omen. The Seabra party resorted to both legal and extralegal means to prevent any further PRB move to stall the gubernatorial election. At the PRD's request, a federal judge issued an injunction to force the interim governor to withdraw the state police from the capitol and to forbid the transfer of the legislature to Jequié.[47] The Seabristas argued that a constitutional amendment was required for transferring a branch of the government out of Salvador. Unimpressed by this argument, the interim governor responded that a federal judge lacked jurisdiction on state "premises"; therefore, the order was null and void. In the meantime, the PRD mobilized the urban masses, or the "black riff-raff" in the words of the American consul in Bahia, to disrupt the city. The New Year's celebration of the Festa dos Navegantes turned into a shooting match between the terrorists of the two rival parties when the determined governor authorized an emergency budget of 300 *contos* for traveling expenses of the complacent PRB deputies and senators.[48] The majority of those who went along with the scheme were the Marcelinistas, the stronger of the two groups in the PRB. In so doing, they made the fatal error of leaving the capitol in the hands of the Seabrista and anti-Marcelinista legislators.

THE BOMBARDMENT OF SALVADOR

The events of January 1912 were to be viewed as the most infamous in Bahian political history. The Seabristas were determined to enforce the federal court order. The commercial quarters in the lower city closed in anticipation of a bloody

45. Pang, "The Politics of *Coronelismo*," pp. 114–15.

46. The two candidates for this office were Júlio Brandão (Seabra's candidate) and João Santos (the PRB man) (*A Bahia*, November 13–14, 21, 1911).

47. *Diário da Bahia*, January 12–17, 1912; Franco, *Um estadista da república*, 2:708–10.

48. Mueller to Secretary of State, Bahia, February 27, 1912, no dispatch no., fls. 165–73, Internal Affairs of Brazil, Reel 4, 823.00/51–225, DOS/USNA. Information in the rest of this chapter may be found ibid.

confrontation between the rival parties. The president instructed the federal army in Bahia to enforce the court order at any cost. On January 10, amid random violence between the state police and the riff-raff of the PRD, the federal army commander pleaded with the interim governor to obey the court order. Governor Viana offered a compromise: the state police would remain in the capitol but would not interfere with the sessions. No satisfactory solution resulted from the morning meeting between the governor and the general of the garrison, and by early afternoon, the army began to move into pre-assigned positions to proceed with battle plans. At 1:30 P.M., the artillery unit of the bay fort of São Marcelo began to bombard the city, while the infantry platoons collided with the state police in the lower city. By dusk, the Palace of Government was completely demolished, along with the state library and archives then housed in the palace. The governor agreed to a cessation of hostilities. The following day, Governor Aurélio Viana resigned, passing the office to the next in line, the chief justice of the state supreme court, Conselheiro Braúlio Xavier.

The second interim governor, untainted by partisan strife, was an honest jurist with impeccable credentials. A native of the Lavras Diamantinas, Braúlio Xavier preferred a judicial career to an unstable political one. By a quirk of fate, he came to occupy the office of the governor and was well aware of his mission: to hold the election on January 28 as planned and to turn over the governorship to the winner. Exactly ten days after he took office, the federal court in Rio reversed the decision of the federal judge in Bahia and ordered the army commander in Salvador to reinstate Aurélio Viana. The minister of war instructed the regional military commander to put Viana back in office as soon as possible.

The following day, when the change of government was announced, Seabrista mobs rioted in parts of the city. The PRD chief was forced to accept the return of Viana, although with strong protest, but his followers would not. Well-armed naval personnel sympathetic to the Seabrista cause were given shore leaves. Along with the street riff-raff who worked as paid henchmen for the PRD, the sailors went on a rampage, killing police officers, looting commercial houses, setting fire to pro-PRB newspaper printing plants, and releasing prisoners from the city and state detention centers. The riots continued for three days. The embarrassed president recalled the commanding general of the federal garrison to Rio, and a frightened Governor Viana took refuge in the French Consulate. The federal army placed a sentry detail at the consulate to protect the governor, but the mob threatened to burn down the building anyway if the governor did not resign a second time. The archbishop of Bahia intervened by persuading Aurélio Viana to sign the letter of resignation at the French Consulate to avoid any further bloodshed. Braúlio Xavier was again called on to take office.

On January 28, 1912, Seabra ran unopposed. A few days later, the state legislature, mindful of the possibility of federal intervention, recognized him the winner. Recalcitrant PRB deputies and senators were constantly reminded of the political successes of General Dantas Barreto in Pernambuco and Colonel Clodoaldo da Fonseca in Alagoas, another "rescuer" who in late December 1911 became governor by defeating the oligarchy in that state. With Seabra's electoral victory, the Bahian Republican Party (1901–12) disintegrated.

4. José Joaquim Seabra and the Taming of the Coronéis, 1912–1919

By MARCH 1912, when Seabra took office, Bahian politics was tempered by the strong personalism of coronéis and by the fragile institutions of fallen and nascent political parties. Bahian coronelismo had already ossified into the mold of a familiocratic oligarchy, firmly entrenched in parts of the state. The political and clan wars which intermittently ravaged the interior municípios after 1889 continued unchecked in the absence of an effective state authority operating in the sertão. The consolidation of coronelista power, therefore, was a natural outgrowth of Bahia's inability to bring "order and progress" to its political house. The dependence of the majority of the backlanders on coronéis had evolved in the absence of basic economic and social change after 1889, further enhancing the coronelista oligarchy's efforts to consolidate its power. By 1912, the biggest challenge any man could face as governor was the taming of coronéis and the restoring of, or rather the imposing of, an organized government as a higher authority in the interior.

Traditionally, the coronéis of the Recôncavo and the cacao country were less difficult to control politically than those in the

Lavras and São Francisco Valley. The two coastal regions depended on the capital for the operation of their export economy. Salvador was Bahia's chief export harbor, the state's banking center, and the seat of the state bureaucracy, all of which exercised a stranglehold on the export economy. Salvador was most of all a place of business, legal business in particular. Merchants and planters frequented the capital, and politicians used the dependence of the sugar and cacao growers on Salvador to create a willing clientele of the state government and the dominant party.

However, the coronelista politics of the Lavras and São Francisco Valley presented a contrasting pattern. After 1889, no governor succeeded in controlling these regions; the internal wars among the coronéis had the effect of readjusting the power status of the leading clans and families at the local level. When the state government did interfere, the general outcome was further inflammation of the wars and the eventual loss of the region to the enemies of the state-ruling cliques in the capital. The Castelo Brancos, the França Antuneses, and the Duques, to cite only the prestigious riverine dynasties, dominated the politics of the valley in alliance with equally powerful coronelista oligarchies in Goiás, Minas, Maranhão, and Piauí. In the Lavras, the Sás, the Gondims, and the Leãos ruled the mining region unchallenged.[1] The power of each of these coronelista clans was in turn reinforced by familial and business ties with members of the political elite of the backlands of other states; thus they established themselves as the rulers of the "states within a state" under the First Republic. Although fragmented into numerous semi-autonomous power enclaves that roughly correspond to a município, these coronelista families became the principal obstacle for Governor Seabra and his PRD in restoring the much-debased authority of the state.

J. J. SEABRA: THE STATE OLIGARCH

The man who was to tame the backlands and to erect one-party rule in Bahia for the next decade or so was born in Salvador in 1855. The son of a moderately rich man, José Joaquim attended

1. For the clan and coronelista division of power in Bahia, see Pang, "The Politics of *Coronelismo*," pp. 121–30.

the Faculty of Law in Recife, where, upon his graduation, he remained to teach. He ran unsuccessfully for the imperial Chamber of Deputies as a Conservative candidate only a few months before the fall of the empire in 1889.[2] In the formative years of the First Republic, Seabra got a reputation as a staunch defender of the democratic principles by attacking the Floriano Peixoto regime, then found himself in exile. Having never secured a proper place within the numerous ruling cliques and parties in Bahia, Seabra drifted in and out of politics until his appointment to the cabinet of President Rodrigues Alves in 1902. Equal in prestige but far more seasoned in politics than Rui Barbosa, Governor Seabra was to become one of the major political figures of Brazil under the First Republic. His hold on the governorship in 1912 served as a point of departure for his steady rise to national prominence over the next two decades. Needless to say, the stress of the Seabra government was on bringing order to state politics, not on good administration.

Seabra's taming of coronéis was to be achieved through monopolistic control of the electoral processes in the state. Strictly speaking, all elections under the First Republic were a two-step process of acquiring votes and having the electoral results canvassed by the state or federal legislature, depending on the nature of the election. In state and municipal elections, the state senate had the final say in the outcome. Whoever controlled the municípios held the key, at least in theory, to corralling votes, but the coronéis lacked the power to validate the results in the senate. Hence, mutual political dependency between coronéis and senators was forged and became a sine qua non in electoral politics. The two-way relationship between the municipal elite and the state (PRs) was the bond that held the two together in the central south. But in the northeast, such an arrangement never provided incentive for developing a strong party system. By his control over the majority in the

2. The standard and official biography of Seabra is written by Barros, *Dr. J. J. Seabra, sua vida, sua obra na república*. This is the first volume of a projected multi-volume biography which was never completed. The political party affiliation of Seabra before 1889 was difficult to label, because he stayed out of politics until then. However, he ran for the imperial Chamber of Deputies as the Conservative candidate from the second district in Salvador, advocating the establishment of the "federation of provinces." For details, see *Diário de Notícias*, August 30–31, 1889.

legislature, the incumbent governor could reject the elected as a means of containing his foes on partisan or personal grounds. Lacking the power to dictate their terms to all the coronéis of the state, governors increasingly resorted to violence (state police) or pre-election arrangements to secure necessary votes.

In many cases, such a quid pro quo accord resulted in a series of temporary alliances between the ruling party or clique in the capital and the coronéis of the backlands. For instance, a governor needed more than the legislature to have his son-in-law elected a state deputy. He needed votes from the coronéis. Conversely, coronéis could not hope to get elected intendentes themselves, or their sons and sons-in-laws deputies, without obtaining recognition from the senate to validate the votes received. Hence, a mutual arrangement by governor and coronéis was required for the proportional distribution of votes and for the determination of which "outsiders" should be allowed to run in a particular backland district. Furthermore, when the electoral results were challenged by the opposition in a duplicata, it became more than ever essential to have the governor's support to assure final victory.

Consequently, the top priority of Governor Seabra in 1912 was control of the state legislature, especially the senate. This would give him the bargaining power to remap the political geography of Bahian coronelismo. By mid-1913, the majority of the state senators abandoned the defunct PRB by crossing over to the PRD. The senators' need for the support of the governor was equally compelling. Traditionally, senators handled matters of electoral arrangements, patronage, and public works for the municípios. With the PRD governor in power, the former PRB lawmakers had no choice but to "play politics" with the new official party, if they were interested in expanding patronage and public works for their districts. Understandably, the first ones to defect were those senators who represented the export zones of the Recôncavo and Ilhéus; but once the exodus was on, such prestigious backland senators as Coronel César Sá of Lençóis and Monsenhor Hermelino Leão of Macaúbas willingly joined the PRD, making Seabra's control of the state legislature a reality. With this political victory, Seabra and his party bosses prepared to face the state and federal elections of 1914.

PINHEIRO MACHADO AND NORTHERN POLITICS

The 1914 presidential election began with an internal power struggle between Pinheiro Machado and his foes. In the northern part of the country, the oligarchic allies of the Gaúcho senator were being ousted one by one by the adherents of "rescue politics," when, in January 1913, Governor Seabra broke with Luís Viana, the chief of the PRC-Bahia, ostensibly over the question of a foreign loan to the state.[3] A year later, General Dantas Barreto, governor of Pernambuco, refused to join the PRC, even under pressure from President Hermes da Fonseca.[4] Events in Ceará in January and February 1914 indicated that the political fortunes of Pinheiro Machado were sagging further: the Gaúcho provoked the wrath of the Acioli oligarchy and his backland sponsor, Padre Cícero, in southern Ceará by initially supporting Army Colonel Franco Rabelo for governor. The private armies of the Acioli-Cícero group stormed Fortaleza and unseated Governor Rabelo. In addition, the officer corps of the army was resentful of Pinheiro's use of federal armed forces for his personal political gain, and some even manifested outright criticism.[5] In short, the prestige of the Gaúcho senator in both the north and the capital was at a new low.

The brief candidacy of Pinheiro Machado was doomed. The political kingmakers forced Pinheiro, who was losing ground in the north, to support the candidacy of Vice President Wenceslau Brás for president. Urbano Santos da Costa Araújo of Maranhão, one of the few states unscathed by the "politics of rescue" in the north, was selected to become the vice presidential candidate. In the opposition, Rui Barbosa began his rousing campaign to become for a second time the candidate for the "outs" of various states. But, due to a lack of general political support, Rui soon abandoned his candidacy, leaving uncontested the election of Wenceslau Brás. Seabra, who would not have backed

3. Birch to Secretary of State, Bahia, January 19, 1913, no. 6, fls. 193–96, Internal Affairs of Brazil, Reel 4, 823.00/51–225, DOS/USNA.
4. Hermes' emissary was José Tomás da Cunha e Vasconcelos. See Griffith to Secretary of State, Recife (Pernambuco), January 30, 1914, no dispatch number, fls. 217–21, ibid.
5. On the situation in Ceará, see ibid.; on the military attitude toward Pinheiro, see Morgan to Secretary of State, Rio, March 10, 1914, No. 334, fls. 225–28, ibid.

Rui's candidacy under any circumstances, was saved from the potential embarrassment of having to oppose a fellow Bahian, who still commanded a following in state politics.[6]

More important to the strengthening of the PRD were the legislative and municipal elections of 1914. At stake were the seats of twenty-two federal deputies, seven state senators, forty-two state deputies, 141 intendentes, and 833 councilmen throughout the state. In the federal congress, the PRD more than doubled its representation by winning fourteen of the twenty-two seats. Among the new Seabrista deputies were Otávio Mangabeira, Antônio Moniz, Moniz Sodré, and the Bahian bancada chief Mário Hermes, a son of President Fonseca. From the opposition (the former PRB and PRC-Bahia), João Mangabeira, Antônio Calmon, Pires de Carvalho, Pedro Lago, and Miguel Calmon were elected. Former PRB senator Severino Vieira, who ran for the chamber of deputies, became a victim of congressional rejection, or degola, forcing the diminuitive politician to retire for good.[7]

The electoral verification power of the state legislature, unlike that of the federal congress, did not become an object of scrutiny by the federal president and therefore was tailored to satisfy the needs of the PRD. In the lower house, the majority of deputies were elected from PRD members and supporters. The senate, already under the domination of Seabra, dutifully endorsed the victory of the intendentes of key municípios to suit the PRD needs. Under the guidance of such Seabra loyalists as Coronel Frederico Costa and Coronel Antônio Pessoa, the existing local coronéis were systematically recruited into the PRD ranks: Aprígio Duarte Filho in Juàzeiro, Janjão Sento Sé in Sento Sé, Ubaldino de Assis in Cachoeira, and Dantas Bião of Alagoinhas lent even more prestige to the ascending power of the official party.

6. *A Tarde* (Bahia), January 2, 1914; for details of the São Paulo–Minas–Pernambuco alliance behind the candidacy of Wenceslau Brás and Seabra's willingness to support the tri-state candidate, see Guerino Casanta, *Correspondência de Bueno Brandão*, pp. 44–45, 178–80, 187. José Bezerra of Pernambuco (its bancada leader in the federal Chamber of Deputies) "leaked" the story that Seabra authorized Mário Hermes (the Bahian bancada leader and a son of the president) to support Wenceslau, not Rui. For details, see *A Tarde*, August 16, 1913; for the abortive campaign of 1914, see João Mangabeira, *Rui, o estadista da república*, pp. 235–36; see also R. Magalhães Júnior, *Rui, o homem e o mito*, pp. 276–88, and Belo, *A History of Modern Brazil*, pp. 226–27.

7. *A Tarde*, December 14–18, 1914.

ANTI-SEABRA OLIGARCHS

Not everyone was willing to knuckle under to Seabra's rule. In the Recôncavo, the traditional oligarchies of the Calmons, the Araújo Pinhos, and the Prisco Paraísos (the historic supporters of the former PRB) remained in the opposition camp. In south Bahia, Coronel Marcionílio Antônio de Sousa, the patrician-fazendeiro in Maracás, stayed out of the PRD. In the São Francisco Valley, where personality and clan politics always intermingled, Anfilófio Castelo Branco and Francisco Leobas, both of Remanso, José Nogueira of Xique-Xique, Franklin Lins of Pilão Arcado, and João Duque of Carinhanha refused to join the PRD. In the Lavras, the rival clans of PRD senators Coronel César Sá and Monsenhor Hermelino Leão rebuffed the governor's party. This left Douca Medrado of Mucugê, Aureliano de Gondim of Andaraí, and Horácio de Matos of Chapada Velha as the important "out" coronéis of the region.

Although the personality of the governor had much to do with enticing or repulsing potential supporters in the backlands, clan disputes played a more important role in a coronel's final decision to join the dominant party. There were several incidences where Governor Seabra mixed two traditional means of persuasion, unleashing the state police and recruiting the victor of a local war, in his approach to building up the PRD. In 1914, he refused to intervene in Maracás where the PRD boss was ruthlessly attacked by Marcionílio de Sousa, who was considered by the governor to be the more effective politician; instead Seabra allowed Marcionílio to chase the PRD coronel out of the município.[8] In Ângical of the São Francisco Valley, Coronel José Joaquim de Almeida, the colorless PRD boss, had failed to produce a good "electoral turnout" and was overthrown by a bacharel, whom the governor swiftly chose as his surrogate. In Nazaré, a district of the capital, the traditional ward boss disappointed the governor with poor electoral results and was tossed out when Seabra and city hall shut off his access to patronage.[9] As a whole, Seabra demonstrated superb skill and flexibility in siding with winners.

Seabra's early dealings with the Matos clan of the Lavras did

8. Ibid., November 13, 1915; for the details, see Pang, "The Politics of Coronelismo," pp. 133–35.
9. A Tarde, January 16, 29, 1915.

not seem out of the ordinary. The Matoses migrated to central Bahia from Diamantinas, Minas Gerais, soon after the discovery of diamonds early in the 1840s. The clan, settled down in Chapada Velha, became the bulwark of the Conservative Party in a region predominantly controlled by Liberals. After the fall of the empire, clan wars spread throughout the backlands, and, in 1893, the Lavras was divided into two warring camps made up of many rival families. The Sá clan, led by Coronel Felisberto, controlled Lençóis and its satellite municípios; Coronel Heliodoro de Ribeiro led another faction. The government supported the Sá group, and, in a series of political and clan wars, the Luís Viana government unsuccessfully intervened in favor of the Sás. In this violent confrontation, Coronel Clementino, the patriarch of the Matos clan, found himself allied with the anti-government party, thus provoking the wrath of the powerful Sá family and the state government.[10] The tradition of opposing the government and its allies was passed on to the next generation of the clan.

SUPERCORONEL HORÁCIO DE MATOS AND THE PRD

In 1913, the patriarch of the Matos tribe died. On his deathbed, Clementino designated his nephew Horácio, not his own sons, to succeed to the clan leadership.[11] Horácio de Quieroz Matos was born in 1882, son of Quintiliano Pereira de Matos and brother of Clementino. Young Horácio grew up unschooled at Capim Duro in the district of Chapada Velha, the clan redoubt. Leaving home to become a merchant, Horácio settled in Morro do Chapeu where he befriended its chief coronel, Francisco Dias Coelho, the leading diamond merchant in Bahia. About 1910, Coelho arranged for Horácio a National Guard commission as lieutenant colonel, a sure indication that the young man was being groomed for future political leadership in Morro. But it was the clan patriarch's call to his deathbed that brought Horácio home. Along with Padre Cícero of Ceará, Horácio de Matos was destined to become one of the most powerful backland political warlords of the First Brazilian Republic, especially in the 1920s.

10. Moraes, *Jagunços e heróis*, pp. 38–43; Américo Chagas, *O cangaceiro Montalvão*, pp. 19–20; Pang, "The Politics of *Coronelismo*," pp. 136–38.
11. Chagas, *O chefe Horácio de Matos*, p. 21; Moraes, *Jagunços e heróis*, pp. 48–49.

In 1914, the ruling Seabrista clique in the Lavras was made up of state senators César Sá and Monsenhor Hermelino Leão and two regional chiefs, Coronel Manuel Fabrício of Campestre and Coronel Militão Coelho of Barra do Mendes. These four dominated local politics as Seabra's handpicked PRD directors. Militão had been embroiled with the Matoses in a clan war; upon his assumption of the clan leadership, Horácio arranged a truce as a show of his good intentions as a peaceful man. Both the clan and Militão, exhausted by the war, consented to a truce. No sooner was peace with Militão restored than another clan war broke out in a post-electoral brawl. Vítor de Matos, a brother of Horácio, was a candidate for a minor local office, but the PRD chief of Campestre refused to accept his candidacy. When the insistent Vítor ran anyway, he was assassinated by PRD henchmen. The chief of Campestre, Manuel Fabrício, was accused of having ordered the killing, and the Matoses demanded that Horácio retaliate.[12]

But the clan chief was reluctant to start another bloodbath. He prevailed over his aggrieved clansmen, persuading them to seek justice through the state government. Months went by without results; Manuel Fabrício was the "law" in the little barony of Campestre, and the state government had no intention of interfering with the PRD coronel's politics. The unwritten rule in the dominant party was that the state not involve itself as long as its coronel was not in danger. As the effort for a peaceful settlement was thwarted, Aunt Casimira, the dowager queen of the clan, ordered the men to seek revenge. Horácio placed himself at the head of the warring clansmen.[13]

After months of fighting, the war persisted without an end in sight. The Sá and Militão groups came to the aid of their ally Manuel Fabrício. Commerce in the region was disrupted and the local economy damaged. The Bahian Commercial Association was besieged with telegrams from regional merchants clamoring for intervention. The PRD state senators from the Lavras, Coronel César Sá and Monsenhor Hermelino, pressed the governor to dispatch the state police in support of Manuel Fabrício. The governor resisted at first but finally acquiesced

12. Moraes, pp. 49–50, 53–56; Chagas, *O chefe Horácio*, pp. 23–26; Olímpio Antônio Barbosa, *Horácio de Matos, sua vida e suas lutas*, pp. 15–26.
13. Barbosa, pp. 15–26; Pang, "The Politics of *Coronelismo*," pp. 139–41.

by sending a police unit to rescue the beleaguered PRD boss of Campestre, a town in Brotas.[14]

By mid-1915, the combined forces of the state police and the local PRD private armies were resoundingly defeated by the Matos clan. The town of Campestre, where Manuel Fabrício and his jagunços had dug in, was under siege by Horácio's forces for forty-two days. Two police expeditions failed to relieve the siege. Both sides were running out of men and matériel. Horácio lost a brother and Manuel Fabrício a son.[15] The police were convinced that the Matoses could not be defeated without further bloodshed. The clan's resolution to fight to the last man and the lack of military success on the part of the local PRD group easily convinced Governor Seabra to reconsider his tactics. The new state strategy was to seek a truce in the Lavras and recognize the status quo there.

Over the vehement protests of Sá and Hermelino Leão, Seabra appointed a truce commission headed by eminent backland chiefs and state officials. Douca Medrado of Mucugê (Horácio's future father-in-law), Aurelino Gondim of Andaraí, José de Sousa Guedes of Rio de Contas, and Padre Antônio Romualdo of Bom Jesus de Lapa were named as truce commissioners. After a series of meetings, the commission consented to Horácio's demands.[16] The state reopened the case of the Vítor's murder, and the Lavras again returned to a shaky armed truce.

STATE VS. CLANS

The clan wars in Brazil had a particular sociopolitical function, historically. The Brazilian clan, in addition to kinship as defined by consanguine ties (*parentesco carnal*), by godchildren (*parentesco espiritual*), and by in-laws (*parentesco de aliança*), also included social and economic dependents.[17] Since the days

14. Pang, pp. 139–41; Moraes, *Jagunços e heróis*, pp. 42–47; Chagas, *O chefe Horácio*, pp. 53–59.

15. The war between Horácio and Militão was recounted in *O Democrata*, August 9, 1919. This paper, the organ of the PRD, consistently referred to Horácio as a "bandit."

16. Chagas, *O chefe Horácio*, pp. 46–47; *A Tarde*, July 7, 1915.

17. Queiroz, "O coronelismo numa interpretação," pp. 164–65; Pierson, *O homem no vale do São Francisco*, 3:29–66. Pierson reports that in Vareda, between the two São Francisco River tributaries of Jacaré and Verde (Bahia), live 4,000–5,000 people with the same surname of Autran (this is a fictitious name),

of the crown vs. donatory conflict over political power, the clan
has served as the champion of such wars. Insulated from outside interference, it was an economic unit, a polity, and a sub-
society. Legal authority was often resisted during colonial
times, and even in the late nineteenth and early twentieth
centuries, the state was virtually powerless over the clan-
dominated backlands. To buttress mutually reinforcing socioeconomic ties, the clansmen came to rally around their patriarch, to whom the group's loyalty was directed. The "state"
remained an abstract notion, at best. Thus private justice prevailed over the king's law, and private revenge struck a faster
blow than the state police. In time, the clan came to defend its
own social, economic, and political interests against outsiders,
whether of another clan in the region or of an organized government. In protracted private quarrels, allied clans often
helped out the beleaguered by directly involving their military
personnel. Under the First Republic, the backland clan war
developed a special sociopolitical function, that of determining
the boundaries of an autonomous state within a state. Administrative federalism notwithstanding, the "clan-state" was further perpetuated by the inability of organized government to
furnish the very services that the clan offered. The chronic
political instability in the northern half of the country considerably weakened the state's authority in the first two decades of the First Republic, and it was during this time that the
major clans of the sertão engaged in wars to redefine the
boundaries of their power against other clans and against the
state. The clan wars in the Lavras in the mid-1910s were
caused precisely by the absence or weakness of the adjudi-
cating power of the state. The clan influence over sociopolitical
matters began to decline only as Brazil entered a phase of
centralization after 1930.

SEABRA'S MUNICIPAL REFORM OF 1915

Governor Seabra found a partial remedy for the clan monopoly
of power in the interior in the centralization of patronage and
the selection of public officials in the municípios. Under the

---

all related to each other (pp. 52-54). Furthermore, one woman who married into
such a big clan said that her relatives numbered 990. Pierson provides a table of
various types of relatives (p. 53).

state constitution of 1891, Bahia permitted each município to elect its intendente. The electoral system for the chief executive could be manipulated easily, as long as politics between governor and coronéis was well regulated by one-party rule and/or strong state power backed up by military forces, as in São Paulo, Minas, and Rio Grande. Here the opportunities for the local coronéis to rebel against the state political leaders were further minimized by expanding economic opportunities that permitted a higher degree of social and physical mobility than there was in the northern half of the country. Consequently, violence was not the sole means of adjusting power relationships between governor and coronéis. The PRs came to serve not only as election enforcers but also as intermediaries for the dominant economic interests in their contact with state and federal governments. In the northern half of the country, such vital functions were assumed not by the party but by individual politicians. The quid pro quo arrangement therefore was not institutionalized on a permanent basis, and as governors came and went, so did the arrangement. The man who dominated the município was inevitably the intendente, and the political support of the coronel-intendente was crucial to Seabra's objective of instituting one-party rule in Bahia.

The Reform Law of August 11, 1915, was enacted to meet the needs of Seabra and his PRD by making appointive the selection of intendentes. Once in office, the intendente would serve four years at the pleasure of the governor. In 1915, the state had 141 of these positions to be filled.[18] Although few realized it at first, the proper implementation of the reform law could, in the long run, lead to a profound change in Bahian politics. It could alter the power relationship between governor and coronéis and between governor and legislators. The centralization of appointments could increase the dependency of the intendentes on the governor rather than on the state senate. Consequently, the political clout of the senate, once based on its power of verification of municipal elections, evaporated overnight. In short, Governor Seabra built a system of equilibrium that called for a new balance of power against the coronéis, circumventing the senatorial power brokers. This change facil-

18. *A Tarde*, October 30, 1915.

itated the rise of partisan rule, the final step toward the taming of the coronéis. The reform law also expanded Seabra's ability to monopolize electoral processes in the state.

During his last four months in office (December 1915–March 1916), the governor took full advantage of the reform law by appointing 135 new intendentes (of a total of 141).[19] Such a sweeping change in the administrative structure at the município level was essential if Seabra were to remain in power after March 1916, even though he ran the risk of provoking another cycle of coronelista violence. The state constitution did not allow him to succeed himself, thus requiring him to sit out one term. During his absence, he had to retain control over the PRD and the intendentes ("the vote-givers") if he were to return to power four years later. Furthermore, once control over the intendentes was secured, Seabra could dictate whatever electoral results he desired, which further enhanced his political prestige at the state and national levels.

PICKING SEABRA'S SUCCESSOR

Seabra's first test of survival as the state oligarch came in 1915 as the question of his successor aroused much discussion in political circles. By July, the names of several frontrunners were mentioned, Federal Senator Rui Barbosa and federal deputies Antônio Moniz and José Joaquim Palma. In theory, the PRD was a unified party, but in reality, it was made up of three major factions, each led by a strong man. Seabra loyalists were in the majority, and Rui's supporters and the Otávio Mangabeira wing of the former PRB constituted two minorities. The governor, aware of friction among the contending currents in his own party, was extraordinarily cautious about his choice as successor. One wrong move could set off the latent factionalism and destroy the unity of the PRD. Rui, a nominal PRD senator, never accepted Seabra as his boss, much less recognized the legitimacy of Seabra's claim as state chief. Mangabeira, although a strong Seabra supporter, was at odds with the Monizes (Antônio and Moniz Sodré). In addition, Mangabeira had strong connections with the anti-PRD ele-

19. *Diário Oficial* (Bahia), October 1, 1915.

ments in state politics—brother João was an opposition federal deputy from Ilhéus.

For the first three weeks of August, Governor Seabra walked a tightrope. The PRD state chieftains pressured him to hold the state convention on August 19; federal deputies from Bahia, meeting in Rio, were deadlocked over the choice among Rui, Antônio Moniz, and José Joaquim Palma. In Salvador, the governor demanded that PRD regulars guarantee their support of his handpicked successor; in return, he promised to appoint the intendentes recommended by local political bosses. This reciprocal arrangement paved the way for passage of the municipal reform law by August 11, 1915. The following day, José Álvaro Cova, the party chief's emissary in Rio, reported that opposition outside the PRD was attempting to persuade Rui to be a coalition candidate.[20] By then, Seabra had won the first battle by gaining control of the state political machine through the reform law.

When Seabra named Antônio Moniz his successor and received the convention's endorsement, the reluctant Otávio Mangabeira went along, but Rui did not.[21] Contrary to the impression that Rui's biographers have created, the Bahian senator was, according to some contemporaries, egotistic, vengeful, and not completely honest.[22] With his oversized head, Rui commanded both national and international prestige as an eminent jurist; but with his equally oversized ego, Rui was shunned by intellectually inferior machine politicians. Ceaselessly pontificating his own grandeur, Rui made more enemies than friends. The frustrated Bahian senator, unable to capture the presidency, became increasingly violent in his attacks on his enemies, particularly Seabra, both as an individual and as the PRD oligarch. The governor dispatched the senator's son, Ruizinho Barbosa, as his emissary to seek endorsement of the Moniz candidacy. The father-son meeting produced nothing more constructive than a charge that Seabra was the usurper of Bahian politics, and, in a typically volatile response, Rui

20. Seabra to Cova, Bahia, August 13, 1915, Cova to Seabra, Rio, August 12, 1915, Arquivo de Gonçalo Moniz, hereafter cited as AGM.

21. Mangabeira to Seabra, Rio, August 13, 1915, ibid.

22. For such a critical view, see Dudley to Secretary of State, Petrópolis, March 4, 1910, no. 500, fls. 6–9, Internal Affairs of Brazil, Reel 4, 823.00/51–225, DOS/USNA; Magalhães Júnior, in *Rui, o homem e o mito*, is, on the whole, not flattering to the Bahian politician.

severed his ties with the governor and the PRD.[23] The vindictive old man could not tolerate Seabra's rise to national prominence through the PRD machine. With a subservient Moniz in Salvador, Seabra could replace Rui as the national spokesman of Bahia. This had to be stopped at all costs, and 1915 was not the last time that Rui Barbosa disrupted the partisan unity of his state for selfish reasons.

In spite of Rui's bolting the PRD, Seabra succeeded in completing his takeover of state politics. He was taming or institutionalizing the political life of Bahia through PRD rule and his strong personalism. The municipal reform of the previous August allowed the Seabrista party to hold 135 intendentes by March 1916, thus assuring the election of Antônio Moniz. Further hold over the state was secured by the expansion of the local patronage army, ranging from state and federal tax collectors to post office clerks and schoolteachers; all these positions were given to the entourage of the dominant coronel. After 1916, intendentes and coronéis had become, for most purposes, synonymous, representing both the PRD and the dominant local elite.[24] José Joaquim Seabra finally became the welder and arbiter of Bahian politics, and for the next decade he was to rule the state as the head of his personalistic oligarchy.

THE MONIZES IN POWER

The first Moniz arrived in Bahia in 1549. A son of this distinguished clan, Antônio, born in 1875, became the first governor educated in the state law school in Bahia. Graduating in 1894, he was briefly a professor at the Escola Politécnica of Bahia, and he entered politics in 1909 as a Seabra supporter. Antônio Ferrão Moniz de Aragão rose steadily in the hierarchy of the Seabrista organization, becoming second in command when Seabra became governor. With Moniz Sodré, his cousin and brother-in-law, he held various state and federal offices and emerged as one of a few nationally important Bahian politicians of the First Republic.[25]

23. Barbosa to Seabra, Rio, August 14, 1915, Pasta José Joaquim Seabra, Arquivo da Casa de Rui Barbosa, hereafter cited as ACRB.
24. It became customary to use the title "coronel-intendente" instead of "intendente," especially when referring to a chief of an interior município.
25. See Costa, "Genealogia baiana," pp. 31-43, on the Monizes; for the

When Moniz assumed the governorship in April 1916, municipal politics of the state was securely in the hands of the PRD, with a few exceptions. The majority of new Seabrista intendentes were loyal party fawners or prospective converts. Only in the south and in the São Francisco Valley did Seabra run into resistance when he chose to name his own men to intendencies, but no major violent confrontations took place. In Belmonte and Itabuna in the cacao country, citizens petitioned the governor to retain the incumbent intendentes, but Seabra appointed his own men (from the local coronéis) who took over the administration with only minor incidents.[26] Seabra was elected, without challenge, to fill the federal deputy's seat vacated by Antônio Moniz. The PRD, now more powerful than ever, was reorganized: Seabra was made president of the executive committee, the decision-making organ of the party; Moniz was made vice president; Coronel Frederico Costa, the senate president, was named party secretary. The committeemen came from various parts of the state, but there was heavy representation from the urban sectors. Unlike the PRB, the mainstream elite of the PRD did not come from the ranks of the rural agrarian aristocracy but rather from Salvador's urban groups and from the ranks of professional politicians. It was an urban party in its makeup, built upon the personal charisma of J. J. Seabra, with the objective of putting together a new coalition of Seabrista loyalists. The party founded its daily paper, *O Democrata*, to assure an independent means of articulating its position.[27] Judging from these developments, it became clear that Seabra was to remain as the chief of Bahian politics with Moniz a mere stand-in.

The first two years of the Moniz government were eventful. The PRD Executive Committee recommended that the four-year term of an intendency be reduced to two years and that each município be required to file its annual financial report with the governor on January 1 each year. The bill passed in the legislature without opposition.[28] Such a measure would further tighten the governor's control over municipal politics, and the absence of overt opposition signified the virtual acceptance of the PRD as the only legitimate party of the state. In order to blunt any sharp reaction to the amendment of the 1915 reform, the governor liberally dispensed the patronage that Seabra had not exhausted, especially judicial appointments of secondary importance such as suplentes.[29]

The significant political development in the first half of the Moniz rule was the emergence of a coalition of Bahia's opposition forces. There were four factions of opposition: the traditional two PRB factions of the Marcelinistas and Severinistas, the former PRC-Bahia group led by Luís Viana, and Rui and his followers who had abandoned the PRD in the wake of the succession question late in 1915. José Marcelino died in April 1917 and Araújo Pinho in June. The federal senate seat of José Marcelino was contested by Seabra and Severino Vieira, and there was no doubt as to the winner.[30] In October, Luís Viana, who with full backing of the PRP in São Paulo called for unity among the opposition forces, judged the moment to be right.[31]

29. From November 5 to December 5, 1916, Moniz appointed a total of 35 suplentes, of whom 22 were coronéis, 8 majores, 2 capitães, and 3 "civilians" (*Diário Oficial*, November 5, 10–11, 22, 24, 30, December 1, 3, 5, 1916). Even in the 1890s in Pernambuco, the holders of National Guard titles often received the appointments as suplentes. Gov. Correia de Araújo made 165 appointments in 44 municípios, or 3 suplentes each. By titles, there were 6 coronéis, 17 tenentes-coronéis, 17 majores, 20 capitães, 10 tenentes (including *alferes*), 6 doutores (médicos), 1 bacharel (law), and 88 with no title. See *Mensagem apresentada ao Congresso Legislativo do Estado em 6 de março de 1899 pelo Governador Dr. Joaquim Correia de Araújo* (Pernambuco [Recife], 1899), pp. 19–25.

30. *Mensagem apresentada à Assembléia Geral Legislativa do Estado da Bahia na abertura da 2ª sessão ordinária da 14ª legislatura pelo Dr. Antônio Ferrão Moniz de Aragão Governador do Estado* (Bahia, 1918), pp. 52–53. José Marcelino died on April 26, 1917, Araújo Pinho on July 23, 1917, and Severino Vieira on September 27, 1917. See *A Tarde* for these dates; brief biographical sketches were given in the obituaries.

31. *A Tarde*, October 2, 1917. Viana's ties with the PRP dated back to the 1890s; it was alleged that he first suggested Campos Sales as the successor to Prudente de Morais. Campos Sales' visit to Bahia after the election was considered as a grateful gesture to the Bahian governor (Bulcão Sobrinho, "O homem do norte—Luís Viana," p. 24). Bulcão Sobrinho argued (p. 31) that, after the deaths of José Marcelino and Severino Vieira, Viana formally broke with Seabra in 1918, joining Rui as a leader of the opposition. In fact, Viana broke with Seabra in 1913 over the question of foreign loans. For details, see Birch to Secretary of State, Bahia, January 13, 1913, no. 6, fls. 193–96, Internal Affairs of Brazil, Reel 4, 823.00/51–225, DOS/USNA. Seabra was also criticized by the Bahian Commercial Association for favoring the French capitalist who planned to establish an agricultural credit bank in Bahia. For details, see *Relatório da Diretoria da Associação Comercial da Bahia lido e aprovado em reunião da Assembléia Geral Ordinária de 28 de fevereiro de 1914 (exercício de 1913)* (Bahia, 1914), Anexo III,

The presidential election of 1918 was approaching, and it was seen as an opportunity for the Bahian opposition to be reinstated in power, especially if it secured a federal cabinet post in the new presidential administration. Moniz was tired of playing second fiddle to Seabra and began to assert his own influence, especially in matters of patronage.

The slowly growing opposition of the commercial community to the Moniz administration was an unexpected but welcome development, linked with events resulting from World War I which were, in fact, beyond the control of the state government. In late 1914, Great Britain imposed an embargo on exports from Brazil to Germany and Austria. In April 1915, the British navy seized a shipment of 1,908 sacks of Bahian cacao and 1,600 sacks of coffee on their way to Copenhagen. The seizure and internment of the Bahian shipment was serious: Wildberger and Co., Ângelo de Araújo and Co., and other prestigious commercial houses in Bahia demanded that Governor Moniz intercede with the Brazilian Foreign Ministry. The governor did so but was not successful in obtaining satisfactory results from Itamarati, though it dutifully protested the seizure. By 1916, even Portugal was engaged in the international game of harassment and seizure of neutral ships carrying Brazilian cargoes, allegedly destined for Germany.[32] The Bahian mercantile colony blamed the ineffectual Moniz government for failing to stop these incidents. Well before Moniz completed his term of office, the Bahian commercial class had become anti-PRD.

MONIZ' ABUSE OF POWER AND BACKLAND CORONÉIS

The opposition found unexpected help coming from none other than the governor. Eager to shed his image as Seabra's crony and to build his own machine, Moniz began to circumvent the PRD Executive Committee for patronage distribution. The more obnoxious Seabra loyalists who were suspected of anti-

pp. 4–10 specifically, Contrato celebrado entre o Governo do Estado da Bahia e o Sr. Dr. Eduardo Guinlé ou Sociedade que organisar para fundação do Banco de Crédito Hipotecário e Agrícola do Estado da Bahia.

32. Cabassu and Lima to Presidente da República, Bahia, October 20, 1914 (Cabassu was the president of the Bahian Commercial Association), Seabra to Muller, Bahia, April 30, 1915, Moniz to Muller, Bahia (n.d.) 1916, all in Bahia: Telegramas Recebidos 1888–1926, 307/4/2, AHI.

Moniz sentiments were summarily dismissed and replaced. Such frequent moves riled the PRD fathers who accused the governor of seriously endangering partisan harmony. Three incidents are worth mentioning.

The first involved the appointment of an intendente in the cacao-rich município of Una, which had been ruled by a Seabrista. In 1917, the governor fired the coronel and named his own bodyguard, a state police lieutenant, to the post.[33] The nomination not only failed to meet the approval of the Una elite but also offended such party chiefs as Antônio Pessoa, the nominal dispenser of patronage in southern Bahia, and Frederico Costa, the senate president. Then Governor Moniz was implicated in a double murder plot. In 1918, one of the governor's nephews, a recent law school graduate, was named to the intendency of Belmonte. In Bahia, nepotism was (and still is) neither a public nor a private sin, but the opposition paper (*A Hora*) condemned the appointment by insinuating that it was designed to peculate the treasury of the rich município. When the governor's nephew ran into the paper's editor in a nightclub, the young man shot at his tormentor but missed. A few days later, a political confidant of Moniz encountered the editor, who he mistakenly thought was about to kill him. The journalist was frightened by the chance meeting, and he panicked and fatally shot the unarmed man.[34] Governor Moniz dispatched state police to burn down the newspaper plant.

The most serious incident involved Moniz' failure to deal in a conciliatory way with the coronéis of the interior. As soon as the clan wars in the Lavras Diamantinas were brought under control in 1915, the state was once again drawn into a political war in the Middle São Francisco Valley. In the town of Pilão Arcado, the traditional ruling elite was the PRD triumvirate of José Correia de Lacerda, Antônio Joaquim Correia, and Adolfo Gomes de Queiroz. Coronel Lacerda served as a state deputy, while Queiroz and Correia ran the politics of Pilão Arcado as intendente and councilman, respectively. Under Moniz rule, the political power of the triumvirate steadily expanded and inevitably led to the merciless persecution of local citizens. By

33. *A Tarde,* February 7, 1917; for details, see Pang, "The Politics of *Coronelismo*," p. 155; José Álvaro Cova, *Relatório apresentado ao Exmo. Sr. Dr. Antônio Ferrão Moniz de Aragão.*

34. *A Tarde,* October 7, 1917.

early January 1918, the local residents approached Coronel Franklin Lins de Albuquerque to ask him to lead an anti-PRD revolt. The coronel accepted the challenge, and the war was on. When the local PRD coronéis were unable to contain the war, the governor sent in state police to bail out the troika.[35]

In spite of state intervention, the war lasted almost a year and spread to other municípios of the valley. Commerce came to a standstill, and police brutality threatened to force the entire valley into political opposition to the state government. In Remanso, the neighboring município, Coronel Anfilófio de Castelo Branco joined the revolt by overthrowing the PRD intendente and effectively neutralized the state police there.[36] By November 1918, the war had practically been won by anti-Moniz coronéis. The ranches and cattle that had belonged to the PRD chiefs were openly taken as booty and divided among the victors.[37] Unlike Seabra, Governor Moniz refused to reconcile with the new elite of the valley by denying them his recognition of their legitimacy. For all practical purposes, the presence of the Bahian government was not felt in the valley for the next two years.

For the remainder of Moniz' term, charged emotion, invective rhetoric, and general civil disturbances in the sertão dominated both the government and the opposition press. In late 1917, Rui Barbosa viciously attacked Governor Moniz, calling him a "worthless devil" and Seabra a "wire-puller." The federal senator named himself as the unifier of Bahian opposition.[38] In the state elections of 1918, the governor further blundered by alienating Seabrista candidates. When the battle

35. Ibid., March 13, 1918; Lins, *O médio São Francisco*, p. 79.

36. Lins, pp. 79 ff.; *A Tarde*, May 1, June 6, October 25, November 23, 1918.

37. After the Revolution of 1930, one official investigating team revealed that Franklin and other coronéis in the Middle São Francisco Valley had been engaged in illegal property-seizing as well as murder and were never prosecuted by the state. For details, see Leopoldo Braga, *Uma sinistra história de roubos, saques, e homicídios*, esp. pp. 9–13; the full report by the state prosecutor was published in *Diário Oficial*, June 3–4, 1931. Wilson Lins, *Os cabras do coronel*, *O reduto*, and *Remanso da valentia* are a trilogy of novels based on the real life of the coronelista world in the Middle São Francisco Valley. The coronel of the novels is a fictionalized version of the author's father, Franklin Lins de Albuquerque.

38. *A Tarde*, September 27, 1917. Rui was soon joined by a new breed of politicians in the movement to oppose the PRD; for details, see Pang, "The Politics of *Coronelismo*," pp. 156–57.

over the nomination of the party's senators and deputies was fought between the Moniz faction and the Seabra loyalists, the governor unwisely chose to remove a few powerful personal opponents. One such victim was Senator Dantas Bião, the political boss of Alagoinhas and an ally of Otávio Mangabeira and Frederico Costa. The deposed Dantas Bião saw his rejection by Governor Moniz as an attempt by the Moniz group to reduce the influence of the Mangabeira and Costa factions.[39]

THE DIVIDED PRD

It soon became clear that the upper echelon of the PRD might split permanently if Seabra, as party chief, further neglected the problem of the rising tide of dissent by entrusting Moniz to manage the party at the state level. It was no secret that the governor and the senate president did not agree on many issues, especially on the method of handling the interior coronéis and patronage. Under the Seabra administration, Frederico Costa had been kept well informed of and consulted on all the political moves and appointments that Seabra had made. In return, the coronel–senate president emerged as the PRD dispenser of favors in the capitol, using his power and influence to ratify Seabra's nominees and to check adversaries.

No such cooperation existed between Costa and Moniz. In the absence of an effective working relationship between the governor and his legislative leaders, Moniz relied more and more on his own judgment and carried out policies that were often opposed by the party hierarchy. Frederico Costa, the leading Seabra loyalist and an open admirer of Rui Barbosa, let it be known that he did not approve of the incumbent governor and vaguely suggested that he might quit the PRD and join the Bahian opposition.[40] By all accounts, this was no idle threat. To keep the PRD united would require far more than mere fence mending.

39. *A Tarde*, December 28, 1918; Seabra to Mangabeira, Bahia, no date (telegram), Arquivo do Otávio Mangabeira, hereafter cited as AOM.
40. *A Tarde*, December 28, 1918.

5. Coronelista Revolts in the Backlands and Consolidation of "States within a State"

THE YEAR 1919 was a momentous time for Bahia. The April presidential election once again divided the state beyond repair, inflaming political hatred between the followers and opponents of Rui Barbosa. A series of coronelista wars in the Lavras Diamantinas and the São Francisco Valley flared up, initially against the local PRD chieftains, to become eventually a collective war of coronéis against the state. As a final blow, the bitterly contested gubernatorial election in December resulted in the escalation of backland revolts and in federal intervention by February 1920. Paradoxically, no one paid much attention to the signs of revolt that had been growing steadily since the administrative reforms of 1915 and 1916 in the Lavras and the São Francisco regions.

Seabra's intrusion into the political autonomy of "clan-states" did not pose serious problems until his handpicked successor embarked upon the policy of confrontation with the backlands by punishing the anti-PRD coronéis and anti-Moniz local chiefs. As a means of coercing the sertão to accept PRD rule, Governor Moniz relied principally on the state police, thus forcing an unfortunate showdown between state and coronéis. Such an unimaginative policy provoked intraparty squabbles that debilitated the PRD and lent welcome support to the gathering opposition. By December 1919, the backland anti-PRD coronéis became de facto partners in the Rui-led opposition in Salvador, thus threatening the balance of power in Bahia. An opposition political victory was prevented only when President Epitácio Pessoa intervened by recognizing the legitimacy of the rebel coronéis through federal peace "treaties" and by preventing the anti-PRD forces from manipulating the revolts.

EPITÁCIO VS. RUI

President-elect Rodrigues Alves of São Paulo died of flu in January 1919, never having assumed the office to which he had been elected for a second time. The entire country was drawn into a series of backroom manuevers, in an effort to find a replacement. The obvious contenders were the governors of rival states—São Paulo, Minas Gerais, and Rio Grande do Sul—and, of course, there was Rui Barbosa.[1] The crucial problem was to find someone acceptable to the collegial oligarchies of the big states. Technically, São Paulo had its "turn" in 1918, and therefore Governor Artur Bernardes of Minas and Governor Borges de Medeiros of Rio Grande were logical choices. But Borges was not interested in the job and suggested that the nomination should go to a man from a smaller state.[2] His proposal was acceptable to the other states, and by the third week of January, a number of politicians from smaller states had been mentioned, José Joaquim Seabra of Bahia, Urbano Santos of Maranhão, Rosa e Silva and Dantas Barreto of Pernambuco, and Epitácio Pessoa of Paraíba the most often named. Seabra was a well-known and prestigious politician of the old school; Urbano had been vice-president of the Republic (1914–18) and was well liked by the politicians of Minas; Rosa e Silva and Dantas Barreto were political arch-enemies, and neither was given much chance of winning the support of his own state. The best choice therefore seemed to be Epitácio Pessoa, a federal senator and Brazilian ambassador to the Paris Peace Conference.

1. Morgan to Secretary of State, Rio, January 21, 1919, fl. 389, Internal Affairs of Brazil, Reel 4, 823.00/51–225, DOS/USNA.
2. Borges de Medeiros to Antônio Azeredo, Porto Alegre, July 24, 27, 1919, Pasta 41, Arquivo de Epitácio da Silva Pessoa, hereafter cited as AESP.

The candidacy of Rui Barbosa initially appeared most promising. Unlike its position in the election of 1910, the army as a whole did not oppose Rui. One general, possibly reflecting the mood of the restive officer corps, had kind words for Rui Barbosa. He recounted Rui's support of the army in the late 1880s, his abolitionism, his service to Deodoro, and his populist views; Rui was never anti-military, he said. If Brazil did not have a Rui Barbosa, it would have invented one.[3] Such a euphony of support simply did not reach the backrooms of the political kingmakers. By early February 1919, the big states of São Paulo, Minas, Rio Grande, Bahia, and Pernambuco had decided on Epitácio Pessoa. The behind-the-scenes brokering was so secretive that is was only after the multi-state accord that the candidate was informed of his nomination.[4] The grateful Epitácio accepted, and the ruling parties of Brazil began to mobilize their resources to formalize the candidacy. In Bahia, the PRD openly declared for Epitácio, denying its support to Rui for the third time in ten years.

The PRD objective in the election was twofold: to keep Rui from becoming a serious contender for the presidency and to shore up the declining fortunes of the ruling party by backing the official candidate. Although the big states had made pre-convention commitments to Epitácio, the opposition fought a final battle on the convention floor. In Rio, Seabra and his PRD delegates were taking no chances. Objecting to the proposal of Governor Bernardes of Minas that each state *elect* its delegates, Seabra managed to have himself and his cronies nominated to the national convention.[5] The Bahian opposition deputies warned that Rui would not accept the results of the convention as a truthful reflection of the "people's will." As far as the PRD was concerned, Rui's defeat would certainly uplift the sagging morale of the party, and in the process Seabra's political prestige would be greatly enhanced. Over the vehement protests of Rui and his followers, the kingmakers gave Epitácio 139 votes

3. *A Tarde*, January 27, 28, 1919. The remark was attributed to General Muller de Campos.

4. Azeredo et al. to Pessoa, Rio, February 25, 1919, Pasta 41, AESP; for details of the back-room brokering, see Pang, "The Politics of *Coronelismo*," pp. 179–80.

5. Moniz Sodré to Antônio Moniz and Seabra, Rio, January 30, 1919, AGM; Pang, "The Politics of *Coronelismo*," pp. 176–77.

Presidents of Brazil

Afonso Augusto Moreira Pena (1906–9)

Nilo Procópio Peçanha (1909–10)

Hermes Rodrigues da Fonseca (1910–14)

Epitácio da Silva Pessoa (1919–22)

Artur da Silva Bernardes (1922–26)   Washington Luís Pereira de Sousa (1926–30)

Governors of Bahia

Virgílio Clímaco Damásio (1889)   Manuel Vitorino Pereira (1889–90)

Hermes Ernesto da Fonseca (1890)

José Gonçalves da Silva (1890–91)

Joaquim Leal Ferreira (1891–92)

Joaquim Manuel Rodrigues Lima
(1892–96)

Luís Viana (1896–1900)

Severino dos Santos Vieira (1900–1904)

José Marcelino de Sousa (1904–8)

João Ferreira de Araújo Pinho (1908–11)

Aurélio Rodrigues Viana (1911–12)

José Joaquim Seabra (1912–16, 1920–24)

Vital Henriques Batista Soares (1928–30)

Juraci Montenegro Magalhães (1931–37)

Frederico Augusto Rodrigues da Costa

Visconde da Oliveira

Barão de Jeremoabo

Antônio Pessoa da Costa e Silva

Manuel Misael da Silva Tavares

Domingos Adami de Sá

Abílio Wolney

Horácio de Queiroz Matos

Hermelino Marques de Leão

Abrahão Cohim

Francisco Dias Coelho

Rui Barbosa

José Joaquim Seabra

Antônio Ferrão Moniz de Aragão

Antônio Moniz Sodré de Aragão

João Mangabeira

Otávio Mangabeira

Francisco Marques de Góis
Calmon

Miguel Calmon du Pin e Almeida

Civilista candidates: Rui (left) and Albuquerque Lins

Rui (left), Antônio Azeredo (middle), and Manuel de Oliveira (right)

Campaign train in 1910 (Rui's left, Washington Luís)

Rui arriving in Bahia (November 1919): Rui's left, candidate Paulo Martins Fontes; between Rui and Fontes, Federal Deputy Pedro Lago

Reception (1919): Rui's left, wife Maria Augusta; Rui's right, Miguel Calmon; behind Maria Augusta, Pedro Lago

Campaign tour (1919) in Salvador

Polyteama Theater: "People's Convention" of
November 1919

Rui crossing Rio Paraguaçu (November 1919): Rui's
right, son Alfredo Ruizinho; Ruizinho's right (in
white), Pedro Lago

Rui preaching democracy in Waterfront, lower city
of Salvador (December 1919)

O coveiro do civilismo

Albuquerque Lins: — Que fatalidade! *Medeiros e Albuquerque:* — Deixemo-nos de fatalismos... Foi um derramamento bilioso complicado com inanição... *Gil Vidal:* — Foi má sorte da *cartada*... *Zé Marcelino:* — Qual! Foi cábula do Cincinato, secretário da Junta Nacional... *Cincinato (coveiro:* — Foi... o diabo que os carregue! *Irineu (ajudante):* — É' isso mesmo, *seu chefe!*

Rui: — Em verdade vos digo: a causa de tôda esta *desgraceira* está no meu manifesto...

Zé Povo: — O meu pressentimento não falhou: o Cincinato seria o coveiro do civilismo. *Cavador* emérito, quis *cavar* a eleição fraudando 20 por cento nas votações do Hermes... Apanhado em flagrante, confessou o crime e... enterrou o civilismo! Que asa negra! Que patife!...

J. R. Lobão   O Malho, de 2 de abril de 1910.

A mudança do Senado

Coleção Corbiniano Villaça

(Rui Barbosa, Soares dos Santos, Lauro Sodré, Urbano dos Santos, João Luiz Alves, Antônio Azeredo, Leopoldo de Bulhões, Francisco Sá, Francisco Sales, Eloi de Souza e Irineu Machado, senadores quando se propôs a mudança do Senado, para um prédio a construir na Praça da República).

J. Carlos — *Careta*, de agôsto de 1916.

A VAGA

Kalixto — D. Quixote,
de 22 de janeiro de 1919.

O NILO — ininteligível.
O ALTINO — incompatível (com Minas).
O RUY — indesiludível.

Em casa de Diógenes

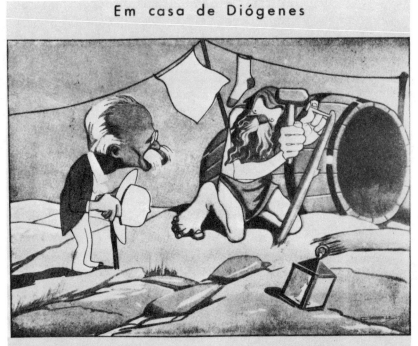

Rui : — É verdade que você está procurando um homem?...

J. Carlos — *Para Todos...*, de 1.º de fevereiro de 1919.

IRRESISTIVEL

Rui (monologando) : — É o suco !

J. Carlos — *Para Todos...*, de 8 de fevereiro de 1919.

A INTERVENÇÃO

Epitacio, o Nacionalista, corre a apagar a fogueira, pelo systema que apprendeu com Clemenceau, na Conferencia da Paz.

Kalixto — *D. Quixote*, de 3 de março de 1920.

TRIPUDIANDO..

O paquete "Ruy Barbosa" conduziu tropas federaes para a Bahia afim de combater a revolução.

RUY — Triste ironia!...

Storni · *O Malho*, de 6 de março de 1920

and Rui 42.[6] A jubilant Seabra concluded his telegram to Moniz with the proclamation "victory is ours, our party's." Moniz Sodré, the governor's cousin and also a delegate, observed that when Seabra cast his vote for Epitácio, thereby rejecting his compatriot for the third time in ten years, some seventy conventioneers gave the PRD chief a standing ovation.[7] Bahia was officially in the winner's camp, and the PRD's position in federation politics seemed more secure than ever before.

THE APRIL ELECTION AND ITS AFTERMATH

On the eve of the election, Rui Barbosa came home. There were rumors that he was not even going to carry his own state as he had done in 1910. On the whole, the election took place without major violence, except for one shooting incident directed against the opposition leaders; one innocent bystander was killed.[8] Epitácio carried many of the interior municípios; Salvador and other coastal cities voted for Rui. In the Lavras, Monsenhor Hermelino Leão, the PRD boss of Macaúbas, "won" the election for Epitácio, and the opposition press alleged that the outcome was a pure fabrication conjured up by the priest.[9] The performance of the PRD machines left something to be desired, but, on the whole, the election was well engineered. Seabra, however, still failed to deliver to Epitácio the promised three-fourths of the state votes. The final tally was Epitácio 28,811, Rui 16,547.[10]

The PRD's retaliation against the supporters of Rui began as soon as the euphoria of the electoral victory wore off. To balance the northern presidency, Epitácio organized a southern-dominated cabinet, drawing all seven ministers from São Paulo, Minas, and Rio Grande. Moniz Sodré, who had been mentioned frequently as a cabinet choice during the election, never received the appointment. The much-humiliated PRD sought an explanation from the president, who pleaded the need for geo-

6. Moniz Sodré to Antônio Moniz, Rio, February 8, 25, 1919, AGM.
7. Seabra to Moniz, Rio, February 25, 1919, Moniz Sodré to Antônio Moniz, Rio, February 25, 1919, ibid.
8. *A Tarde*, March 26, 31, 1919; Lago to Pessoa, Bahia, March 28, 1919, Pasta 41, AESP.
9. *A Tarde*, June 16, 1919.
10. Azeredo to Pessoa, Rio, July 16, 1919, Pasta 41, AESP.

graphical balance as an excuse for not naming a Bahian to the cabinet.[11]

Since 1916, long before the election, armed confrontation between state police, who often served as the executioners of the governor's political wrath, and interior coronéis had been escalating. The Força Pública, then a ragtag army of underpaid and underdisciplined men, lacked a reputation for displaying the morale and conduct expected of officers. To compensate for their long-overdue pay, the police often pillaged the stores and ranches of the anti-Moniz coronéis, action which the state discreetly condoned. In the cacao country, such incidents were becoming more numerous, eventually forcing Governor Moniz to hold an inquiry.[12] The level of police violence did not subside, and by mid-1919 the situation in the backlands had reached a critical point.

The real trouble spots, however, were Carinhanha (the Bahia-Minas border region) and the Lavras Diamantinas. In Carinhanha, Coronel João Duque, who supported Rui's candidacy, had been the dominant force since 1910. The Bahian state police, presumably under orders from the governor, singled out Duque as their target. He was an interstate coronel-warlord with ties to the cattle interests in Minas, hence an ally to some of the leading political clans in that state. On numerous occasions, the state police of Minas bailed him out by crossing the border to join in the fighting. Opposition politicians were quick to point out that the coronel of Carinhanha was victimized by Moniz, and they were eager to turn him into a symbol of police persecution.[13]

In the ever inflamed Lavras, the allies of Horácio de Matos were up in arms again, this time to fight the tribal PRD oligarchy of César Sá, Militão Coelho, Manuel Fabrício, and Monsenhor Hermelino Leão. The shaky armed truce of 1915 was broken when the jagunços of Coronel Militão attacked the ranch

11. *A Tarde*, July 28, 1919; *O Democrata*, July 29, 1919. For the regional balance of federal offices in the executive and legislative branches, see Azeredo to Pessoa, Rio, June 19, 1919, Pasta 41, AESP. This telegram obviously influenced Epitácio to appoint a Gaúcho to the cabinet.

12. The first official investigation of the "Crime of Jequié" was conducted in October 1916, but the "whitewashing" led to no prosecution; for the report, see *Diário Oficial*, December 7, 1916. Police abuse continued to mid-1919; see *A Tarde*, July 28, September 8–9, 12, 23, 1919; Pang, "The Politics of Coronelismo," pp. 171, 184.

13. Pang, "The Politics of *Coronelismo*," pp. 171–72.

of Horácio's aunt Casimira, thus showing that the truce was first violated by the PRD coronéis. By mid-1919, the intermittent war was two years old; numerous but ineffectual police interventions had failed to defeat Horácio. In June and July, two additional police expeditions were sent to silence Horácio and his allies. It was seen that the backland warlord could not be beaten but was instead gaining popular support among the *sertanejos.* The Matos clan was determined to fight until the last of the rival clans was completely wiped out of the region.[14]

The backland war even became a concern of the federal congress where Moniz Sodré sought to defend the violent policies of Governor Moniz by condemning Horácio as a "bandit."[15] No amount of verbal assault on Horácio in the hall of the federal congress could turn the tide against the warlord. By early September 1919, the name Horácio evoked the image of a living legend in Bahian backlands. Consequently, he emerged as the strongest of all the opposition coronéis, and his military prowess was unrivaled; one popular myth had it that Horácio had a *corpo fechado* (literally, a closed body, i.e., he was bullet-proof).[16] Desperate for a solution, Governor Moniz chose to capitulate by seeking a truce again, for, after all, it had worked once.

The governor named a well-known politician from the Lavras, José Joaquim Landulfo da Rocha Medrado, kin to Coronel Douca Medrado of Mucugê, to head the state truce commission, his mission to restore law and order in the sertão at any cost. The emissary arrived in the small town of Descoberto in mid-September to find the entire region devastated by war. Large and small armed bands roamed freely. The state mediator convened the truce meeting with the two antagonists present. Horácio demanded that Militão be removed from local politics and that the county seat of Barra do Mendes be transferred from Militão's stronghold to Jordão, the Horacista enclave. Medrado accepted the demand ad interim, agreeing that fuller implementation of the terms would be worked out upon his

14. *O Democrata,* August 9, 1919, condemned Horácio as a "bandit" (on August 13, the same newspaper published the PRD chieftain Militão's appeal for help to save his family from "Bandit" Horácio); Chagas, *O chefe Horácio,* pp. 71–81; Morães, *Jagunços e heróis,* pp. 65–72; *A Tarde,* June 27, July 30, August 18–20, 1919.

15. *A Tarde,* September 9, 11, 1919.

16. See Neill Macaulay, *The Prestes Column: Revolution in Brazil,* p. 216, on the "corpo fechado."

return to the capital.[17] By early October, the Lavras had returned to peace, at least for the time being.

The truce offered by the state government to Horácio had far-reaching ramifications for the future of state politics in general and the nature of coronelismo in particular. The terms of peace were meager but invited other coronéis to extract concessions from the state by violence. Such concessions showed the failure of the PRD to institutionalize or tame interior coronéis, as shown so well in the case of Horácio de Matos who had managed successfully to flout the official party and the state *twice* in four years. The state government had set a dangerous precedent by acquiescing to the demands of a rebellious coronel of a clan-state, especially in a gubernatorial election year.

THE RALLYING OPPOSITION

In the months of August and September, while war and truce negotiations alternated in the Lavras, the opposition began to gear up its unity movement. In addition to backland revolts, there were other signs that augured well for the Rui-led movement. First, the Bahian federal senator and the loser of the April presidential election was anxious to forge a united opposition movement of the bacharéis in Salvador and the coronéis in the sertão to overthrow the Seabra-dominated PRD. The multicephalous factions of Luís Viana, Pedro Lago, João Mangabeira, and others gingerly rallied behind a Rui mellowed by age but as belligerent and revengeful as ever.[18] The president, whom the PRD had supported in the April election, seemed to remain deliberately aloof to regional politics. For instance, his cousin, Coronel João Pessoa de Queiroz, broke off with Governor Manuel Borba and allied with Estácio Coimbra, thus setting off a power struggle in Pernambuco. In this shifting alliance, Epitácio Pessoa chose not to interfere by aiding his kinsman. Instead, the president asked Dantas Barreto to resolve the conflict.[19] Such an indirect intervention might be repeated in Bahia. Additionally, the president was a friend to neither Seabra nor Rui.

17. *A Tarde*, September 24, 30, 1919; Pang, "The Politics of *Coronelismo*," pp. 172–73.

18. *A Tarde*, August 5, 1919.

19. Ibid., August 21, 1919.

Second, Bahia was also experiencing one of the first incidents of major urban labor unrest in the twentieth century. The politics of the capital was traditionally manipulated by such charismatic leaders as Rui, Seabra, César Zama, and others whose humble background had a special appeal to the urban sectors. In the 1910s, the state politics of Bahia was beginning to bring both class and regional interests into focus. The PRB leadership as a whole represented the dominance of rural agrarian interests under the two governors, José Marcelino and and Araújo Pinho. By contrast, the PRD was born of urban mass support in Salvador; its leaders came from the ranks of liberal professionals. Not surprisingly, Rui was always popular in the cities. In the capital, numerous working-class unions and and lower-middle-class professionals staged strikes in sympathy with the opposition. City employees, teachers, and dock workers joined the strike, the first of its kind in the state. The immediate causes of dissatisfaction were unpaid salaries and bad working conditions. Related to their grievances was the collective support of the backlanders' struggle against the PRD and the state police oppression. Many of Salvador's poor came from the interior and identified readily with the sertanejos' revolts. Newspapers in Rio and Salvador supported the striking working class by crusading against the Seabra party.[20] The liberal professions and commercial class in the capital were equally critical of the PRD and the Moniz government. The state's failure to intercede with Britain and other allied powers to relax the embargo on Bahian shipments during the First World War gave the mercantile-financial colony a new cause. The record flood of 1919 had destroyed much of the cacao crop, causing the worst harvest in years.[21] Under these conditions, Bahia faced the potentially most divisive gubernatorial election in its history.

Between August and October, the ruling party was also going through drastic changes. The governor's attempt to secure the nomination for his cousin Moniz Sodré set off stiff opposition among Seabra loyalists. The four-day front page build-up of Moniz Sodré by O Democrata in late August was effectively neutralized by Seabra's personal victory when he was elected

20. Ibid., September 9, 11, 1919; John W. F. Dulles, Anarchists and Communists in Brazil, 1900–1935, pp. 92–95.
21. A Tarde, January 13, 15, 1919.

party president.[22] Governor Moniz was replaced by a Seabra loyalist as party vice-president; Frederico Costa was re-elected party secretary. The arduous, grueling power struggle over the party's key positions was fought by the Monizes and the Seabra loyalists. By early November, the Seabrista coronéis began to take over the party directorates in major municípios by easing out the Moniz followers and restoring the balance of power in favor of Seabra. With this move, the Monizes lost any hope of holding the governorship for another four years.[23]

THE OPPOSITION AND THE COMMERCIAL CLASS

By mid-October, the opposition still had no candidate for governor and no party organization. Rui Barbosa, more interested in revenge than in the governorship, would have been denigrating himself to seek the job. Other younger politicians—Pedro Lago, the Calmon brothers, Simões Filho, and the Mangabeira brothers (Otávio had left the PRD the previous July)—were more or less contemporaries and were of similar political stature. The selection of any one of these men would destroy the existing fragile unity. The problem was solved, however, when the commercial-financial community in Salvador offered the candidacy to Federal Judge Paulo Martins Fontes; the opposition, including Rui, swiftly accepted, leaving only the formal endorsement of the candidate at the convention.[24]

The opposition rally of November 18, 1919, was a show of tripartite political unity among the commercial class, the opposition bacharéis, and the anti-PRD coronéis of the sertão. Called the "People's Convention" (Convenção Popular), it was organized principally by the stewards of the civilista campaign of ten years earlier. In addition to the usual crowd who gath-

22. *O Democrata*, August 27, 30, September 2-3, 1919.
23. Ibid., September 12, 17, 21, 25, October 2, 7, 10, 23, 25-26, 29-30, November 1, 5, 11, 15, 18-19, 22-23, December 2, 5, 12, 23, 1919. These articles published the complete roster of new PRD directors in Salvador and other municípios.
24. *A Tarde*, July 13, October 18-20, 1919; interview with Fiel Fontes, Rio, September 8, 1971. The late Fiel Fontes was a son of Judge Paulo Fontes; Fiel served as a federal deputy in the mid-1920s, representing the northeastern part of Bahia. According to Fiel, his father was most reluctant to accept the nomination, for the judge never held an elective office and lacked experience as a politician. For details of the nomination, see Pang, "The Politics of *Coronelismo*," pp. 186-87.

ered around Rui, the leading anti-PRD chieftains from the backlands and the Recôncavo attended: Coronéis Anfilófio Castelo
Branco and José Nogueira represented the Middle São Francisco Valley; the Visconde da Oliveira and José Wanderley de
Araújo Pinho represented the sugar interests of the bay area.
From the cacao country came Coronéis Domingos Adami and
Pedro Lavigne Catalão. The convention put on one of the most
colorful shows since the 1910 campaign and rubber-stamped
the candidacy of Judge Fontes. A few days later, the PRD held
its low-key convention to nominate Seabra as its candidate. On
November 23, barely five weeks before the election, Seabra
accepted the nomination as the standard-bearer of the much-
battered ruling party.[25]

Judging from the publicity in the press, the contest was fought
by the candidate Seabra and the non-candidate Rui; the opposition campaign was eye-catching. Like a conquering medieval
pope, Rui toured the Recôncavo municípios in an attempt to
vindicate his name and honor, and incidentally to campaign for
the candidate. It was the finest hour of his political career: a
farewell bid to Bahia, to whom he was both a demigod and an
enigma. He orated endlessly about himself, God, the sea, the
sertão, Bahia, and Brazil, in that order.[26] The emphasis of the
campaign was on Rui, on his desperate attempt to seek a
proper place in Bahian history by reminding the citizens of his
existence, his power, and his prestige in national politics. Many
emotion-choked admirers threw flowers on the path Rui walked,
somewhat vulgarly recreating the return of Jesus. Amid this
fanfare, there was a tragic sense of sadness and ennui: everyone
knew that this was going to be the last political campaign for the
seventy-two-year-old Rui.

ELECTORAL VIOLENCE

The December 29 election was preceded by conflicting partisan
claims and armed confrontations. In Salvador, the PRD organ,

25. *A Tarde*, November 17, 1919; Pang, "The Politics of *Coronelismo*," pp.
188–90; *O Democrata*, November 1, 1919. Originally, the convention was
planned for the Day of the Republic (November 15), but Rui was late in arriving
in Bahia so it was postponed until the seventeenth.

26. Rui Barbosa, *Uma campanha política: a successão governamental na
Bahia 1919–1920*, is a collection of Rui's speeches; also, *A Tarde* carried Rui's
speeches daily between the third and twentieth of December 1919.

O Democrata, claimed the support of the prestigious Ilhéus
Commercial Association for Seabra, while the opposition paper,
A Tarde, counterclaimed that the association had backed the
Fontes candidacy.[27] Once again, for the second time in three
months, the city government employees, streetcar conductors,
textile workers, and dock workers staged anti-government
strikes.[28] In the São Francisco Valley, João Mangabeira and
Pedro Lago were said to be attempting to bribe the state police
detachment there and to supply money and arms to anti-PRD
coronéis.[29] In the Lavras, the opposition won handily the support
of Coronel Horácio and his followers. Rui Barbosa personally
wrote to the warlord of the Lavras, urging him to support Judge
Fontes.[30] Horácio de Matos informed Governor Moniz, in a blis-
tering telegram, that in the Lavras, Fontes was going to be the
winner.[31]

Violence broke out before December 29. In Remanso, a município in the Middle São Francisco Valley, Coronel Castelo Branco
took over the town, canceling the election. The opposition deputy
demanded that the governor send in the police. In the Lavras, the
Horacista supporters were attempting to produce a greater turnout by forcibly taking over the elections in those municípios that
César Sá controlled. In Barreiras and in Rio Preto, a western part
of the valley, Abílio Wolney and Abílio Araújo guaranteed
Fontes' victory. In Salvador, the desperate state government
asked the federal president to allow the use of the federal army to
"combat the banditry" (i.e., to suppress the anti-PRD coronéis),
but Epitácio refused.[32]

When the so-called election was over, each side predictably

27. *O Democrata*, December 12, 1919; *A Tarde*, December 15, 1919.
28. *A Tarde*, December 12, 20, 22, 1919; Dulles, *Anarchists and Communists*,
pp. 92–95.
29. *O Democrata*, December 23, 1919, January 25, 1920.
30. Barbosa to Matos, Bahia, December 19, 1919, Arquivo de Horácio de
Queiroz Matos, hereafter cited as AHQM. The man who was instrumental in
winning Horácio's support for the Rui camp was Coronel Manuel Alcântara de
Carvalho, planter, diamond merchant, and *A Tarde* correspondent in the Lavras,
and he and Rui had previously exchanged telegrams and letters: Carvalho to
Barbosa, Lençóis, April 10, 1919, Pasta Manuel Alcântara de Carvalho, ACRB;
Barbosa and Lago to Carvalho, Bahia, November 22, 1919, AHQM; interview
with Manuel Alcântara, Lençóis, June 29, 1968.
31. *A Tarde*, December 23, 1919.
32. Ibid., December 18, 1919; Pessoa to Moniz, Rio, December 25, 1919, Pasta
53—Bahia—Eleição do Governador—Conflagração—Intervenção Federal,
AESP.

claimed victory for its candidate. But from the opposition's standpoint, the electoral dispute should have been kept out of the legislature that was dominated by the PRD. The only way to win the election seemed to be armed resistance to the PRD and dramatizing its significance nationwide. Many factors were in the favor of the anti-PRD forces: the military successes of the coronéis in the sertão, the total anarchy reigning in the state, the labor strikes in the capital, the ever plummeting popularity of Antônio Moniz, and finally the political neutrality of President Epitácio Pessoa. If these conditions continued to hold constant, the Bahian state government could be overthrown.

FLOWERING OF THE REVOLTS

Officially, the Moniz government denied the existence of coronelista revolts in the sertão. *O Democrata* and PRD politicians continued to talk about the "banditry" in the backlands. One headline of the PRD organ cried, "Where is the honor of Mr. Rui Barbosa?" blaming the backland revolts and urban unrest in Salvador squarely on his agitation and exhortations.[33] As the revolts in the interior gradually consolidated the power base for the opposition coronéis, the state government began to reconsider its policy. The situation had become too unstable for the state police to handle alone. Such a staunch PRD coronel as Douca Medrado of Mucugê began to join the revolts. In the Lavras, Douca's defection turned the tide. In the São Francisco Valley, the revolt was quickly won by the opposition in mid-January. River navigation came to a halt.[34] In the central south Marcionílio de Sousa and his allies effectively beat the PRD elements. The coronel was even considering the expansion of his sphere of influence beyond the traditional boundary of his fief.[35] In the cacao country of southern Bahia, which had so far

33. *O Democrata*, January 15, 22, 1920; the headline said, "Onde está a honra do sr. Rui Barbosa?" On February 28 (two days after the federal intervention was proclaimed), *O Democrata* called Rui "o pai saturno da constituição."
34. *A Tarde*, January 19–21, February 18, 1920.
35. Sousa to Matos, Machado Portela (Bahia), January 31, 1920, AHQM. In this telegram, Coronel Marcionílio asked on behalf of Pedro Lago, Simões Filho, and himself if Horácio could march toward Salvador. The coronel of Maracás recommended that Horácio march "east" first taking Sítio Novo or Paraguaçu, either of which would be a convenient jumping-off point to "Caxoeira" (Cachoeira) and São Felix, only hours from the capital by car or by ship.

been uninvolved, coronéis on both sides were amassing jagunços, ready for violence.

By February 1920, the electoral results had yet to be verified
by the legislature, which had been in recess and showed no
interest in holding sessions. The state of Bahia had already
been in civil war for three months, and politically savvy
deputies and senators wanted to wait for the time being. There
was talk of an invasion of Salvador by the rebels; Bahian
politicians remembered well the fate of the Franco Rabelo
government of Ceará brought about by the invading horde of
Padre Cícero's jagunços in 1914. The state police had about
2,600 men, most of them poorly armed. The commander of the
federal garrison in Bahia calculated that the combat strength
of the state police would be around 1,500. Rebel Coronel
Horácio de Matos alone was believed to have more than 2,600
men in arms. Castelo Branco and his allies commanded at least
1,500 men.[36] In addition, the valley's coronéis could count on
substantial help from Piauí, Goiás, Pernambuco, and Minas if
the protracted conflict spread to Salvador. With such a precarious balance of power between contending forces, no legislature was going to hold sessions and deliberate the election
results.

It is not necessary to repeat full details of the federal intervention of February 23, 1920; they have been treated elsewhere.[37] However, the political ramifications of federal interventions in general and those in Bahia in 1920 should be
considered.

THE ROLE OF FEDERAL INTERVENTIONS

Historically, federal intervention was the state's last resort
when it was unable to resolve political and civil conflicts.
Under the Federal Constitution of 1891, the president of the

36. *Diário Oficial*, January 15, 1920; Aguiar to Pessoa, Bahia, February 21,
1920, Pasta 53, AESP. For details on the interior revolutionary development,
see Pang, "The Politics of *Coronelismo*," pp. 195–99.

37. Pang, "The Revolt of the Bahian *Coronéis*." The American chargé in Rio
mistakenly thought that the opposition was against the intervention (Wadsworth to Secretary of State, Rio, February 25, 1920, Telegram, fl. 248, Internal
Affairs of Brazil, Reel 4, 823.00/51–225, DOS/USNA); contrary to Wadsworth's
analysis, the opposition sought federal intervention. See Aguiar to Pessoa,
Bahia, March 6, 1920, Pasta 53, AESP; Pang, "The Politics of *Coronelismo*," p.
204; Alberto Cardoso de Aguiar, *A intervenção na Bahia*.

republic (with or without the request of state governors) was empowered to intervene to restore law and order ("tranquillity") in the federation. Politically, federal intervention became a handy tool for the federal president to use to shore up his supporters and to punish his foes. Frequently, interventions were designed either to bring the candidate of the president's choice to power or to retain his man in power. It was the Fonseca administration that refined the use of both declared and undeclared interventions for this purpose. The cases of Pernambuco in November 1911 and of Bahia in January 1912 were such undeclared interventions. In 1914, President Hermes refrained from formally intervening in Ceará, where the private armies of Padre Cícero attacked the constitutionally elected regime of Governor Franco Rabelo, which was on the brink of collapse. The federal army in Fortaleza was ordered to stay out of the civil war, giving Cícero's jagunços a free hand. The Rabelo regime fell and the Acioli tribal oligarchy returned to power. In the 1920s, the use of federal presidential intervention in state politics was increasing.

The intervention of 1920 in Bahia defied the usual pattern. It was not intended to save the PRD regime from collapsing, although that was a result. Epitácio Pessoa was more interested in maintaining order and tranquillity in Bahia than in aiding either Seabra or Rui Barbosa. He did not owe a political debt to either, though Seabra claimed presidential support by virtue of having placed the PRD on the winning side in the April election.[38] The president's rationale was based on his impartial role as the defender of law and order. To this end, he strove to force both parties to a compromise: a new election. The proposal was welcomed by the opposition, but Seabra flatly rejected it.[39] Having failed to secure the political compromise that would have spared intervention, Epitácio Pessoa sought to prevent further bloodshed by seeking a separate solution from the backland coronéis. His military commander

38. Seabra to Pessoa, Bahia, March 9, 1920, Pasta 53, AESP; Epitácio Pessoa, *Pela verdade*, 1:123–24; Laurita Pessoa Raja Gabaglia, *Epitácio Pessoa (1865–1942)*.

39. Pessoa to Seabra, Rio, February 19, 20, 1920, Seabra to Pessoa, Bahia, March 9, 1920, Pasta 53, AESP. President Pessoa told Seabra that the Bahian chief should stay in federal politics and nominate his own candidate for governor, just to avoid all the unpleasant circumstances leading to federal intervention.

in Bahia was instructed to deal with the sertanejo insurgents *only*, without involving the PRD government and the opposition. The president, as well as his army commander, reasoned that the political demands of the backlanders were different from the objectives of the Rui-led opposition. The coronéis sought to legitimize their hard-earned status as a new power elite, while the Rui faction hoped to utilize the military might of the coronéis to unhorse the Moniz regime. To Epitácio, these two objectives were not compatible, and any potentially dangerous alliance should be defused before it exploded. The Moniz government would not, and could not, grant such legitimacy to the coronéis without destroying itself. Therefore, the president chose to ignore the politicians in Salvador and proceeded to sign three separate peace treaties with the insurgent coronéis, granting them multiple political and administrative concessions that the Moniz regime could not.

Toward the end of the first week of March, the backland coronéis accepted the federal terms of the peace treaties, and the state legislature met to proclaim José Joaquim Seabra the next governor. The president grudgingly accepted the final outcome. The federal garrison kept the city in order, and the soldiers never ventured near the legislature to influence the verification results.[40]

"STATES WITHIN A STATE"

By the terms of the treaties, Epitácio Pessoa had in fact created independent states of coronéis in Bahia. The treaty coronéis were exonerated from any wrongdoing, were immune from state prosecution, were allowed extensive political powers in the matters of state and federal patronage, and were permitted to manage elections. In the case of Coronel Horácio de Matos, the federal government specifically allowed the warlord of the Lavras to elect (that is, name) one state deputy and one state senator to present his personal and regional interests.[41] The coronéis were

40. *A Tarde*, March 8, 1920; Aguiar to Pessoa, Bahia, March 20, 1920, Pasta 53, AESP; Boletim da V Região Militar, no. 60 (March 12, 1920), no. 63 (March 15, 1920), no. 65 (March 17, 1920), no. 99 (April 22, 1920), Arquivo do Quartel General da 6ª Região Militar, hereafter cited as AQG6RM. The last holdout (Horácio) was counseled by his lieutenant (Olímpio Barbosa) to accept the federal peace terms without further delay and to avoid a showdown with the army at all cost (Barbosa to Matos, Palmeiras [Bahia], March 1, 1920, AHQM).
41. José Lapa to Matos, Mundo Novo (Bahia), March 8, 1920, Simões Filho to

permitted to keep their arms, thus establishing a new balance of power between the state military forces (Força Pública) and the coronelista jagunços in the sertão.

Two significant changes in federal-state political relations resulted from the treaties. First, direct access opened between the federal president and the backland coronéis; this subsequently undermined the role of the state government and its dominant party as intermediaries. During the 1920s, the pattern of direct communication between the president and the coronéis was continually strengthened and refined through federal deputies elected by the coronelista states, who in turn replaced the governor and other power brokers as regional spokesmen. Second, the coronelista politics of Bahia, and to a certain extent of other northern states, was subject to modification as the coronel's political ties with one or more dominant PRs in São Paulo, Minas, and even Rio Grande strengthened or weakened his position. In short, the fortunes of Bahian coronéis was much influenced by federal and interstate political considerations. The more powerful and prestigious a coronel, the less dependent he was on the state governor. Thus, the head of the coronelista state became a full-fledged national politician, an indispensable ally to the president and the dominant PRs in the central south. As will be shown, the federal presidents after Epitácio Pessoa actively courted the coronéis of Bahia, often bypassing the state governors.

This perspective reinforces the subsequent rapport between Seabra and the treaty coronéis and the argument that the coronelista revolt was a movement against Salvador's interference in local affairs; that is, it was a manifestation of an opposition directed toward a specific group, in this case, the Moniz faction, but not necessarily against the ruling party as a whole. It was irrelevant who ruled Salvador. What mattered was who opposed the coronéis. After 1920, the new oligarchy of the treaty coronéis constituted the new supporters of the PRD in the sertão. It was ironic that federal intervention served as the means of revamping Bahia's oligarchic structure at the expense of state authority. Throughout the 1920s, the state never recovered its luster and prestige in the backlands.

Matos, Bahia, March 10, 1920, AHQM; the original draft of the peace agreements is found in the Pasta 53, AESP; Documentos Parlamentares, *Intervenção nos estados*, 14:606–11.

6. The Fall of Seabra's Oligarchy and the Zenith of Bahian Coronelismo, 1920–1924

THE BASIC changes in coronelismo and state politics after 1920 were easily recognizable. The traditional pattern of the state governor serving as intermediary between the coronel and the federal president was effectively broken. As the arbiter of regional and local politics, the president replaced the governor. Political centralism considerably dissolved the administrative federalism of the state government as the familiocratic oligarchies gained direct access to and recognition by the president as the legitimate local elite. Also, for the first time in Bahian history, the federal government sanctioned power by violence. This further coerced the state government into accepting the independence of the coronelista states of the sertão as rival institutions of power and authority. In a curious way, Bahia was fragmented into numerous states within the state, the kind of federalism that the writers of the Constitution of 1891 had failed to envision.

While the treaties of 1920 indirectly assured the PRD of its superficial control over the state government, the power of the Seabrista personalistic oligarchy was considerably reduced in reality. As the personal prestige of Seabra was tarnished in the wake of federal intervention, the effectiveness of the PRD proportionately declined. More significant politically, Seabra's attempt to institutionalize the coronéis into obedient pawns of the PRD simply collapsed. Bahia once again retrogressed to a state without a dominant party; the hope disappeared of building a collegial oligarchy by fusing the personal charisma of Seabra and by taming the coronéis. The administrative reforms of 1915 and 1916 had not produced the desired effects in the long run, and whatever power base Seabra had managed to build was destroyed by the incompetent Moniz. Thus, the creation of a one-party system, though ambitiously conceived and executed, met sudden death in its first serious test.

SEABRA'S PEACE CONCESSIONS

When José Joaquim Seabra assumed office in April 1920, coronelismo in Bahia had just entered its golden age. The governor, not oblivious to the terms of the federal treaties, began to implement his own peace offerings. Horácio de Matos, the unchallenged warlord and the de facto "governor general" of the Lavras Diamantinas, was made the regional police delegate (*delegado regional*), a post normally reserved for a bacharel.[1] The unusual aspect of the appointment was Horácio's extensive power to rule twelve municípios (the same jurisdiction guaranteed in the 1920 treaty and later extended to fourteen), although the delegado was in charge of one comarca. The Comarca of the Lavras Diamantinas was then comprised of two municípios, Lençóis and Campestre. Horácio had a monopoly of municipal, state, and federal patronage in his coronelista state. As a whole, the prosecutor (*promotor público*) and the judge (juiz de direito) were the righthand men of the governor. The police delegate, the wielder of violence, was subordinate to these men. They often worked as a team in elections, dealing with the governor's political opposition and doling out favors to party hacks. In many regions, where no strong coronel existed, either the judge or the prosecutor acted as de facto and de jure ruler. In Horácio's case, the title was of a lower grade, but in fact he chose judges and prosecutors for the fourteen municípios that constituted the Horacista tribal oligarchy of warlords. To complete his honor, the governor appointed the warlord as the regional director of the PRD.

1. *Diário Oficial*, April 4, 1920.

In various parts of the interior, Seabra offered similar concessions to the treaty coronéis. In the São Francisco Valley, the coronéis settled down comfortably with a series of state and municipal posts. Anfilófio Castelo Branco and Chico Leobas alternated as intendentes and presidents of the council in Remanso; Coronel Franklin Lins ruled Pilão Arcado in the same way; Antônio Honorato de Castro was the intendente of Casa Nova; Janjão was still the chief in Sento Sé; in Rio Preto, Abílio Araújo began his second decade as the ruler; and in Barreiras, the Goian-born Abílio Wolney was completely integrated into the local power structure. In Lapa, the Moacir brothers finally gained control of the region as the new PRD directors, one serving as state senator and another as intendente.[2]

In the cacao country, Antônio Pessoa, the indefatigable state senator, was still the PRD chief in Ilhéus. Violence and intrigue continued to be the principal tools in politics, and no man emerged in the 1920s as the sole regional lord. Sons of the coronéis began to enter politics. The management of cacao exports required much legal work, and the university-trained sons and sons-in-law gradually took over family and clan businesses. Young bacharéis dabbled in politics, commerce, and banking. Thus, Astor and Mário (sons of Antônio Pessoa), Gileno Amado (son-in-law of Misael Tavares), and Ramiro and Epaminondas (sons of Ramiro Ildefonso Araújo de Castro) came to represent cacao interests in municipal, state, and federal politics.[3] Only thirty years removed from violence, banditry, and crime, these second-generation politicians of Ilhéus and Itabuna exhibited refinement in manner, urbanity in outlook, and conservatism in philosophy. Europe ("Oropas"), Rio, and São Paulo replaced Salvador as the sources of pleasure, education, and retirement.

THE PURGE OF PRD HACKS

Seabra's purge of the incompetent PRD cadres and the foes of the treaty coronéis was swift and brutal. In São Francisco municípios, officeholders who had been thrown out during the

2. Ibid., October 15, 1920; interviews with Bolívar Sant'Ana Batista, Salvador, June 1, 1968, and Wilson Lins, Salvador, July 25, 1968.

3. Interviews with Renato Berbert de Castro, March–August 1968, and Otto Seligsohn, July 30, August 3, 1968. Seligsohn is the author of *Bahia-kakao*.

revolt of 1919–20 were kept out. In Xique-Xique, a Seabrista federal tax collector returned to reclaim his office; the new ruling coronel refused to allow him to have the old job, vigorously protesting to Seabra that the governor was obliged to uphold the terms of the federal treaty. Seabra backed off.[4]

In the Lavras Diamantinas, the four key PRD chiefs were dislodged from power and forced to leave the region. Monsenhor Hermelino Leão of Macaúbas was banished to another part of the state to start a new life as a pastor.[5] Coronel Militão Coelho of Brotas, a long-standing enemy of the Matos clan, made repeated attempts to regain his power, but failed; in his last days, he languished as a house guest of Franklin Lins in Pilão Arcado. Coronel Manuel Fabrício of Campestre was resettled in northeastern Bahia as a state employee. Finally, State Senator César Sá, the chief of PRD organization and the dynast of the Sá clan, was forced to leave Lençóis and settle in a Recôncavo town.[6] By the end of July 1920, the political situation in the region had gelled as a new Horacista elite took over.

The in-house purge in Salvador was equally swift. State Police Chief José Álvaro Cova was fired because he was held responsible for the police expeditions in the interior. Another hard-core Moniz man, Júlio Brandão Rocha Leal, was the intendente of Salvador; he was also sacked and replaced by Coronel Manuel Duarte de Oliveira, the political boss of São Francisco do Conde's PRD. The cleaning out of the city ward bosses resulted in the eviction of many Moniz men. In the district of Brotas, one of the most populous residential sections of Salvador, Coronel Frederico Costa, the powerful state senator and Seabra loyalist, was made the new ward boss.[7]

The status of the top leadership in the PRD was also unstable. The original cardinals of the party—Seabra, Antônio Moniz, Moniz Sodré, and Otávio Mangabeira—were no longer in unity. The Monizes and Seabra remained in the party, but the relation-

---

4. *A Tarde*, July 24, 1920.

5. Ibid., August 7, 1920. Monsenhor Hermelino sold his properties in Macaúbas after the revolt of the coronéis and moved elsewhere; for details, see Matos to José Matos, Macaúbas, June 17, 1920, AHQM. In this telegram, Horácio told his brother that Hermelino and Pedro Marques (a brother of the monsenhor) were given safe conduct to enter, leave, and/or reside in Macaúbas.

6. Geraldo Rocha, *Nacionalismo político e econômico*, p. 368; *A Tarde*, March 3, June 1, 1920; Pang, "The Politics of *Coronelismo*," p. 223. César's brothers and other kinsmen were permitted to live in Lençóis.

7. *A Tarde*, March 24, 25, 26, April 10, 1920.

ship between Antônio Moniz and the governor soured when Seabra supported the candidacy of Moniz Sodré as his successor to the federal senate. Normally, the outgoing governor would have been rewarded, but Seabra had to mollify the personal foes of Moniz within the PRD.[8] Otávio Mangabeira left the party months before the 1919 election, and his departure cost the PRD many followers. Arlindo Leoni and Raul Alves, two other second-level PRD chieftains, were energetic politicians with moderate followings of their own, but neither was of the caliber of Seabra, the two Monizes, and Mangabeira. In brief, the PRD was deprived of good leaders and cadres, forcing the governor to seek the support of the interior coronéis.

For the third time in Bahian history, Seabra planned to change the geopolitics of the sertão through an administrative reform. It had worked twice, in 1915 and in 1916. Partly to fortify the party's position and partly to put his relationship with interior chiefs in more realistic terms, he chose to restore electoral autonomy to the município—the autonomy he had taken away in 1915. The peace treaties of 1920 not only superseded the administrative reform of 1915 but also nullified in one swift stroke the governor's appointive power over the treaty coronéis. Seabra's decision to restore electoral autonomy to the municípios was not as grand a concession as it seemed. Political reality called for it. By doing so voluntarily, the governor demonstrated his willingness to observe the terms of the treaties between the coronéis and the federal government, while at the same time he enticed the backlanders to support him. It was a gamble, but it was worth the risk.

Under the new law of 1920, the intendentes were to be *elected* for a term of two years and would be permitted to serve two consecutive terms. The intendente of Salvador and of those municípios which depended on state financial assistance for their operation and upkeep would continue to be appointed by the governor.[9] The state senate would review the electoral results as before. Those intendentes who have been appointed by Moniz in 1919 were quickly removed by Seabra before the new law became a reality. The first election under the new law took

8. Ibid., May 13, July 29, 1920.

9. Bahia, *Leis do Estado da Bahia no ano de 1920*, pp. 16–60; Lei no. 1387 of May 24, 1920, contains seventeen chapters or articles, and Article 14 specifically deals with the method of electing intendentes.

place in August 1920, and by then Seabra had already worked out his choices for the majority of the municípios, picking either party stalwarts or, in the cases of the municípios controlled by anti-Seabra forces, rival coronéis. In those "treaty municípios," the federally designated coronéis were authorized to manage the election.

THE NEW INTENDENTES

Once the August election of intendentes was over, Governor Seabra was determined to bridge the political gap between his PRD and the new interior intendentes. The electoral autonomy granted in 1920 successfully transferred the potential causes for friction from the governor to the coronéis since the governor no longer exercised direct control over the selection of municipal chief executives. However, as shown in several municípios during the August election, this autonomy bred further violence as the power struggle intensified among rival groups. As early as April 1920, Coronel João Duque of Carinhanha, for example, was challenged and dethroned by a rival who managed to secure the support of the federal army commander in Bahia. During the election itself, both groups were once again embroiled in war. As expected, the governor was still being dragged into these conflicts. To redefine his role in backland politics and to delineate clearly the limits of state and município power relationships, Governor Seabra chose to call a meeting of intendentes.

The Congress of Intendentes was the first of its kind in Bahian history. It had two specific purposes: to acquaint Seabra with the new interior elite and to give the governor the opportunity to pacify the backland chiefs by listening to their grievances and recommendations for improving commerce and agriculture. Fittingly, the congress was as much a political as a diplomatic summit conference for the heads of the coastal and coronelista states. Seabra was intrigued by the prospect of revising the pre-1919 alliance with the rulers of the sertão. Douca Medrado of Mucugê, Franklin Lins of Pilão Arcado, Castelo Branco of Remanso, and Marcionílio of Maracás were among a host of luminaries attending the meeting. As expected, the congress produced few tangible benefits for the coronéis, but politically, it paved the road to détente between Seabra and the coronéis.

The governor promised not to intervene in the internal affairs of the sertão, and the coronéis assured him of their support.[10]

SEABRA AND THE PRESIDENTIAL ELECTION OF 1922

Having cemented a political rapprochement with the backlands, Governor Seabra turned his attention to the presidential election of 1922. As early as June of that year, rumors were circulating that the rival states of São Paulo and Minas had resolved their differences by agreeing on the candidacy of Artur Bernardes of Minas, thereby avoiding a repetition of the events of 1919. Governor Washington Luís of São Paulo, along with Borges Medeiros of Rio Grande and former President Hermes da Fonseca, was also mentioned, but he had less chance of success while Epitácio Pessoa was president. The autocratic governor of São Paulo antagonized Pessoa by criticizing presidential policies on public works, especially drought control projects for the northeast. The tribal chief of the Batatais district of São Paulo was deeply disturbed by the president's neglect of the coffee stabilization program, which had been sacrificed to save the northeast.[11] Epitácio's failure to respect the political autonomy of the ruling oligarchies of the northeast and to pacify the restive junior officers and intellectuals pressing for broad social and political reforms made him appear an unaccommodating politician. In view of the tense relationship between Washington Luís and Epitácio Pessoa, Governor Bernardes stood to benefit, serving as their principal go-between. Thus, the candidacy of Bernardes was given credibility from the outset.

In spite of Bernardes' early lead, the election of 1922 was one of the most controversial in Brazilian history. The balancing of the ticket with a man from the north was favored by the kingmakers, but that posed a serious problem for the Bernardes candidacy. Four men were frequently mentioned as good vice-presidential candidates: José Joaquim Seabra of Bahia, José Bezerra of Pernambuco, Urbano Santos of Maranhão, and

10. *A Tarde*, February 11–12, 23, March 24, 1921.
11. Franco, *Um estadista da república*, 2:969–70. For conflicting views on the financial policies of Washington Luís and Epitácio Pessoa, see Carone, *A república velha II*, pp. 324–27. For a concise description of Washington Luís' financial philosophy, see Ernest Donald Oates, "Washington Luís and the Brazilian Revolution of 1930," pp. 40–72.

Lauro Sodré of Pará. The first three were the governors of their respective states, the fourth a federal senator.[12] Bahia and Pernambuco led other northern states in their attempt to capture the vice-presidency. Raul Soares, the campaign manager and a prestigious politician of Minas, sought ways to keep the support of Seabra and Bezerra intact: he reasoned that the nomination of Urbano Santos would be a satisfactory compromise and would avoid offending either of the other governors by a choice between them.[13] Urbano, an establishment politician, had other qualifications that satisfied the PRM. He was vice-president for 1914–18 and was named to the portfolio of minister of justice by Rodrigues Alves, president-elect for 1918–22. The politician from Maranhão was removed by Epitácio Pessoa to make room for a southerner in a northern presidency.[14] Urbano was a political virtuoso and a club member who understood and played well the rules of big state politics.

THE REPUBLICAN REACTION

The Urbano Santos candidacy was intended to produce harmony in the northern bloc but had the opposite effect. Governor Seabra denounced the selection and moved to form an opposition ticket. With the tacit support of Governor Bezerra of Pernambuco, Seabra invited Nilo Peçanha, former president of the republic and the mulatto strongman of the state of Rio de Janeiro, to become the presidential candidate. Peçanha accepted the nomination and, with Seabra, founded the Republican Reaction (Reação Republicana) alliance to be joined by Bahia, Pernambuco, Rio, and Rio Grande. The first two had native son candidates; Rio Grande refused to support the Bernardes candidacy for the superficial reason that the Mineiro politician had no platform; Rio rejected the candidacy as a concoction of the federal kingmakers rather than a popular selection.[15]

12. *A Tarde*, June 8, 1921.
13. Antônio Gontijo de Carvalho, *Raul Fernandes, um servidor do Brasil*, pp. 177–78; Brígido Tinoco, *A vida de Nilo Peçanha*, p. 236; *O Democrata*, July 19, 1919. For a brief biography of Urbano Santos, see Abranches, *Governos e congressos da República dos Estados Unidos do Brasil*, 1:207–9.
14. *O Democrata*, July 19, 1919, published this story which had been supposedly told to Seabra by Epitácio Pessoa.
15. Morgan to Secretary of State, Rio, June 12, 1921, no. 1816, fls. 616–18,

Peçanha and Seabra were nominated for president and vice-president, respectively, as the candidates of the "Four Allies." Bezerra secretly fretted over the Seabra selection but honorably remained with the alliance. The campaign was badly financed and lacked coordination among the opposition groups of various states. Seabra campaigned in the southern states while Nilo toured the north. Nilo's campaign, strapped by a shortage of funds, was financed by chartering a Lloyd Brasileiro ship whose space was obviously rented out to political sympathizers "to cover the expenses of his [Nilo's] expedition."[16] Despite these valiant efforts and the sympathy shown by urban masses in Rio and São Paulo, the opposition candidates lost. Marshal Hermes da Fonseca demanded the establishment of the Tribunal of Honor to scrutinize the electoral results in an attempt to keep the federal congress from having the final say, but this proposal was rejected. On June 9, 1922, the federal congress declared Bernardes the winner.[17]

"THE BERNARDES LETTERS" AND HERMES

The military's involvement in the presidential election was partly triggered by an incident called "the Bernardes letters," but the deep-seated motive for the interference was the general instability that plagued postwar Brazil. In late 1921, candidate Bernardes is supposed to have written two letters to his campaign manager denouncing Hermes and ridiculing the army. The military called for an investigation. The Clube Militar under the presidency of Hermes set up a special committee to study the incident; under pressure, the committee rendered a judgment in early January 1922 that the letters were genuine, although many of the club officers believed them to be forgeries. Bullied by Hermes and his cohort, the club reluctantly decided that the nation should be the judge.[18] The issue and ensuing furor became so explosive that the neutral Epitácio found it

Internal Affairs of Brazil, Reel 4, 823.00/51–225, DOS/USNA; Belo, *A History of Modern Brazil*, pp. 242–44; Carone, *A república velha II*, pp. 332–41.

16. Morgan to Secretary of State, Rio, August 24, 1921, no. 1844, fls. 745–57, Internal Affairs of Brazil, Reel 4, 823.00/51–225, DOS/USNA.

17. Crosby to Secretary of State, Rio, June 14, 1922, no. 1914, fls. 117–19, Internal Affairs of Brazil, Reel 5, 823.00/226–399 [823.022/51–226–399?], ibid.

18. Morgan to Secretary of State, Rio, January 7, 1922, no dispatch no., fls. 1–6, ibid.; Carone, *A república velha II*, pp. 344–48. A handwriting expert wrote

prudent not to vote in an effort to avoid "an expression of preference for either candidate."[19]

Closely following this incident was the federal army's involvement in Pernambucan politics. In the fall of 1920, Governor José Bezerra succeeded in uniting various political factions in the state, hoping to maximize his prestige in the competition for netting the vice-presidential nomination. No fewer than five tribal and personalistic oligarchies complicated state politics: the Rosistas, Dantistas, Borbistas, Pessoistas, and Bezerristas. Governor Bezerra persuaded others to join him in an alliance known as *paz e concórdia* (peace and harmony), which broke down when the governor died in late March 1922. The oligarchic compact failed to agree on a suitable candidate to succeed Bezerra, and by mid-April two new factions emerged from the original five. The *coligados* (the coalition group) consisted of the followers of Dantas, Pessoa de Queiroz (Epitácio's cousin), Estácio Coimbra, and Rosas. The coligados ran Coronel Eduardo Lima de Castro, then the mayor of Recife, as their candidate, while the official party (the Borbistas) put up Federal Senator Henrique Carneiro da Cunha.[20] The federal army in Recife was in sympathy with the coligado candidate; the state police obviously backed the Borbista. The election results were disputed by both sides, and the state legislature, under pressure from Manuel Borba and the state police, granted the victory to Carneiro da Cunha.

This situation brought about swift confrontations between the coligados and the Borbistas, between the federal army and the state police, and between the president and the former president. The fighting between the federal army and the state police intensified in June as both sides were reinforced by private armies of jagunços and bandits from the interior. As president of the Clube Militar, Marshal Hermes dispatched a telegram to the federal garrison in Recife, urging it not to obey the federal government. The famous telegram "politics passes,

---

a book on the subject: Edgard Simões Correia, *As cartas falsas atribuidas ao snr. dr. Artur Bernardes e a prova da verdade.*

19. Morgan to Secretary of State, Rio, March 9, 1922, no. 1914, fls. 32–34, Internal Affairs of Brazil, Reel 5, 823.00/226–399, DOS/USNA. Epitácio was registered in Petrópolis and was in that city on election day.

20. Cameron, "Report on Political Disturbances in Pernambuco since March 26, 1922," Strictly Confidential, fls. 160–98, ibid.

the army stays" provoked President Epitácio Pessoa, whose political sympathy lay with the coligados, to order the house arrest of the former president, but he was released July 3.[21]

Tenentismo AND THE MODERNIST WEEK

Only two days later, the Fort of Copacabana and the Vila Militar in Rio revolted, initiating the first cycle of the famous junior officers' "revolution" of the 1920s. The awakening of the military, especially the junior grade officers, or tenentes, was enhanced by the political crisis caused by the presidential election, an unpredictable economy of falling exports and violently oscillating foreign exchange rates, and the infusion of new ideologies, especially communism. Swept into the vortex of an awakening New Brazil, the junior army officers resorted to armed violence to press for broader social, economic, and political reforms on behalf of the lower and middle classes. In the mid-twenties, urban areas such as Rio and São Paulo were stirring in an effort to organize class parties such as the Brazilian Communist Party in 1922 and the Democratic Party of São Paulo in 1927. At least one communist was elected to the city council of Rio, and the Democratic Party captured the office of mayor and a number of seats in the city council of São Paulo.[22]

Equally cogent in the presentation of the concept of a New Brazil was the Week of Modern Art of February 11–18, 1922, an adept summary of recent major trends in the arts and literature. Philosophically kin to tenentismo, the Modernist Week was considered a revolt against the traditionalism of a Brazil so willingly submissive to and imitative of Europe. A host of artists, writers, musicians, and architects joined a collective search for a new identity: Vila Lobos and Guiomar Novais in music, Victor Brecheret in sculpture, Mário de

21. Crosby to Secretary of State, Rio, July 5, 1922 (telegram), fl. 127, ibid.; Hélio Silva, *1922—sangue na areia de Copacabana*.

22. Lester Baker, Major, GS (Military Attaché), "Communism in Brazil," November 8, 1929, Internal Affairs of Brazil, Reel 8, 823.00B, DOS/USNA; Dulles, *Anarchists and Communists in Brazil*, is a thorough and informative work on the subject, with an extensive bibliography on communism. The standard work on the Democratic Party is Paulo Nogueira Filho, *Ideais e lutas de um burguês progressista: o Partido Democrático e a revolução de 1930*, the first edition of which appeared in 1958. Of the two communist aldermen in the City Council of Rio, Major Baker identified one as Minervino de Oliveira, who "may be head of the Brazilian Communist Party."

Andrade and Ronaldo de Carvalho in literature, Anita Malfatti and Di Cavalcanti in painting, and A. Moya and Georg Przyrembel in architecture were among the most stimulating proselytes of this new generation.[23] As the participants rejected the old values that had permitted blind worship of Europe and abjured things Brazilian, so too did the advent of a new era of tenentismo mark the beginning of the end of oligarchic Brazil.

FURTHER SETBACKS FOR SEABRA

Adding fuel to the already explosive political situation was the sudden death of the vice-president-elect, Urbano Santos, in May while he was en route to Rio. Seabra immediately claimed the vice-presidency on the grounds that he received the second highest number of votes. The federal lower court upheld Seabra's contention, to the dismay of the Bernardes camp, but the Federal Supreme Court reversed the decision in time to select Urbano's successor.[24] Bernardes looked to Pernambuco for his vice-president, Estácio Coimbra, the leader of the coligados and a political ally of Epitácio Pessoa. In August, Coimbra was elected unopposed. The chagrined and heartbroken Bahian chief saw Coimbra's ascent to the vice-presidency as a personal affront and Bernardes' revenge.

The failure to capture the vice-presidency was not the only price that Seabra had to pay in the election of 1922. The nomination of the Bahian governor as the vice-presidential candidate of the Republican Reaction group spurred the PRD hierarchy to split further, not over the nomination itself but over the constitutional successor to the governor. Senate President Coronel Frederico Costa suddenly found himself in a position to influence the power alignment within the PRD. As acting governor during Seabra's absence, Frederico Costa fired some Moniz men from state jobs, thus further undermining the political power of the already diminished group. The efforts of the party cadres in the municípios and capital districts were stifled by the top-level power struggle in the PRD at a most vulnerable time: the municipal election of late October 1921 for the term of

23. Araci Amaral, *Artes plásticas na semana de 22*, p. 130.
24. Crosby to Secretary of State, Rio, May 8, 1922 (telegram), fl. 38, July 25, 1922, fls. 245–55, Internal Affairs of Brazil, Reel 5, 823.00/226–399, DOS/USNA.

1922–24. The Bahian opposition cliques, well aware of the PRD's internal struggle, chose to attack.

The demoralized PRD cadres failed to run a tight election, especially in the coastal municípios. In Cachoeira, an opposition candidate trounced the incumbent PRD intendente. In Ilhéus and Itabuna, the PRD coronéis retained their seats but by a narrow margin. Santo Amaro, Muritiba, and São Felix all defected to the opposition. In the central west and in the São Francisco region, a few key municípios fell into the hands of the opposition. Coronel João Duque triumphantly returned to power in Carinhanha by defeating the PRD coronel there. Itaberaba, the important "gateway" município to the Lavras, was now in the hands of the anti-PRD forces.[25] The overall performance of the PRD candidates was viewed as good, but the slow disintegration of the party was definitely under way.

The dominant Bahian party suffered still further setbacks when Bernardes took office in November 1922. The new president had a reputation as a gutsy political fighter: he remembered his friends and never forgot his foes. As it turned out, Bernardes was just beginning to unveil his plans for revenge. In the organization of his cabinet, he picked an opposition deputy from Bahia, Miguel Calmon, to be his minister of agriculture. As a former cabinet minister in the Afonso Pena presidency (1906–9), Calmon had been the boy wonder of Brazilian politics and had come to represent the pro-PRM Bahian politicians. His entry into the Bernardes cabinet laid the groundwork for the founding of a new opposition party in Bahia and paved the way for Seabra's downfall two years later when he made his brother Góis Calmon the governor.[26]

In the state of Rio, the gubernatorial election in July 1922 was fought between a supporter of Nilo Peçanha and a Bernardista candidate. The election, coming immediately after the formal announcement by the congress of Bernardes' victory in June, inevitably resulted in a duplicata. The anti-Nilo candidate contested the results, and the federal president promptly proclaimed federal intervention in early 1923.[27] Both events only

25. *A Tarde*, October 23, December 10, 16, 27, 1921, March 1, 1922.

26. Carone, *A república velha II*, p. 361; Pang, "The Politics of *Coronelismo*," pp. 232–33.

27. *A Tarde*, May 23, 1923. The political retaliation against the Nilistas (Nilo's supporters) had begun before the governor's election in the State of Rio

encouraged the Bahian opposition to renew its efforts to unseat Seabra.

With the outspoken support of the federal president and Minister Calmon, Bahian opposition politicians began to negotiate an alliance. In January 1923, Pedro Lago, Vital Soares, Simões Filho, and others held a plenary meeting where they resolved to found the Bahian Republican Concentration (Concentração Republicana da Bahia). "Concentration" was political parlance for confederation, meaning that there remained a few obstacles to be overcome among the factions before a party could be forged. Soon the CRB was reinforced by such politicians as the Calmons, the Mangabeiras, Alfredo "Ruizinho" Barbosa, and José Álvaro Cova, Moniz' police chief of 1916–20. From the backlands, Geraldo Rocha, the leading power broker of the interior municípios and counsel to many coronéis of the São Francisco region, defected from the PRD and joined the CRB, taking with him many backland chiefs of the valley and the Lavras.[28]

CRB's New Backland Elite

The acquisition of Geraldo Rocha by the opposition alliance was as significant as winning over the Calmons in the Recôncavo: it encouraged other backlanders to join the CRB also. The Rochas originally settled in Barra in the early nineteenth century but later moved farther west to Barreiras, where the clan prospered as the elite of an important commercial center in the far west of Bahia. One of the largest landowners and cattle ranchers, the Rochas not only ruled the western part of the São Francisco Valley but also were influential in state and national politics.

The clan was represented politically by brothers-in-law Francisco and Geraldo. By the late 1910s, physician Geraldo and

in July 1922. As a Nilista deputy, Raul Fernandes was excluded from his place on the Finance Committee in the Federal Chamber of Deputies, one he had held before Bernardes became the president. Fernandes was opposed in the July 1922 gubernatorial election by Army Major Feliciano Sodré. The election resulted in a duplicata; the elections for the offices of municípios went overwhelmingly Nilista, forty of forty-eight municípios. For details of the events leading to the federal intervention, see Carvalho, *Raul Fernandes*, pp. 187–99.

28. *A Tarde*, January 12, 29, 1923; interviews with Bolívar Sant'Ana Batista, Salvador, June 2–4, 1968, and Morgan Duarte, Salvador, July 29, August 2–3, 5, 1968. Geraldo Rocha talks about the coronelista politics of Bahia's backlands in his *Nacionalismo*.

engineer Francisco emerged as political advisors to such coronéis as Horácio de Matos, Franklin Lins, and João Duque, among others. Geraldo Rocha was especially astute and skilled in managing the coronéis. As a brother-in-law of Coronel Antônio Balbino de Carvalho of Barreiras, one of the most prestigious men in the valley, Geraldo moved easily in corone-lista political circles. In the presidential election of 1922, Artur Bernardes tapped Geraldo as his emissary to the Bahian back-lands. On one occasion, candidate Bernardes approached Horácio de Matos, obviously at Geraldo's suggestion, to ask this warlord of the Lavras for electoral support.[29] Bernardes' victory only enhanced the prestige of Geraldo and Francisco Rocha in Bahian politics. With the Calmons and the Mangabeiras from the coast and the Rochas from the sertão, the Bahian Republican Concentration was well equipped to challenge the Democratic Party (PRD) in the elections of early 1923.

"Política dos Presidentes"

In the federal election, both the PRD and the CRB claimed victory for their candidates. President Bernardes gave half (eleven) of the Bahian delegation to the CRB in the federal Chamber of Deputies and assigned the opposition deputies to important committees while the PRD solons were removed from them.[30] The state legislative election also ended in a duplicata, and by April the chamber of deputies was holding two separate sessions. The CRB deputies met at Campo Grande, another section of the capital, while the PRD group held its session at the state capitol.[31] Encouraged by Bernardes' favoring the CRB

29. Horácio refused to go along with Bernardes: Matos to Reis, Lençóis, September 8, 1921, and Matos to Seabra, Lençóis, August 4, 1921, AHQM. Horácio's telegram to Bernardes' aide (Antônio Marques Reis) states, "Sciente vosso telegramma. Sinto não poder apoiar candidatura eminente Dr. Arthur Bernardes por estar filiado Partido Democrata ao qual hypotheco solidariedade" ("received your telegram. I am sorry that I am not able to support the candidacy of the eminent Dr. Arthur Bernardes, for I am tied to the Democratic Party [of Seabra] to which I pledge solidarity"). Since telegrams between politicians were routinely censored, this message might have been meant to deceive the Seabra side. It is highly possible that Horácio supported Bernardes in spite of the tele-gram, since the two became allies after 1922. See note 49.
30. *A Tarde*, May 12, 1923; for details, see Pang, "The Politics of Coro-nelismo," pp. 239–40.
31. *A Tarde*, April 20, 1923.

federal deputies, the opposition appealed to the president to resolve the impasse in the state legislature.

With the advent of Artur Bernardes, Brazilian politics entered a new phase—the politics of presidents. In contrast to the politics of governors, the politics of presidents signified the ascending role of the federal chief executive as the final arbiter in state political conflicts. The direct involvement of the president occurred frequently in the Hermes da Fonseca administration (1910–14), especially under the tutelage of Gaúcho Senator Pinheiro Machado, who sought to dominate state and regional politics of the north. The counterforce to this attempt, or the politics of rescue, ironically contributed to fuller development of presidential interventionist politics. The death of the Gaúcho *caudilho* in 1915 briefly ended this trend until Epitácio Pessoa came to power. An ambitious and independent-minded president from the northeast, Epitácio intervened in state politics out of necessity, in particular in the northeast. In Bahia, the federal intervention of 1920 and its resultant peace treaties with the backland coronéis effectively terminated the existing function of the governor as an intermediary between the federal president and coronéis, on the one hand, and as the legitimate interpreter of state political will, on the other. Direct access was established to bind the president and the coronéis politically, and, after 1922, the two authoritarian presidents (Artur Bernardes and Washington Luís) carried this pattern even further. In 1923, the CRB maximized the interdependency between the highest and lowest levels of government in an effort to destroy the middle, the PRD government of Seabra.

In order to blunt the impact of the new politics of presidents, Seabra had been considering a compromise with the CRB. In January and February 1923, the governor attempted to persuade the PRD directorate to bend with the wind.[32] His party was divided into two factions, Seabra loyalists and the Moniz group. As Seabra analyzed the situation, the gubernatorial election of that year held the key to the PRD's survival. The reverses suffered by the official party in the legislative elections (federal and state) convinced the governor of an impending need for compromise. On municipal, state, and federal levels, the PRD was no longer in a dominant position.

32. Ibid., January 30, February 28, 1923.

Under normal circumstances, Governor Seabra would have picked Federal Senator Moniz Sodré as his successor. Antônio Moniz had succeeded Luís Viana as Bahia's federal senator in 1921, when the latter's nine-year term expired. But in 1923, with a vindictive president in power, the PRD could hardly afford another move that would accelerate its decline. When the party hierarchy was unable to agree on a suitable candidate, Seabra himself proceeded with a compromise. He asked an eminent physician-historian, Brás Hermenegildo do Amaral, to serve as a go-between for the PRD and the CRB. After some arduous negotiations, Brás do Amaral reported to Seabra that a compromise candidate had been found, Francisco Marques de Góis Calmon. On February 28, the governor formally revealed his candidate. Judging from initial reactions, the choice was an excellent one.[33]

The selection of Góis Calmon was well considered. As president of the Bahian Economic Bank and the Bahian Bar Association, he was the least controversial of the three Calmon brothers. Miguel was not interested in a state job; Antônio, the most cunning and best politician of the family, kept to his interests in federal politics. In addition, Miguel and Antônio were the key directors of the CRB, and, as such, neither would be a good choice as a compromise governor. More important, Miguel and Antônio had been militant anti-Seabristas for a decade or so, and the PRD could never accept either of them. In a sense, the nomination of Góis Calmon was Seabra's way of admitting his defeat. On March 2, the governor informed Rui Barbosa by letter that he had decided to name Góis to succeed him, because he wanted "to avoid a political fight." On that very day, Rui Barbosa died, never having seen his dream fulfilled. The note that announced the imminent fall of Seabra was never shown to him.[34]

Although Góis Calmon was a good choice, he offered both advantages and disadvantages as a candidate. His career as a banker-lawyer was impeccable. He was a key backer of the commercial class in the election of 1919, and neither the dominant economic elite of the state nor the CRB could reject a Calmon. He could keep the commercial-financial community

33. Ibid.; Pang, "The Politics of *Coronelismo*," pp. 240–42.
34. *O Imparcial* (Bahia), March 2, 1923.

from blatantly opposing Seabra. Since he was a potential healer of Bahian politics, the PRD hierarchy could find no valid reason for denying the candidacy to the least political Calmon, but there were possible drawbacks. Seabra was aware of Góis' indecisive character and his reliance on Miguel and Antônio for advice, yet he thought that these weaknesses were far outweighed by his strengths. Antônio Moniz had shown somewhat similiar characteristics—a good family, no charisma, and blind loyalty to Seabra—but once in power, he had become ambitious, self-reliant, and independent of Seabra and of the party. Góis Calmon had been Seabra's student in the Faculty of Law in Recife and might accept his mentor as a political master and not depend on the CRB politicians. By the same token, he might ignore the PRD, and Seabra in particular. All in all, the governor thought it was worth the gamble.

Góis' Candidacy and PRD New Hopes

The initial reaction in the CRB and PRD rank and file was enthusiastic. President Bernardes was said to have approved the compromise and promised to remain neutral. In case of a duplicata, the president said, the court should decide the outcome. The Archbishop of Bahia endorsed Góis Calmon, as did the PRD local leaders in Ilhéus and the Recôncavo. Federal Deputy Otávio Mangabeira arrived in São Paulo to confer with Governor Washington Luís on the question of the Bahian succession. From the Lavras Diamantinas, a Horacista state deputy, Coronel Manuel Alcântara de Carvalho, announced his support of Góis Calmon and urged his chief to do the same. The warlords of the sertão, Douca Medrado of Mucugê, Franklin Lins of Pilão Arcado, Chico Leobas of Remanso, Marcionílio of Maracás, and Duque of Carinhanha openly embraced the candidate. Once Seabra won major commitments for his candidate from key coronéis and bacharéis, he seemed more optimistic about his party's future.[35]

By July, the governor chose to embark on a political trip to the backlands. The occasion was appropriate: Horácio de Matos, the PRD chief of the Lavras and the key man in coronelista politics,

35. *Diário de Notícias*, March 8, 10, 11, 1923; *A Tarde*, March 19, April 28, 1923.

had just married a daughter of Douca Medrado, the legendary chief of Mucugê, thus reinforcing the political alliance between these two warlords and catapulting Horácio to the fore as the most powerful man in the Bahian sertão.[36] The summit conference between Horácio and Seabra was arranged in Lapa, a neutral territory. Making his way upstream from Juàzeiro, Seabra paid courtesy calls on the coronéis of the valley and reinforced his contacts with them. In Lapa, the governor met the warlord of the Lavras, their first face-to-face encounter. Among other matters discussed was the political future of the fallen PRD state senator from the Lavras, Coronel César Sá. The governor agreed to sack the senator and offered Horácio the vacant seat. In August, two weeks after his return from Lapa, the governor ordered the PRD directorate to remove the senator on the grounds that he was absent from the legislature too often. Speaking for the PRD executive committee, Federal Senator Antônio Moniz, one-time nemesis of the backland coronéis, announced the nomination of Horácio as the new PRD state senator.[37] It was one of few egregious political announcements that Moniz had made in years.

Seabra's trip to Lapa and the announcement of the Góis candidacy should have produced political rapprochement between the PRD and the CRB, but little progress was made toward conciliation. Bernardes continued to be hostile to the PRD and, in particular, to Seabra. The senatorial election to fill the seat previously held by Rui Barbosa was set for July. The PRD ran Arlindo Leoni and the CRB matched him with Pedro Lago. No concrete formula for sharing public office had been reached by the two parties, and therefore no one was certain of the outcome of the election. But one thing was certain: President Bernardes would make the final choice. The routine duplicata was referred to the federal senate, which promptly declared Lago the winner.[38] In view of its second defeat in the federal congress since May, the PRD—especially the Moniz faction—was convinced that the compromise candidacy of Góis would not save the tottering party. Furthermore, it was President Bernardes, not the CRB, who was the reluctant conciliator. By September the disillusioned Moniz faction was demanding the cancellation of

36. *A Tarde*, August 2, 1923; Barbosa, *Horácio de Matos*, pp. 57–58.
37. *O Democrata*, August 29, September 6–7, 11, 1923.
38. Ibid., September 5, 1923.

the compromise candidacy and threatening to boycott the convention if the wish was not honored.[39]

The PRD met on October 15, 1923, to nominate Góis Calmon as its candidate, without the Monizes in attendance. A total of 120 delegates from various municípios came and appeared unperturbed, at least on the surface, by the Monizes' rebellion. Senate President Frederico Costa presided over the convention that hurriedly nominated Góis Calmon.[40] While the Monizes were brooding, the president of the Republic, Minister Calmon, and other national politicians of the PRM and the PRP enthusiastically endorsed the candidate. The problem of a merger between the two groups remained to be solved.

THE PRD VS. THE CRB

The long-awaited merger of the PRD and the CRB never happened. As was the PRD, the CRB was fragmented, unable to present a united front. Soon after the campaign was under way, a pro-Bernardes (but anti-Calmon) wing of the CRB alleged that the Calmons were attempting to take over the party by fortifying their position on the municipal level through the destruction of their foes within the CRB. Furthermore, the anti-Calmon faction, like the Moniz group, doubted the utility of a possible marriage of the two parties. To arouse more friction within and without the CRB, they accused the Calmons of conspiring to cooperate with Seabra and to become masters of Bahian politics. Minister Calmon was said to have told brother Antônio "to do anything to get the nomination for Chico [Góis Calmon]." A further disconcerting accusation was that the Calmons were not loyal to Bernardes. To substantiate this, the anti-Calmon wing pointed out that Wanderley Pinho, a son-in-law of Góis, had succeeded in eliminating the Bernardista power elite of Santo Amaro. Similar Calmonista coups were taking place elsewhere, all to shore up the victory of Góis at the sacrifice of the CRB's unity.[41]

The anti-Calmon wing did not stop here. Medeiros Neto, one of the leaders of the group, informed the PRD that Góis had promised Bernardes that he would "extirpate Seabrismo" once he was elected governor. The governor immediately questioned

39. *A Tarde*, September 25, 28–29, 1923; for details of the Monizes' opposition, see Pang, "The Politics of *Coronelismo*," p. 244.
40. *A Tarde*, October 10, 13, 16, 1923.
41. Ibid., November 20, 1923.

the president about the alleged remark, and when Bernardes failed to deny it, Seabra was reportedly wavering on his commitment to the candidate.[42] Medeiros Neto and his group presented Francisco Prisco de Sousa Paraíso as their candidate and asked the PRD to support him, but only the Moniz wing of the PRD joined them.[43]

A few days later, on November 27, Seabra announced that he, too, was withdrawing his support for Góis Calmon. In an attempt to bring the PRD to his side, the governor called a meeting of the Executive Committee; only one member showed. At a later meeting, two members came, one bearing a letter signed by those absent demanding that the PRD continue to back Góis. Virtually deserted by his loyalists, the briar fox of Bahian politics was more than ever determined to go down fighting Bernardes and the Calmons rather than committing political suicide.[44]

Seabra's turnabout was certainly influenced by the unreceptive attitude of Bernardes as well as by his undying loyalty to the Monizes. Nonetheless, it produced electrifying results. The anti-Moniz faction of the PRD responded to the governor's rash action by bolting the party and joining the CRB. Frederico Costa, the Pereira Moacir brothers, Antônio Pessoa, and other Seabra loyalists parted ways with the chief. The enraged Seabra responded by removing from office those state PRD officials who continued to identify with Góis Calmon.[45] In the interior, similar party-switching was taking place. Horácio de Matos, who had pledged his support the previous August in Lapa, remained with Góis.[46] With Horácio standing firm, the Lavras Diamantinas became Calmon country. In the São Francisco Valley, the Pereira Moacir brothers and the Rochas

42. Brett to Secretary of State, Bahia, November 27, 1923, no. 34, fls. 712–13, Internal Affairs of Brazil, Reel 5, 823.00/226–399, DOS/USNA.

43. *A Tarde*, December 15, 1923.

44. Ibid., November 27, 1923; Brett to Secretary of State, Bahia, December 3, 1923, no. 36, fls. 714–15, Internal Affairs of Brazil, Reel 5, 823.00/226–399, DOS/USNA; Pang, "The Politics of *Coronelismo*," p. 248.

45. *A Tarde*, December 1, 4, 1923; Barbosa, *Horácio de Matos*, p. 61; Brett to Secretary of State, Bahia, December 4, 1923, no. 37, fls. 716–17, Internal Affairs of Brazil, Reel 5, 823.00/226–399, DOS/USNA.

46. Horácio supported Góis. See a document marked "Exposição de Motivos: Horácio de Queiroz Matos aos Seus Correligionários e Amigos" (dated) December 1923, in Barbosa, *Horácio de Matos*, pp. 129–31. Seabra attempted to persuade Horácio to withdraw his support of Góis but failed; see Moraes, *Jagunços e heróis*, pp. 145–47.

(Geraldo and Francisco) persuaded the coronéis to stay with the Calmons. In the capital, candidate Prisco Paraíso formally withdrew from the race and pledged his support to Góis.[47]

In spite of the snowballing popularity of Góis, the PRD was not going to concede gracefully. The Seabrista party picked a last-minute, face-saving candidate, fully realizing the futility of the move. Arlindo Leoni, the defeated senatorial candidate and a loyal Seabrista, was to oppose Góis Calmon. Leoni was promptly dubbed the "dead cat" (gato morto), a scapegoat and an ineffective prop for the faltering PRD.[48] Smelling defeat in the air, the CRB moved to secure its victory for Góis. As expected, Bernardes' attitude in the election was a decisive factor, in spite of his public utterance about neutrality. He had made up his mind about punishing Seabra in November 1922, and only a year later the vindictive chief of state had a magnificent opportunity to implement the "politics of presidents." Bernardes ordered the federal army in Bahia to patrol the capital and dispatched a naval squadron to back up the army, all ostensibly to maintain a fair atmosphere for the forthcoming election.[49] In an equal show of enthusiam, Minister Calmon and Federal Senator Pedro Lago sent a circular telegram to the state politicians and coronéis to vote for Góis. Bernardes, for the second time in two years, requested Horácio de Matos and other backland chiefs to elect Góis as the next governor of Bahia.[50] On December 29, 1923, Bahia was to witness the demise of the official party for the second time since 1911, the victim of the politics of presidents.

47. A Tarde, December 5, 10–11, 1923.
48. Barbosa to Matos, Bahia, March 24, 1924, AHQM; Pang, "The Politics of Coronelismo," pp. 250–51. The American consul in Salvador reported that Seabra offered the candidacy to Prisco Paraíso before the PRD cardinals chose Arlindo Leoni (Brett to Secretary of State, Bahia, December 14, 1923, no. 40, fls. 718–19, Internal Affairs of Brazil, Reel 5, 823.00/226–399, DOS/USNA). He stated further that Seabra, who was seventy years old, could have been "bullied" by the Monizes to withdraw his support of Góis and to put up Arlindo Leoni as the PRD candidate.
49. A Tarde, December 8, 1923; Melo Franco, Outubro, 1930, pp. 90–91. The Bernardes government put on pressures in other areas. The American consul reported that the minister of transportation ordered the São Francisco Company not to carry any arms for the Seabra government, and the National Telegraph Service required its Bahian manager to make copies of all telegrams to and from Seabra (Brett to Secretary of State, Bahia, December 27, 1923, no. 43, fls. 734–35, Internal Affairs of Brazil, Reel 5, 823.00/226–399, DOS/USNA).
50. A Tarde, December 15, 1923; "Exposição de Motivos," in Barbosa, Horácio de Matos, pp. 129–31.

7. The Balance of Power Restored: The *Entente Cordiale* between Coronéis and Bacharéis, 1924–1930

J OSÉ BEZERRA, the governor of Pernambuco who master-minded the paz e concórdia alliance (1920–22), made a profound observation on the nature of elections in general: "being elected is one thing, being recognized is another."[1] Both the PRD and the CRB claimed victory in the December election, forcing the Bahian state legislature to "recognize" the winner. The pro-PRD papers, including *Diário Oficial*, awarded Leoni a two-to-one edge, while *A Tarde*, chief mouthpiece of the CRB, granted Góis an incredible seven-to-one victory. The discrepancy in the total number of the votes cast as claimed by the two parties was so glaring that an impartial observer had to conclude the purported results were fraudulent: *A Tarde* reported a total of 92,236 votes cast, *Diário Oficial* 72,096. The discrepancy of 20,000 votes was never explained, although it was assumed that the bico de pena was responsible.[2] Whatever the conflicting

1. Adélia Pinto, *Um livro sem título (memórias de uma provinciana)*, p. 181. The original in Portuguese is "Eleito é uma coisa, reconhecido é outra."

2. *A Tarde*, January 7, 1924. *Diário de Notícias*, January 3, 1924, gave Góis Calmon 70,059 and Leoni 12,730. *O Democrata* and *Diário Oficial* reported the "official count" filed by PRD State Senator Wenceslau Guimarães as Leoni 47,575 and Góis Calmon 24,521.

claims, it was the politics of presidents that resolved the impasse.

The American consul in Salvador reported that Seabra and his party were using government funds to buy senators for political support.[3] Between January and March of 1924, both the PRD and the CRB applied fresh pressures to state legislators for recognition of their respective candidates. A group of independent-minded legislators of both groups asked President Bernardes to intervene so that the legislature could process the election results without violence.[4] The chamber of deputies was about evenly divided; the supposedly PRD senate was wavering. At least thirteen of the twenty-one senators had promised to recognize Góis the winner in spite of Seabra's bribery; only three or four could be counted on to support Leoni. With such dim prospects, Seabra and his party chiefs resolved to resort to violence to make Leoni the next governor.

Since November 1923, the capital had been patrolled by the federal army, and the state police had in fact been neutralized, indicating little desire for a confrontation. The commander of the state police was ordered by its constitutional commander, the governor, to lock up the legislators when the legislature met to review the election results, but the outpowered state police chose to disobey.[5] The federal army was still stationed in key sectors of Salvador, and, at the request of the state legislators, President Bernardes placed the army on alert and had important state buildings occupied so that the police could not interfere with the recognition process. By the end of the first week of March, the state legislature declared Góis Calmon the winner.[6] There were rumors that Seabra and his henchmen

3. Brett to Secretary of State, Bahia, February 13, 1924, fls. 783–84, Internal Affairs of Brazil, Reel 5, 823.00/226–399, DOS/USNA.

4. Barbosa, *Horácio de Matos*, pp. 61–63.

5. Pang, "The Politics of *Coronelismo*," pp. 253–54.

6. In the recognition battle at the state senate, Wenceslau Guimarães spoke for the PRD and Pereira Moacir for the opposition. Olímpio Barbosa reported to Horácio that Raul Alves and "ZéCarlos" were cooking up some sinister plots to keep the victory for Arlindo Leoni and to unseat Coronel Frederico Costa, the incumbent president of the senate and a PRD leader/supporter of Góis. For details, see Barbosa to Matos, Bahia, March 24, 1924, AHQM. The American consul also reported that in spite of Góis' victory, "the Seabra administration means to turn over the state government to sr. Arlindo Leoni on March 29, regardless of the opinion of the legislature unless federal interference comes before that time" (Brett to Secretary of State, Bahia, March 6, 1924, no. 58, fls. 794–97, Internal Affairs of Brazil, Reel 5, 823.00/226–399, DOS/USNA).

were preparing to ignore the decision and were going to turn over the government to Leoni. President Bernardes proclaimed a state of siege on March 20 to ensure the orderly transition of government from Seabra to Góis Calmon.[7]

THE PATTERNS OF BAHIAN OLIGARCHIES

Such important families as the Calmons, the Monizes, the Mangabeiras, and even the Araújo Pinhos produced a number of politicians, but none succeeded in building a statewide network of political clientele. The diversified economy, the isolation of scattered economic activities, and difficult communication and transportation links were some factors that discouraged the rise of a familiocratic oligarchy to the state level in Bahia. In its place, tribal and personalistic oligarchies emerged, and from time to time they succeeded in transforming themselves into a primitive form of party. During the First Republic, no political party in Bahia levied membership fees; general expenses for party operations were assumed by the state government. Each clique or party made and unmade its own patronage army, which in turn manned the field operations of the ruling group. In 1912, when the PRD lost control of the state government, it dissolved into numerous personality-dominated factions, quickly losing the cohesiveness that the financial and patronage resources of the state government had forged. Similarly, in 1924, the PRD that had ruled the state for twelve years quickly disintegrated into factions as the governorship was seized by the Calmons of the CRB. It was only then that Bahia witnessed the rise of the first collegial oligarchy of the state.

When Francisco Marques de Góis Calmon became the penultimate elected governor of Bahia on March 29, 1924, the Calmons emerged as an enduring political dynasty of Brazil whose influence spanned more than a century. Under the monarchy, the Calmons distinguished themselves in Conservative politics. The Marquês de Abrantes (Miguel Calmon du Pin e Almeida) was a great-uncle to Góis; the Barão de Araújo Góis was a maternal great-uncle to the governor. The governor's father was an admiral of the imperial navy. The Calmons were

7. Gaulin, "State of Bahia under Martial Law," March 21, 1924, fls. 798–99, ibid. The American consul in Rio added that Seabra "will offer only verbal resistance."

also senhores de engenho in Santo Amaro and São Francisco do Conde, intermarrying with such equally aristocratic clans as the Araújo Pinhos, the Costa Pintos, and the Vilas Boases, to name a few blue-blooded latifundistas of Bahia. When "Chico," oldest of the three brothers, became governor, he represented a vast network of Bahia's economic elites, whose collegial interests extended from sugar to banking. In the words of the American consul in Bahia, Góis was the first businessman to become governor, and "Bahia will be regenerated financially, politically and morally"[8] as a consequence. In a way it was fitting to have the businessman-banker Chico in the governor's office to represent the complex economic interests of companies and clans, instead of either of the politician-brothers, Miguel and Antônio.

Miguel, named after great-uncle Abrantes, was the family star. At twenty-two, engineer Miguel became the state secretary of agriculture. At twenty-eight, he became a federal minister, assuming the role of power broker in state and national politics. His meteoric rise slowed only when the PRB disintegrated over the election of Araújo Pinho as governor in 1908 and when his patron Afonso Pena died the following year. The years of PRD rule (1912–24) were a long political winter for Miguel who emerged from hibernation to become a federal minister in the Bernardes cabinet. Miguel's return to the locus of power in Rio laid the foundations for unification of Bahian opposition cliques as well as political recovery of the agrarian aristocracy in the Recôncavo.

Older brother Antônio was reputed to be the family politician.[9] Although his political career was less spectacular than the youngest brother's, he was an effective organizer. It was Antônio who negotiated with Seabra for the nomination of his oldest brother Chico for governor. Although he never held an office higher than that of federal deputy, Antônio nevertheless emerged as the political Calmon of the clan in the last six years

8. See Brett to Secretary of State, Bahia, October 13, 1923, fls. 706–7, ibid.; according to this dispatch, Bernardes made it clear that he would support Góis for governor and so instructed the CRB leaders. Peixoto et al., *Góis Calmon in memoriam*, is a short biography of Góis. For biographical information on the Calmons, see Costa, "Genealogia baiana," pp. 153–55.

9. Interview with Fiel Fontes, Rio, September 8, 1971. Fiel Fontes, son of Judge Paulo Martins Fontes, served in the federal chamber of deputies with Antônio Calmon.

of the First Republic. Thus, with the three brothers in politics (a federal minister, a federal deputy, and the governor), the Calmons established a formidable hold on state politics at the head of Bahia's first collegial oligarchy.

OTHER CONFEDERATE MEMBERS

The politicians of the ruling CRB were not house pets of the Calmons. Countering the influence of the agrarian dynasty was the bourgeois upstart Mangabeira family. The sons of a pharmacist in Salvador, João and Otávio were born into a middle-class family. João moved to the cacao frontier where he first practiced law and later became a local politician, serving as mayor of Ilhéus, federal deputy, and finally federal senator-elect in 1930. A political maverick and socialist, he was also a born opposition politician, emerging as an "in" party deputy in the last six years of the First Republic. One of the few politicians of the First Republic still active in the 1960s, João Mangabeira capped his career by serving as a cabinet minister for the Goulart administration.[10]

Younger brother Otávio was more cautious and conservative than João, but he did lead the Mangabeira group in state politics. A civil engineer, Otávio began his political career as a councilman in Salvador in 1908. In 1910, he supported Hermes da Fonseca and became one of the founders of the Seabra party of the PRD. He was chief of Bahia's bancada in the chamber of deputies when Góis became governor; in 1926 Otávio was named to the portfolio of foreign affairs by President Washington Luís. In the 1920s, Otávio was the spokesman for Bahia's Bernardistas. At one time, he told Raul Soares, governor of Minas and Bernardes' confidant, that in a showdown with the Calmons, at least eighteen of the twenty-two Bahian deputies would vote with him.[11] Like Seabra and Rui Barbosa, the Mangabeiras rose to political prominence as bourgeois statesmen of urban origins. Their socioeconomic backgrounds were in contrast and even counterweight to the dynastic rural agrarian politicians. This diverse nature of confederate politics of the oligarchy accounted for the CRB's inability to become a cohesive party at the outset.

10. Jaime de Sá Menezes, *Vultos que ficaram. Os irmãos Mangabeira (Francisco, João e Otávio),* pp. 77–157, esp. pp. 82–83.
11. Mangabeira to Soares, Rio, May 26, 1924, AOM.

The political relationship between the littoral and the sertão still needed to be redefined.

THE POLARIZATION OF CONFEDERATE POLITICS

Outside Salvador and the Recôncavo, polarization of the Calmon and Mangabeira factions was taking place. In the cacao country of southern Bahia, Antônio Pessoa was still in charge. He had supported Góis in the election and was a long-time companion of Frederico Costa in the state senate. Advanced in age, he was content to be a state senator while delegating the local political mantle to his son Mário, the intendente of Ilhéus.[12] In other cacao municípios, coronéis were split along the two major streams of politics. Federal Deputy João Mangabeira, who represented southern Bahia, commanded a substantial following of his own. Aside from these considerations, the traditional jealousy of cacao planters and merchants toward Salvador's coveted status as the economic capital hardly helped to turn the region toward the Calmons.

In the São Francisco region, the Calmons did not fare well. In Juàzeiro, Coronel Aprígio Duarte Filho, a Seabrista second-term intendente, was replaced by a Calmon man, Coronel Leonidas Torres, in 1924. As it turned out, the change was only temporary: Duarte Filho returned to power two years later. In Sento Sé, where the Seabristas had a strong hold through Federal Deputy Raul Alves, Tenente Romualdo Leal Vieira was elected intendente by the people for the term 1924–26. He never completed his term; instead, Governor Góis Calmon "imposed" his intendente, Luís Antônio de Lacerda, who served until 1928.[13] In Pilão Arcado, the redoubt of Franklin Lins, the governor was powerless. The coronel served as intendente from 1920 to 1924 and then assumed the presidency of the municipal council. During this time, Franklin was provoked on numerous occasions by the state government but successfully defended his position. Soon, he was pushed to the Mangabeira faction, and he remained anti-Calmon until 1930.[14] In Remanso, Chico Leobas,

12. *Diário Oficial*, December 4, 1924. Coronel Virgílio Calasans de Amorim, an ally of Coronel Antônio Pessoa, was president of the Electoral Board of Ilhéus.

13. Ibid., January 17, 1924; Romualdo Leal Vieira, *Sento-Sé rico e ignoto*, pp. 69–76; interview with Bolívar Sant'Ana Batista, Salvador, June 1, 1968.

14. Albuquerque to Mangabeira, Pilão Arcado, February 23, 1920, AOM;

owner of a famous harem of the valley and political ally of Francisco Rocha, was staunchly anti-Calmon.[15] The Castelo Branco clan, rival to Chico Leobas, remained with the government, switching from Seabra to Góis Calmon.[16] In Barreiras, Coronel Antônio Balbino de Carvalho and brother-in-law Chico Rocha had seized control of the município in 1920. In 1922, Chico Rocha was elected to the federal congress, and Antônio Balbino, president of the municipal council, assumed Rocha's unexpired term as intendente. Coronel Abílio Wolney was "elected" in Antônio's place.[17] With Chico and Geraldo Rocha working as a team in Rio de Janeiro, Antônio Balbino and Abílio Wolney dominated the politics of Barreiras and its vicinity until 1930 and beyond. These coronelista oligarchs were pro-Mangabeira.

The upstream municípios leaned more to the Calmons. In Lapa, Federal Deputy Antônio Pereira da Silva Moacir and his brother had been political chiefs for some time. As former directors of the PRD in that region, the Pereira Moacir brothers built up an impressive clientele among the upstream valley's coronéis. Until 1920, Lapa had lacked the tradition of strongman rule, but after that year, Antônio emerged as the unchallenged ruler. By 1924, he was made the governor's man and a federal deputy in that part of Bahia as a reward for his famed defection to the Calmons in the 1923 election. In Carinhanha, João Duque, in turn, remained friendly to the Calmons, serving as the intendente until 1928.[18] With Miguel Calmon in the cabinet of the Mineiro president, Duque's relations with the Calmons in Salvador were obviously tempered by his traditional ties with Minas.

---

interview with Wilson Lins (a son of Coronel Franklin Lins de Albuquerque), Salvador, May 14, 1968.

15. Coronel Chico Leobas once told Governor Góis that the state government could not remove a state tax collector from the job without his permission: "tomei a resolução de pedir a V. Exa. para que isso não se dé": França Antunes to Góis Calmon, Remanso, February 4, 1926, AFMGC.

16. Simões Filho to Góis Calmon, Salvador, telegram, no date, AFMGC. Simões advised to Góis to appoint Anfilófio Castelo Branco suplente de juiz municipal.

17. *Diário Oficial*, November 24, 1920, January 24, 1922.

18. Orlando M. Carvalho, *O rio da unidade nacional: o São Francisco*, pp. 102–3, lists Duque, Franklin, and Janjão as "donos do rio"; *Diário Oficial*, January 24, 1922.

CHICO CALMON VS. HORÁCIO DE MATOS

The major challenge that the Calmons faced in their rise to political supremacy came from the Lavras coronéis. Between December 1924 and February 1925, the private armies of the coronelista state of the Lavras collided with the combined forces of the Força Pública da Bahia and anti-Horacista coronéis. In this war, the role of the federal president was crucial as the final arbiter in the restoration of peace and the eventual establishment of the entente cordiale between the sertão and Salvador. In Bahia, the war between the Calmons and Horácio de Matos was the first major test of the viability of the politics of presidents. The outcome of the so-called Battle of Lençóis illustrates perfectly the workings of the coronel-president relationship, on one hand, and the diminished role of the governor in local affairs, on the other.

There were several factors that came into play, precipitating the Calmon-Matos showdown in 1924–25. As part of the concessions granted to the treaty coronéis of 1920, Horácio de Matos was made the Lavras state senator by the PRD, replacing the traditional oligarch, César Sá. César's uncle, Francisco Sá, was an important Cearense politician, who transplanted his political roots from Minas by marrying a daughter of the state oligarch, Acioli. In 1922, Francisco Sá was nominated for a cabinet position in the Bernardes government. César Sá's political career could have been more secure than ever, but this was not the case. Seabra was a political foe of President Bernardes, and the political expediency of the PRD chief forced César's ouster from power. In 1924, Seabra was out of the governorship and once again in exile, and the supporters of César in the capital and in the Lavras were eager to restore their lost power by riding the coattails of Minister Francisco Sá.

The opportunity seemed ideal. Horácio was away from the Lavras during much of 1924, marking time as a state senator in Salvador. The political influence of César Sá in the capital, especially with the business community, was still pervasive, for the former senator was one of the leading diamond merchants of the state. Góis Calmon, the businessmen's governor, sympathized with César Sá and looked the other way when the merchants of Salvador supplied weapons and ammunition to

César's allies in the Lavras. The relations between Góis and Horácio were cordial, although some speculated that the warlord of the Lavras had not been an enthusiastic supporter of the banker-governor in the 1923 election.[19] Furthermore, the Calmon group was intrigued by the prospect of unseating Horácio, and once the warlord could be reduced to a mere plebeian coronel, the entire interior of Bahia could be turned to the Calmons. The presence of Miguel Calmon and Francisco Sá in the Bernardes government could be the critical mass in the strategy of the conquest of the sertão.

The first step in unhitching Horácio was to remove him from the state offices that he held: the state senate and regional delegacy. Góis Calmon summarily removed Horácio from the delegacy and named to it one Coronel Otávio Passos, a crony of César Sá and his war chief.[20] When Horácio opposed his dismissal and prevented Passos from taking office, the governor dispatched a police unit to enforce his appointment. About one thousand men, a combined group of Passos' jagunços and the state police, were armed at the expense of the Sá-Passos factions.[21] The governor went one step further and deputized his aide-de-camp to lead the punitive expedition.[22] In anticipation of the Passos–state police attack, the residents of Lençóis were evacuated, and Horácio and his men dug in. In the first skirmish, the commander of the police was killed, and the men dispersed in all directions.[23] By the end of February 1925, the

19. Barbosa to Matos, Bahia, April 3, 1924, and Andrade et al. to Matos, Lençóis, April 24, 1924, AHQM. The second letter was signed by Lençóis merchants, who complained to Horácio that Coronel Otávio Passos, a Sá man in the Lavras Diamantinas, harassed people and even inspected all the political telegrams going in and out of Lençóis.

20. Olímpio Barbosa warned his chief that the Sá faction was trying to bring federal support through César Sá's brother-in-law, Coronel Viveiros of the Brazilian army, who was also a good political friend of Minister Francisco Sá of the Bernardes administration. See Barbosa to Matos, Bahia, March 31, 1924, Andrade et al. to Matos, Lençóis, March 21, 1924, AHQM; Ângelo Francisco da Silva to Góis, Lençóis, January 28, 1926, AFMGC (this document is a lengthy report on the state police expedition to Lençóis).

21. Moraes, *Jagunços e heróis*, p. 6; 1925: Chefia de Polícia—Inquérito Policial, April 13, 1925, by Otávio César de Sales Pontes, AFMGC.

22. It was Manuel Alcântara de Carvalho who first introduced Mota Coelho, then a captain of the state police, to Horácio (visiting card of Manuel Alcântara, AHQM).

23. Barbosa, *Horácio de Matos*, pp. 69–72; Moraes, *Jagunços e heróis*, pp. 162–63; Chagas, *O chefe Horácio*, pp. 157–77; Boletim, no. 56, February 25, 1925, Arquivo do Quartel General da Polícia Militar do Estado da Bahia, hereafter

armed confrontation between the Góis Calmon government and Horácio de Matos was over, with the state having failed to enforce its law by placing Passos in power.

BERNARDES' INTERVENTION IN THE LAVRAS

Judging from the reactions of the Mangabeira and Bernardes supporters in Salvador and Rio, not all was well with the governor's policy. Góis and his advisers grossly miscalculated the strength of the political ties between Bernardes and Horácio. The coronel "elected" Francisco Sá Filho (a son of Minister Sá) to the federal chamber of deputies from the Lavras, although the young Sá was a stranger to local politics. The Mangabeira faction, unable to contain its glee at the Calmons' setback, was the first to call for a truce. Bernardes pressured Minister Calmon to prevail on his brother to abandon the confrontation policy toward Horácio.[24] The humiliated governor, at the behest of brother Miguel, named a peace commission headed by the chief justice of the state supreme court and Coronel Auto Medrado, Horácio's brother-in-law. The secretary-general of the Bahian Commercial Association was added to the commission to lend an air of impartiality. The governor, licking his wounds, went through the motion of organizing a second police expedition, but the state police were in no condition to mount another assault.[25] It was an empty gesture that served only to save face.

As in the peace treaty of 1920, Horácio dictated his terms like a Tokugawa shogun dealing with the envoys of the power-

cited as AQGPMEBa; Brett, "Political Occurrences in Bahia," March 12, 1925, no. 21, fls. 573–76, Internal Affairs of Brazil, Reel 6, 823.00/400–567, DOS/USNA. The American consul in Bahia reported, "A major of state troops who tried to enter the town [Lençóis] was killed and it is rumored that a squad of fourteen men who tried to rescue his body was wiped out. Four soldiers of the state troops were carrying a wounded comrade to the American mission hospital at Ponte Nova but all were slaughtered on the way."

24. A Tarde, February 26–28, 1925; Relatório apresentado ao Exmo. Snr. Dr. Governador do Estado pelo Tenente Coronel da Força Pública Ângelo Francisco da Silva por intermédio do Exmo. Snr. Dr. Secretário da Polícia e Segurança Pública da Bahia: Ano de 1925, AFMGC; Pang "The Politics of Coronelismo," pp. 259–60.

25. The Bahian state police units were fighting in southern Brazil against the tenentes. For this reason, Góis was in no position to mount a second assault on Horácio. The American consul cited a Diário Oficial report that Bahia sent at least 650 men to southern Brazil and had plans to build up its police force to 4,000 men (Brett to Secretary of State, Bahia, November 1924, fls. 440–41, Internal Affairs of Brazil, reel 6, 823.00/400–567, DOS/USNA).

less emperor. He was to continue as state senator, and the governor withdrew the Passos nomination as the regional police delegate.[26] With this accord sealed, César Sá's ambition of returning to Lençóis was permanently shelved. The Calmon-Matos conflict showed two important changes that had taken place in the coronelismo of the First Republic. First, the existence of the coronelista "states within a state" became a reality, but not in isolation, divorced from the politics of the capitals of the state and the federation. On the contrary, the survival of a Bahian coronelista state was determined in Rio, not in Salvador. The politics of presidents was not in fact a key component in control of the coronéis of the municípios by the dominant parties of the central south (the PRM and the PRP), but it was for the survival of coronéis of secondary states, who in a short time became clients of the PRP or the PRM. Second, the entente cordiale between the coronéis and the bacharéis did not result in dichotomizing state politics but rather in setting up a triangular power relationship of a working alliance of coronéis, presidents, and the PRs. This trend continued throughout the 1930s and into the 1960s, as the presidents increasingly relied on, and even bargained with, local political chiefs for electoral votes. Seen in this context, the importance of coronelismo as a local power institution did not decline after 1930 but continued as a new factor in national politics.

THE PRESTES COLUMN AND THE CORONÉIS

The relationship between presidents and coronéis in Bahia was further strengthened by the latter's participation in the defense of legality and in the campaign against the Prestes Column in 1925–27. The army revolts of 1924 and 1925 in São Paulo and Rio Grande do Sul evolved into protracted guerrilla warfare. Out of these movements a marching column was formed, known

26. *A Tarde*, February 27, 1925; 1925: Inquérito Policial, AFMGC; Associação Comercial da Bahia, *Relatorio da 84ª Diretoria da Associação Comercial da Bahia 1925* (Bahia, 1926), pp. 88–100; José Honório Rodrigues, *Conciliação e reforma no Brasil*, pp. 83–87; *Mensagem apresentada pelo Exm. Snr. Dr. Francisco Marques de Góis Calmon Governador do Estado da Bahia à Assembléia Geral Legislativa por ocasião da abertura da 1ª reunião ordinária da 18ª legislatura em 7 de abril de 1925* (Bahia, 1925), pp. 100–101, 135–38. The American consul reported that Góis made a grave mistake: "It is now glaringly apparent that the attempt to overthrow Matos and to oust his adherents was a blunder" (Brett, "Political Occurrences in Bahia," March 12, 1925, no. 21, fls. 573–76, Internal Affairs of Brazil, Reel 6, 823.00/400–567, DOS/USNA).

as the Prestes Column. About 1,500 men and women, both civilian and military, made up this marauding column that trekked 25,000 kilometers of the backlands from Rio Grande to Maranhão, from Pernambuco to Mato Grosso, and from Bahia to Bolivia. During this two-year march, the regular army proved ineffective dealing with the guerrillas.[27]

Throughout the country, not surprisingly, the federal president turned to the coronéis of the Brazilian backlands for military help. In São Paulo, Washington Luís and Fernando Prestes (no relation to Luís Carlos Prestes) organized an armed posse of jagunços.[28] In Ceará, Padre Cícero and his lieutenant Federal Deputy Floro Bartolomeu da Costa grouped their men to fight the column.[29] In Maranhão, Piauí, Pernambuco, and other northeastern states, local coronéis mobilized their personal bands to confront the column. Nowhere in the country did the coronéis show more enthusiasm in heeding Bernardes' call than in Bahia. By early 1926, about ten "patriotic battalions" (batalhões patrióticos) were organized by the coronéis of Bahia. Of these, three came to play a prominent role in the campaign: the Lavras Diamantinas Battalion commanded by Horácio de Matos (about 1,500 men), the Franklin Lins Battalion from the Middle São Francisco Valley (about 800 men), and the Abílio Wolney group made up of jagunços of Barreiras and Goiás (about 1,000 men). These units were furnished with federal money and weapons, and officers and men were given ranks of the regular army.[30] The story of the campaign need not be told

27. There are a number of works on the Prestes Column and its implications in Brazilian history: Macaulay, *The Prestes Column*, is based on the diaries and memoirs of column members; A. B. Gama [pseud. of Afonso Rui de Sousa], *Coluna Prestes (2 anos da revolução)*, was the first nonparticipant's view; Lourenço Moreira Lima, *A Coluna Prestes (marcha e combate)*, is the official diary of the column by its secretary; Jorge Amado, *O cavaleiro da esperança (vida de Luís Carlos Prestes)*, is an idolized biography of Prestes; João Alberto Lins de Barros, *Memórias de um revolucionário*, is a biography of one of Prestes' deputies, and Glauco Carneiro, *O revolucionário Siqueira Campos*, is a biography of another; Juarez Távora, *Uma vida e muitas lutas*; Hélio Silva, *1926–a grande marcha*.

28. Carone, *A primeira república*, pp. 86–87, and *A república velha*, p. 254.

29. della Cava, *Miracle at Joaseiro*, pp. 166–67; *Boletim do Exército*, no. 298, March 20, 1926. For an interesting biography of the Bahian adviser to Cícero, see Nertan Macedo, *Floro Bartolomeu: o caudilho dos beatos e cangaceiros*.

30. Tasso Fragoso, "A Revolução de 1930," *RIHGB* 211 (April–June 1951): 10, deals with the conflict between the two commanding generals, João Gomes and Álvaro Mariante, in charge of the campaign against the column; Lourival Coutinho, *O general Góis depõe . . . .* p. 33 (Captain Góis Monteiro was General Mariante's aide-de-camp in Bahia); Boletim do Quartel General do Grupo do

here in view of the recent publication of a first-rate English-language chronicle of the column.[31] What is needed here is an examination of the political aspects of coronelista participation in federal military campaigns.

At the end of the campaign in early 1927, the coronéis of Brazil emerged to claim a special place in state politics. As mobilizers of personal armies that were loyal to the president, the coronéis effectively bypassed state governors in political and military decision-making. Federal army commanders consulted backland chiefs for the induction of jagunços and channeled money and matériel directly to the coronéis, not through the state government. By 1927, the military might of the Brazilian backlands reached new heights, and in Bahia, the Força Pública never fully regained the power it lost in 1925 at the Battle of Lençóis. Except for a few isolated cases, the coronéis of the Bahian sertão became powerful rivals to the state government in their dealings with the federal president. An increasing number of federal deputies and senators preferred to bargain directly with coronéis, often speaking for the president, thus making the oligarchic party system useless as the articulator of the state's collective political will and turning it into an edifice to house divergent interest groups. The founding of a new political party in 1927 in Bahia would reflect the latter.

PRB II—Collegial Oligarchy

Since 1925, Bahia had been dominated by a new coalition of Calmons, Mangabeiras, and former Seabra loyalists. The mixture of the traditional agrarian interests of the Calmons and the urban populist forces of the Mangabeiras, not to mention the former ward bosses of the Seabra PRD, was a precarious

---

Destacamento "Mariante," no. 2 (February 28, 1926), no. 11 (March 9, 1926), and other issues of the Boletins, AQGPMEBa. For the Wolney group's activities, see "Conferência Telegráfica entre o Major Taborda e Cap. Costa Neto," March 3, 1926 (Margem do São Francisco), Revolução no Norte da República 1924–1926, Cx IV, no. 24, AME. For Horácio de Matos' solidarity with the legality, see the statement by Alfred Miguel, in Serviço Prisioneiros: Depoimentos Enviados a Esta Seção 1925–1926: Termo de Declarações de Alfred Miguel 30 anos de idade, civil, Revolução no Norte da República, 1924–1926, Cx V, no. 30, AME. For fuller details of the Bahian coronéis' involvement in the campaign, see Pang, "The Politics of *Coronelismo*," pp. 264–66.

31. Macaulay, *The Prestes Column.*

balance of power. The previous August, of the total 144 municípios, 131 participated in the meeting, called by the governor, that selected Bahia's delegates to the presidential convention in Rio. The Calmons won two of the three delegates, the Mangabeiras the other.[32] Miguel Calmon, an earlier favorite for vice-president, was replaced by Melo Viana, governor of Minas Gerais (who was also briefly considered for president), and when Otávio Mangabeira became minister of foreign affairs in Washington Luís' government, this upstaged the Calmons for the last four years of the First Republic. The frequent juxtaposition of victories and defeats in the state and federal capitals taught the Calmons to be more tactful in their pursuit of power. The following episode illustrates such a case.

Cônego Manuel Leôncio Galrão had been political boss of Areia for over three decades when Góis became governor. Fully a year before the monarchy was overthrown, Padre Galrão began his career as a village priest in Areia. His energetic, imaginative organization of social services earned him quick recognition from his superiors, who rewarded him with the title of canon. By 1892, he was elected to the municipal council of Areia, and that was the beginning of a long and distinguished political career that ended in 1944. By 1906, the priest had replaced Araújo Pinho as state senator, and from 1906 to 1924, Galrão managed to be on the winning side. Throughout his career, the coronel-priest changed political parties no fewer than four times.[33]

In the election of 1922, the PRD federal deputy supported the Nilo Peçanha–Seabra ticket, and, as a result, his re-election to the federal Chamber of Deputies in 1924 was blocked by Bernardes.[34] This was only the first of his political troubles with the Calmons. Reading the danger signs, the priest joined the CRB. By 1925, Galrão had been elected to the Aréia city council and had led the município to the Mangabeira faction. Otávio and João Mangabeira had been colleagues in the federal Cham-

32. *A Tarde*, August 27, 29, 31, 1925. Antônio Calmon received 131 votes, Vital Soares 123, and Celso Spínola 123.

33. See Bulcão Sobrinho, "Relembrando o velho senado baiano," p. 194, on Galrão's political career; Galrão to Mangabeira, Areia (Bahia), August 12, 1924, Pasta—Para Otávio Mangabeira—Década de 1920—Pires do Rio, Dantas Bião, Virgílio de Lemos, Fiel Fontes, AOM.

34. Bulcão Sobrinho, "Relembrando o velho senado," p. 194; Pang, "The Politics of *Coronelismo*," pp. 266–67.

ber of Deputies, and Otávio had been especially close to Galrão since their days in the PRD. Governor Góis Calmon wanted to remove Galrão altogether from Areia when the priest turned anti-Calmon. The governor had his own candidate, one Barbosa Sá, who was promptly put in charge of municipal politics. The irate priest refused to bow to Calmon's pressure and mobilized his supporters to oppose Barbosa Sá. When the governor's candidate failed to pass muster in Areia, Góis Calmon introduced an administrative reform that halved the município, one part for Galrão and another for Barbosa Sá. The priest did not mind that he was given the smaller area of the two, as he was still political chief of Areia, though it had been reduced in size and population.[35] By the end of 1927, Bahia had 151 municípios, an increase of six from 1925. The case of Galrão in Areia demonstrated the final mastering of political gerrymandering of the state by the Calmons.

The Bahian Republican Party (organized in January 1927) was a compromise from the outset. The Calmons sought to dominate the convention by absorbing former Seabra loyalists. The Mangabeiras objected to the Calmonista move, which led to a deadlock. The chiefs of the factions agreed to request that Washington Luís mediate. By the end of January, Miguel Calmon and Otávio Mangabeira signed a document celebrating the compromise with presidential approval.[36] Officially, Washington Luís recognized only two factions in the new party, Mangabeira and Calmon. The Mangabeira faction would receive three of the nine seats in the PRB Executive Committee and would also be given a third of the forty-two state deputies; Minister Calmon would be the new PRB federal senator in 1927; the Mangabeira faction would be entitled to eight of twenty-two federal deputies; and the next governor of Bahia would be a Calmonista, Vital Soares.[37] The Seabra loyalists were left out of

35. Galrão to Mangabeira, Areia, August 12, 1924, AOM.

36. *A Tarde*, January 15–17, 1927; information on the Mangabeira brothers from an interview with Dona Maria Helena de Pinho Gama, Rio, September 5–7, 1968; *A Tarde*, January 31, 1927.

37. *A Tarde*, January 31, 1927; Governador Góis Calmon, Presidente Comissão Executiva, Partido Republicano, Bahia (unsigned telegram which listed the conditions of compromise), Pasta—Telegramas até 1930—Góis Calmon, Seabra, et al., and João Mangabeira to Góis, n.p., n.d., Pasta—Para Otávio Mangabeira—Telegramas de Góis Calmon, Vital Soares, e Outros e de Otávio Mangabeira aos mesmos políticos anterior a 1930, AOM.

this compromise but were soon absorbed by the two dominant factions. The party document had a secondary implication in that it was also a compromise between the traditional, rural agrarian aristocracy and the urban, bourgeois politicians, to share power in state politics. Bahian politics in the 1920s had left an era of power monopoly by a particular class or regional interest group. The new modus vivendi (entente cordiale) balanced conflicting interests between rural and urban, commerce and agriculture, coronéis and bacharéis, littoral and sertão. The second Bahian Republican Party was built on such a shaky foundation that it failed to serve as a party of cohesive groups.

With the edification of the PRB, Bahian politics of the late 1920s began its third phase of "one-party" rule with tribal cliques intact; these were loosely clustered into one party. Thus in the São Francisco region, Francisco and Geraldo Rocha of Barreiras represented the Mangabeira faction in the backland *coronelato*, while Antônio and Francisco Pereira Moacir served as spokesmen for the Calmon wing. Virtually, no change was reported in the factional lineup in the Middle São Francisco Valley and the Lavras. Franklin of Pilão Arcado, Chico Leobas of Remanso, Antônio Balbino and Abílio Wolney of Barreiras, and Horácio de Matos of the Lavras were closely tied to the Mangabeira faction and, by extension, to the Washington Luís regime and the PRP.[38] By contrast, the Calmonista coronéis ruled the municípios of Lapa (Pereira Moacir), Correntina (Juvenal Magalhães), and Santa Maria da Vitória (Clemente de Araújo Castro), to cite well-known cases.[39] As a rule, it could be stated that while the traditional delineation of littoral-sertão was becoming blurred after 1927, the Mangabeiras had an edge in the backlands; the Recôncavo and the capital became more pro-Calmon.

38. Barbosa to Matos, Bahia, March 24, 1924, Arlindo Sena to Matos, Bahia, August 2, 1929, AHQM; Aurélio Roiz Mascarenhas to Frederico Costa, Riachão do Jacuípe (Bahia), July 12, 1926, AFMGC; memo signed by Pereira Moacir, indicating who ruled the São Francisco Valley, dated April 12, 1924, AFMGC.

39. Municípios sob a responsabilidade de Homero Pires (a document which listed the municípios where Homero Pires had representation), Pereira Moacir and Homero Pires to Góis Calmon, Rio, July 12, 1924, Pereira Moacir to Góis, Bahia, August 30, 1924(?), Pereira Moacir to Góis, Lapa (?), November 10, 1924, Francisco Rocha to Góis, n.d., n.p., AFMGC. According to Nelson de Sousa Sampaio, the compartmentalization of power enclaves continued to the 1960s. Furthermore, the dichotomy of "backland coronéis" and "coastal bacharéis" persisted in Bahian politics. See his *O diálogo democrático na Bahia*, pp. 16 ff.

THE CONSOLIDATION OF PRB RULE

The elections of 1927 were prima facie evidence that the PRB factional compromise between the Mangabeiras and the Calmons was working. Also playing a role was the intermingling of nepotism and political clientelism. One federal deputy from the Lavras approached Horácio to arrange the re-election of Francisco Sá Filho, grandson of Ceará's Acioli and son of a Bernardes cabinet minister. The first election of Sá Filho in 1924 had been arranged in the spirit of political friendship between the coronel and the president. His re-election in 1927 was used as a lure in the economic development of the region, according to the intermediary. The Lavras needed only a 200-mile railroad to link it to the capital. Horácio was told that the minister of transportation (Francisco Sá) had already taken measures to build the vital rail link and that this line would hook the major municípios of the Lavras to Salvador.[40] Sá Filho was re-elected to the federal chamber of deputies without campaigning for a single day in the Lavras. In addition to Sá Filho, Horácio had two other mouthpieces in the federal congress, Francisco Rocha and Afrânio Peixoto.

The elections based on political clientelism also had room for nepotism. For the state legislature, Horácio picked two of his relatives to serve as state deputies, Olímpio Antônio Barbosa, a lawyer, for the term of 1924–28 and Arlindo Sena, a dentist, for 1928–30. They faithfully served the personal interests of Horácio in Salvador. Similar examples abound. Fiel de Carvalho Fontes, whose father, Paulo Martins Fontes, ran unsuccessfully for governor in 1919, was re-elected to the federal congress at the order of Góis Calmon.[41] Fiel was not a member of the Calmon clan but was related to the Costa Pintos who were interrelated with the Calmons. Sons and sons-in-law of prominent coronéis and bacharéis were being elected to the state and federal legislatures.

40. Américo Pinto Dantas to Matos, Bahia, January 7, 1924, Lago to Matos, Bahia, February 9, 1923, AHQM. Pedro Lago, speaking for the CRB, presented to Horácio four men: Francisco Sá Filho, Francisco Joaquim da Rocha, Homero Pires, and Antônio Pereira da Silva Moacir. The fifth candidate, to be chosen by Horácio, was Américo Pinto Dantas, an old family friend. All five were "elected" and recognized by the federal chamber, then firmly under the control of the Bernardistas.
41. Interview with Fiel Fontes, Rio, September 8, 1971.

It was in this spirit of a new compromise between the two dominant factions that Bahia elected its first PRB governor. Vital Henriques Batista Soares was a native of Valença, a Recôncavo town. The second graduate of the Bahian Faculty of Law to become governor (the first being Antônio Moniz), Vital Soares briefly dabbled in city politics in 1908–10, but soon after the advent of the PRD in 1912, he dropped out and devoted his life to law and business. A protégé of Góis Calmon, the confirmed bachelor Vital Soares was also a banker. Returning to politics in 1924, he became a state senator and two years later was made the chief of Bahia's bancada in the federal congress, replacing Otávio Mangabeira. In a confidential conversation with the American consul, Governor Calmon made it known fully two months before the January 1927 compromise with the Mangabeiras that Vital would be his successor and brother Miguel would succeed Moniz Sodré as Bahia's federal senator.[42] Vital Soares made up for his lack of dynamism and charisma by being a loyal political serf to the Calmons.

THE CALMONS IN CHARGE

In spite of a few serious reverses, the Calmons of the PRB seemed firmly ensconced in power. Their relations with Horácio de Matos were still somewhat unsettled but showed no obvious signs of worsening. Geraldo Rocha, a political ally of Washington Luís, was piqued at Góis, who had failed to deliver to him the promised monopoly contract of the São Francisco navigation company, but he made no serious move to undermine the Calmons. Miguel Calmon, who had supported the presidency of Melo Viana instead of Washington Luís in 1926, was nonetheless recognized as federal senator from Bahia in May 1927, and Otávio Mangabeira, Bahia's bancada leader in the lower house, was tapped as minister of foreign affairs in 1926 by the Paulista president. The Mangabeira nomination definitely hurt Calmon interests in Bahia, but the January 1927 compromise allowed only a third, not a half, of the federal and state legislative positions to be held by the Mangabeira faction. Over half of the

42. Dawson, "Political Notes, Bahia Consular District October 1926," Bahia, November 8, 1926, fls. 381–84. "Bahia Political Notes, November 1926," December 13, 1926, fls. 443–48, Internal Affairs of Brazil, Reel 7, 823.00/568–652, DOS/USNA.

Seabra loyalists under the masterful Frederico Costa fell in line with the Calmons. Thus, with guarded optimism, Góis Calmon returned to the Bahian Economic Bank as its president for the second time, leaving Vital Soares and his siblings Miguel and Antônio in charge of state politics.

With the PRB in command, Bahia would exert a greater role in the 1930 presidential election. The state with the third largest population could have mustered more influence than it did in national politics in the manipulatory democracy of the First Republic. Economic underdevelopment notwithstanding, the diminished role of Bahia in the first three decades of the republic can be blamed largely on its image as projected by Rui Barbosa, who perennially opposed the dominant parties of the central south in his frustrated pursuit of the presidency four times between 1910 and 1919. It was ironical that in no time in Bahian history did Rui ever come close to the real power center as a builder of parties. His oratorical prowess, national and international fame as a jurist, and renowned intellect became valuable but exaggerated assets for Bahia's ruling parties, the first PRB (1901–12) and the PRD (1912–24). Rui was a political loner, never fully "in" with the ruling cliques of his own state. Including the election of 1910, he never received the unqualified support of his state, and in each election, his disruptive electoral rhetoric further inflamed partisanship, divided Bahia, and weakened its political prestige at the national level. The situation in 1929 was radically different from that of previous years, however. Rui had been dead for over five years, and since 1924, Bahia had been accepted by the PRM and PRP as a junior partner.

CAFÉ CONTRA LEITE: THE ELECTION OF 1930

As early as May 1927, President Washington Luís was grooming Júlio Prestes as his successor. When Governor Carlos de Campos of São Paulo died in late April, a full year before his term expired, preparations for the presidential succession in 1930 were in fact being made. Coronel Fernando Prestes, lieutenant governor of the state and father of Federal Deputy Júlio Prestes, was persuaded by Washington Luís to refuse the governorship.[43] According to the state constitution, a relative of

---

43. Morgan to Secretary of State, Rio, April 29, 1927, fls. 631–45, ibid.; Bruno de Almeida Magalhães, *Artur Bernardes, estadista da república*, pp. 210–11.

a governor could not succeed him; thus, Coronel Fernando gave up his right of succession to enhance his son's political career. With the intervention of Washington Luís, the PRP picked Júlio Prestes as the governor of São Paulo and, thereby, an heir to the presidency of the Republic.

Throughout 1928, Governor Antônio Carlos Ribeiro de Andrada of Minas Gerais was frequently mentioned as a successor to Washington Luís. A scion of the aristocratic family that had produced leaders of Brazilian independence, Antônio Carlos was one of the most masterful politicians of the country. Having served in the state senate and federal congress and as minister of finance, Governor Antônio Carlos was a natural contender for the presidency. But when Washington Luís became president in 1926, he invited the bancada leaders of major states to serve in his cabinet, except for José Bonifácio, Minas' bancada leader and a brother of Antônio Carlos. Instead, the cabinet post went to another Mineiro. To further slight the prestige of the Mineiros, Washington Luís awarded the chairmanship of the senate finance committee, long held by a Mineiro, to a Paulista.[44] The president despised the governor of Minas, who, according to his contemporaries, was an intellectual, aristocrat, and elegant bon vivant—everything that Washington Luís was not. Repeated peace offers by Antônio Carlos were ingloriously dismissed as gestures of weakness.

By early June, Washington Luís had made it clear that Governor Prestes would be his successor. None other than Getúlio Vargas, governor of Rio Grande do Sul, supported the candidacy.[45] But there was a more tangible reason for Washington Luís to turn over the presidency to a fellow Paulista. His well-known financial reform of 1926 called for monetary sta-

44. Magalhães, *Bernardes*, p. 210.
45. Morgan to Secretary of State, Rio, June 14, 1929, fls. 842–44, Schoenfeld to Secretary of State, Rio, August 12, 1929, no. 3207, fls. 488–512, Internal Affairs of Brazil, Reel 8, 823.00B, DOS/USNA. The second memo contained a copy of Vargas' letter to Washington Luís, dated July 29: "The choice of my name by the State of Minas and its acceptance by Rio Grande do Sul, however, implicate no hostility towards Dr. Júlio Prestes, whose candidacy had not been mentioned up to that time, nor towards Your Excellency whose viewpoint in the case was likewise unknown. I did not accept the indication of my name by the State of Minas as a candidacy of combat; I do not desire this precisely as no good Brazilian can desire it. . . . If after consultation with Your Excellency the Minas Republican Party declares itself satisfied with the formula found and expressly acquaints me therewith, *I shall have no hesitancy in relieving it from the engagement which it voluntarily assumed*." This quote is from fls. 502–3 and the italics are added.

bilization of a fixed exchange rate and convertibility, and the introduction of gold coins to replace paper *milréis*.[46] A long-time believer in fiscal conservatism, Washington Luís was convinced that the plight of the Brazilian coffee economy lay in the fluctuating exchange rate. By attacking the core of this problem through reform, he sought a long-term solution to the Achilles heel in the Brazilian economy. His successful budgetary policies had produced surpluses in 1927 and 1928, and he was not convinced that Antônio Carlos was the right man to continue his financial programs.[47] The autocratic president was more comfortable with Júlio Prestes, his own political creature, and with Prestes in power, Washington Luís could "retire" to Batatais and boss state and national politics from there. Furthermore, the money-conscious president and his fellow PRP directors had much resented the equal status that Minas had been seeking in national politics, although over half of the federal revenues were collected in the state of São Paulo.[48]

THREE AGAINST SEVENTEEN

By July 1929, Antônio Carlos had offered the candidacy to Governor Vargas of Rio Grande to form an opposition ticket. With a nod from former president Epitácio Pessoa, the three states of Minas, Rio Grande, and Paraíba chose to challenge the candidates supported by the other seventeen states led by São Paulo and Bahia.[49] As expected, the September convention in Rio nominated Júlio Prestes of São Paulo and Vital Soares of

46. Oates, "Washington Luis," p. 42.
47. Morgan to Secretary of State, Rio, June 5, 1928, fl. 148, May 8, 1929, fl. 357, Internal Affairs of Brazil, Reel 8, 823.00B, DOS/USNA.
48. "Current Political Situation in Brazil" (military attaché), September 10, 1929, fls. 849–54, Internal Affairs of Brazil, Reel 7, 823.00/568–652, ibid.
49. Schoenfeld to Secretary of State, Rio, September 7, 1929, no. 3227, fls. 519–23, Internal Affairs of Brazil, Reel 8, 823.00B, ibid. The American chargé commented on the dim prospects of the Liberal Alliance candidates in these words: "Their [Bernardes' and Melo Viana's] enthusiasm for the dissident candidacy or an extremist policy is likely to be but lukewarm at best." Much has been written on the presidential campaign of 1930: Skidmore, *Politics in Brazil,* pp. 4–5; Aurino Moraes, *Minas na Aliança Liberal e na revolução;* Hélio Silva, *1930–a revolução traída;* Sertório de Castro, *A república que a revolução destruiu;* John W. Dulles, *Vargas of Brazil: A Political Biography;* Franco, *Outubro, 1930;* Pessoa, *João Pessoa—Aliança Liberal—Princesa;* Oates, "Washington Luís"; and Barbosa Lima Sobrinho, *A verdade sobre a revolução de outubro.*

Bahia for president and vice-president, respectively. The opposing three states organized the Liberal Alliance with Governor Vargas of Rio Grande and Governor João Pessoa of Paraíba for president and vice-president. Thus the last presidential campaign of the First Republic began.

In Bahia, the candidacy of Governor Vital Soares was to reinforce the rising prestige of the PRB. With the exception of Rui Barbosa and Seabra (both opposition candidates), no Bahian since Manuel Vitorino Pereira had been elected to the vice-presidency. Teaming up with São Paulo made the victory seem inevitable, and the ascent of the governor to the vice-presidency would certainly strengthen Bahia's position as a major voice in the council of federation politics. Such a euphoric state was short lived, however, when the sertão once again erupted into violent wars against the state government.

INTERSTATE CORONÉIS' WAR

What began as an innocuous municipal electoral dispute in Carinhanha rapidly evolved into a violent confrontation between Bahia and Minas. Late in 1928, when his second term of office had expired, Coronel João Duque ran illegally for a third term as the intendente of Carinhanha. Serving as president of the electoral board himself, he shamelessly validated his own reelection. An outraged Vital Soares rejected Duque's claim and instead awarded the senatorial recognition to rival Coronel João Alkmim.[50] Duque and his allies in Bahia and Minas retaliated with violence to keep the victorious Alkmim from taking office. The situation reached a critical point as Alkmim's kinsmen in northern Minas decided to join the dispute. Thus the proxy war between Minas and Bahia began.

Normally, such an interstate war could be contained, if the governors wished to do so. But in 1929, neither Vital Soares nor Antônio Carlos was anxious to suppress the war. It served as a sort of pre-election test to determine each one's strength in the Upper São Francisco Valley. Also, Vital Soares could not tolerate Duque and his Mineiro cohort overthrowing his hand-picked Alkmim, at least not in an election year. Antônio Carlos was caught in the intra-PRM power struggle over the choice of

50. *A Tarde*, July 5, 1929; *Diário Oficial*, December 28, 1927, January 1, 1928; for details, see Pang, "The Politics of *Coronelismo*," pp. 280–81.

his successor and was eager to destroy Alkmim, a known supporter of the Paulista faction of the PRM headed by Minister of Justice Viana do Castelo, Lieutenant Governor Alfredo Sá of Minas, and Carvalho de Brito, all partisans of Washington Luís and the Prestes candidacy. The PRM Executive Committee in Belo Horizonte was helplessly deadlocked, failing to nominate Bias Fortes, Governor Antônio Carlos' first choice; instead the committee offered the position to former presidents Wenceslau Brás and later Artur Bernardes. The PRM finally resolved to name compromise candidates, Olegário Maciel, a seventy-four-year-old state senator, and Pedro Marques de Almeida, also a state senator but in addition a henchman of the incumbent governor. It was suspected that Olegário was not going to complete the term, considering his advanced age and ill health, and therefore, Lieutenant-Governor Pedro Marques would take over as governor and serve as a front for the Andrada tribal political machine.[51] This succession struggle divided the state into factions, and João Duque was a faithful foot soldier in the Antônio Carlos camp.

The leading Bahian coronéis of the Middle São Francisco Valley, in particular those of the anti-Calmon group, were directly and indirectly involved in the Duque-Alkmim war. Franklin of Pilão Arcado and Chico Leobas of Remanso, both of whom Vital Soares (and Góis Calmon) had personal reasons to persecute, readily took stands in behalf of Duque.[52] Others sent personal armies to aid Duque. By November and December 1929, several sharply phrased letters were exchanged between Vital Soares and Antônio Carlos. At President Washington Luís' instructions, the federal prosecutor in Bahia decided to indict Duque, Franklin, Leobas, and other coronéis implicated in the so-called crime of Carinhanha. The state police of Minas quickly withdrew Duque from Bahia.[53] Once he was safely out of the

51. Magalhães, *Artur Bernardes*, p. 214; Manuel Tomás de Carvalho Brito, *Concentração Conservadora de Minas Gerais*.

52. Albuquerque to Mangabeira, Pilão Arcado, February 23, 1930, Pasta—Lauro Sodré et al., AOM.

53. Pang, "The Politics of *Coronelismo*," pp. 281–82; Arlindo Sena to Matos, Bahia, January 1, March 7, July 4, 9, 1929, AHQM; Pericles Madureira de Pinho, *Orientação e prática da polícia na Bahia: relatório de 1929*, pp. 10–40. Sena, Horácio's state deputy, informed his chief in numerous letters of the state government's attempt to implicate Franklin to Duque so that the federal government could prosecute both. In one letter, Sena stated that the state police

state and immune to prosecution, the Vital Soares government unleashed its Força Pública to punish the coronéis of the middle valley. Thus, months before the election, war between the coronéis and the state was provoked, and by January 1930, the Bahian coronéis needed little persuasion to support the Liberal Alliance in the election.

PRB's POST-ELECTION POWER ADJUSTMENT

The breakdown of the political entente cordiale between the state government and the interior coronéis had little effect on the official vote count. By the federal government's count, Júlio Prestes received 1,091,877 votes and Vital Soares 1,079,360. The opposition candidates received fewer than a million votes. The Brazilian congress dutifully ratified the official count, formally declaring the victory of the governors of São Paulo and Bahia for the term 1930–34.[54]

In Salvador, the principal factions of the PRB gathered to quietly resolve the problems of a successor to Vital Soares. The Calmon-Mangabeira compromise of January 1927 did not go beyond the founding of the PRB, and a new arrangement was required for 1930. The vice-president-elect favored Ernesto Simões Filho, the publisher of *A Tarde* and the chief of Bahia's bancada in the lower house. The Mangabeiras immediately rejected the Simões candidacy. Miguel Calmon pushed Pedro Lago as his candidate; Góis preferred Otávio Mangabeira. Coronel Frederico Costa, for his faction, stated that he would accept anyone whom Washington Luís named. By mid-June, a multiple compromise was wrought, with the full approval of the president and the president-elect: Pedro Lago would be the next governor; João Mangabeira would replace Lago as Bahia's federal senator; Frederico Costa would serve as interim governor until Lago was formally elected and ready to take over.[55]

Governor Vital Soares formally resigned from office in August and left for Europe. Coronel Frederico Costa, the state senate

---

chief (Madureira de Pinho) showed several telegrams from Carinhanha linking Horácio to Duque.

54. Brasil, Tribunal Superior Eleitoral, *Dados estatísticos: eleições federais e estaduais*, p. 19; *A Tarde*, May 23, 1930.

55. *A Tarde*, May 5, 20, June 12, 17, 19–20, 1930; Vital Soares to Washington Luís, Bahia., n.d., Pasta—Lauro Sodré et al., AOM.

president, became the new governor. In a festive mood, the governor temporarily shelved the government's plan to prosecute the coronelista perpetrators of the Crime of Carinhanha, and ordered the state police to stop the war against the coronéis. Each political tribe in Salvador was too busy to savor the rewards of the compromise of June 1930, and no one cared about the disposition of the case against the backland oligarchs.

8. The Revolution of 1930
and the Coronéis
of Bahia

PREPARATIONS FOR the Revolution of 1930 were among the worst kept political secrets in Brazilian history. In spite of the diligent work by Oswaldo Aranha of Rio Grande, the Liberal Alliance leadership as a whole was not convinced of the feasibility of a military coup d'état. Borges de Medeiros and, to a certain extent, the defeated candidate Getúlio Vargas were not completely in favor of a revolution. Minas Gerais was just emerging from an internal power struggle over the gubernatorial succession and the devastating degola of its congressional seats by Washington Luís and became, therefore, a reluctant partner in the conspiracy. Governor João Pessoa of Paraíba was in the middle of a full-blown civil war between the governor's party and the backlanders of Princesa, the redoubt of Coronel José Pereira and his supporter, former governor João Suassuna. The Washington Luís government had secretly been lending a hand to the rebels while the other two partners of the Liberal Alliance offered their material support to the beleaguered João Pessoa.

It was not until July 1930, when Governor Pessoa was assassinated in Recife, that the Liberal Alliance found a martyr and a cause for renewed unity. The Gaúcho conspirators, led by Aranha, immediately moved to secure firmer commitments from Borges and Vargas within their own state, from Governor Antônio Carlos of Minas Gerais, and from the entire Pessoista administration in Paraíba.[1] The first contact between the Liberal Alliance and the tenentes took place in mid-1929, and as soon after the election as April 1930, the military conspirators led by Juarez Távora, Siqueira Campos, and João Alberto laid plans for a coup. By mid-May, their former comrade-in-arms Luís Carlos Prestes, now a communist, denounced the whole scheme as a "bourgeois" adventure, dismissing Távora's emissaries with a firm "no."[2] Juarez Távora complained of the "incredible pusillanimity" of the Liberal Alliance leaders and proposed that the tenentes proceed with the revolution alone, should Rio Grande come to terms with the Washington Luís government. By the end of July, after the assassination of João Pessoa, Juarez Távora had completed recruiting the junior officers in the federal garrisons in the northern part of the country, principally Bahia, Pernambuco, Paraíba, and Ceará.[3] Thus the revolutionary bond between the tenentes and the civilian politicians of the Liberal Alliance was forged once again, a tenuous partnership in their common pursuit to overthrow the Washington Luís government and to prevent the inauguration of Júlio Prestes.

TWO REVOLUTIONARY CONSPIRACIES IN BAHIA

In Bahia, there were separate groups of "revolutionaries" entangled with the Liberal Alliance. The first was a small cadre of junior officers in the Sixth Military Region. Two officers, Lieutenants Humberto de Sousa e Melo and Joaquim Ribeiro Monteiro, were on their way to a new assignment in Bahia when they were approached by a group of lieutenants sailing for Paraíba on the same ship. They were Juraci Magalhães, Jurandir Mamede, and Agildo Barata. The "Paraiban group" persuaded the Bahian contingent to join the revolution and to serve as the recruiters in the federal garrison

---

1. Ademar Vidal, *1930—história da revolução na Paraíba*, p. 437.
2. José Calasans, "A primeira fase da conspiração no norte: abril–maio, 1930," p. 56.
3. Ibid., pp. 45–46, 51; Távora, *Uma vida e muitas lutas*, 1:241–63, 2:6–8.

in Salvador. After months of work, the Bahian group was able to recruit only ten junior officers and sergeants. They were discouraged by lack of progress, and at one time the two principal leaders (Sousa e Melo and Monteiro) considered pulling out of the conspiracy altogether. As it turned out, neither played a key role in the revolution: on the day of the revolution, October 3 (October 4 in the north), Monteiro was in Ilhéus on a temporary assignment, and Sousa e Melo had broken his leg in a horseback accident, dashing whatever hope the revolutionaries had for mobilizing the Bahian garrison.[4] Colonel Ataliba Osório, commander of the garrison, resisted the revolutionary cause, and as his position was made known, whatever sympathy had prevailed covertly among the officer corps dissipated.[5]

Predictably, stronger support for the Liberal Alliance came from the ranks of the coronéis in the São Francisco Valley. The electoral dispute over the intendente of Carinhanha in 1928 and the subsequent conflicts between Duque and the state police of Minas and Alkmim with the Bahian state Força Pública paved the way for the eventual bond between the anti-Calmon coronéis in the valley and the conspirators of Minas Gerais. Skillfully cultivating Duque's discontented allies, Governor Antônio Carlos arranged a series of strategy sessions between the PRM directors and the Bahian coronéis. By February 1930, Duque had become the chief recruiter on behalf of the Liberal Alliance in the valley. A group of Bahian coronéis led by Durval Marinho Paes of Ângical visited Antônio Carlos in Belo Horizonte; following the Ângical group to Minas were Deraldo Mendes of Conquista, Mário Teixeira of Caetité, and one coronel "Rabello" of Lapa, all joining the Mineiro conspirators.[6] By March, Franklin Lins of Pilão Arcado was securely in the hands of the PRM and was advising Minas to ship small arms and at least 30,000 rounds of ammunition. By June, the PRM designated Franklin the key recruiter for the revolution

4. Interview with General Humberto de Sousa e Melo, Rio, November 20, 1967; Távora, *Uma vida*, 1:288.
5. Interview with Sousa e Melo; Boletim da 6ª Região Militar, no. 232, October 12, 1930, AQG6RM; Boletim das Forças em Operações no Norte do Brasil, no. 1, October 18, 1930, AQGPMEBa.
6. Paes and Almeida to Aranha, Ângical (Bahia), August 26, 1931, Mendes and Lacerda to Aranha, Conquista (Bahia), July 6, 1931, Pasta—Ministério da Justiça—Telegramas Recebidos—Bahia, Arquivo de Oswaldo Aranha, hereafter cited as AOA.

in the middle valley and selected Mário Brant, Odilon Braga, and Tenente Djalma Dutra as the chief organizers of the revolutionary conspiracy in Bahia. Mário Brant and Odilon Braga were PRM operatives, and Djalma Dutra was one of the tenente-revolutionaries. To coordinate communications between the PRM and Franklin, Governor Antônio Carlos named Colonel Herculano Leite of the Minas state police as the liaison officer. With Franklin signing on in the north and Duque in the south, the entire valley slipped into the revolutionary camp well before October. Their strategy was to dispatch Franklin and his army to Salvador to take over the state government while Duque came slowly downriver to clean out pockets of resistance of recalcitrant coronéis.[7]

THE REVOLUTION UNDER WAY

In the first two weeks of September, both sides were reassessing their preparedness. On September 8, Governor Júlio Prestes, the president-elect, sent a handwritten letter to the incumbent Washington Luís; he wrote in a relaxed way, "It seems that with the coming of the new government in Minas we will be heading to a new phase, [one] of more tranquillity. The measures taken in relation to Rio Grande do Sul proved very opportune and will produce good results. . . . Tomorrow or the day after, I will be going to my fazenda in Itapetininga, where I will stay for a week. My telephone there is good: 'Itapetininga 107.' There I have all the security, [and] I can talk to you every day when I want to, and in case of need, I can get back to São Paulo in two and a half hours by automobile."[8] Only five days later, Oswaldo Aranha made it clear that all was not well in the revolutionary camp. In his status report to Vargas, the Gaúcho chief of the conspiracy pointed out that the Liberal Alliance had not secured the total commitment of the army and navy brass whose loyalty was essential for success. Army garrisons in the north pledged their support to the revolution, but those in Amazonas, Sergipe, and Alagoas continued to hold out, remaining with the Washington Luís govern-

7. Brant to Albuquerque, Rio, November 7, 1931, Leite to Albuquerque, Belo Horizonte, June 18, 1930, Arquivo de Franklin Lins de Albuquerque, hereafter cited as AFLA.
8. This letter is found in Pasta—Washington Luís, AOA.

ment. Lindolfo Color, a Gaúcho federal deputy, had already won support of key army and navy officers, including General Tasso Fragoso, the army chief of staff, and General Malan d'Angrogne, who became Vargas' first army chief of staff after the revolution. The commitment of the naval officers was more tenuous. Minas Gerais could mobilize 10,000 men, if the four army and police battalions continued to adhere to the revolution. The federal army in Mato Grosso could also be counted on. Rio Grande alone could mobilize 60,000 men, but Aranha emphatically pointed out that "the revolution will be easy in the rest of the country, only with the [first] success of the golpe in Porto Alegre."[9] In short, what the Liberal Alliance conspirators had managed was a series of warm to lukewarm, even tentative, commitments that could easily be broken and disavowed if Rio Grande failed to secure victory within the first forty-eight hours.

It is important to note that no mention of northern states, especially civilian supporters, was made in the September 13 situation report. It was possible that the Bahian coronelista conspirators were counted in "the 10,000 men" of Minas, but it was more probable that the Gaúcho leaders were not informed of the Bahian involvement. It was most likely that the Gaúchos were placing bets on their own success, not on a simultaneous strike from the south and north. Only a blitz-like military victory in the state of Rio Grande would set off a snowballing effect among the reluctant states, and this was precisely what happened. The government of Washington Luís fell not because of its defeat in the north but because of its inability to contain the upsurge of revolt in the central south. Timely defection of the army and navy chiefs in the crucial hours dealt the fatal blow to the First Republic.[10]

When the revolution was formally launched on October 3, 1930, the three major centers of the movement were Rio Grande do Sul in the south, Minas Gerais in the center, and Paraíba in the north. By the end of the first day, Rio Grande fell to the rebels by prearranged agreement as well as by the

9. Aranha to Vargas (Situação Geral), Porto Alegre, September 13, 1930, Pasta—Getúlio Vargas, AOA.

10. A colorful description of the exchange of heated words between President Washington Luís and the military chiefs on October 23, 1930, at Catete Palace is found in Oates, "Washington Luís," pp. 142–47.

physical takeover of the federal units by the rebels.[11] In Minas Gerais, rebel forces were not having much luck. The federal army put up a tenacious fight. Governor Olegário Maciel, reporting to Oswaldo Aranha on the situation there, relayed that one federal unit had already surrendered and that the Eleventh Infantry Regiment in São João del Rei was expected to surrender at any hour. On October 15, Aranha received a report from Minas that the Eleventh Infantry had indeed surrendered. For the next few days, rebel forces in Minas were racing toward the borders of Rio and Espírito Santo.[12]

In the north the revolution's pace was sluggish. Juraci Magalhães and the state civilian authorities had little trouble securing control of Paraíba by the end of October 4.[13] That same day Piauí fell into the revolutionaries' hands. The state republican party there had been in the throes of anarchy, and it was not until late August that Washington Luís was able to mediate the restoration of a political truce between the Pires Ferreira faction and his foes, who had overthrown the state government and joined the revolution.[14] By October 6, Juarez Távora had gained complete control of Pernambuco. Governor Estácio Coimbra and Governor Juvenal Lamartine of Pernambuco and Rio Grande do Norte, respectively, were escaping on board a Lloyd Brasileiro ship.[15] Ceará, the native state of Juarez Távora, was still in the hands of the legalist forces, who drove the small group of revolutionary tenentes to an interior town on October 4.[16] On the eighth, Alagoas was still in the hands of Governor Álvaro Paes, an adherent to the Washington

11. Franco, *Outubro, 1930*, pp. 212–13.

12. Maciel to Aranha, Belo Horizonte, n.d., Cristiano Machado to Sousa Filho, Belo Horizonte, October 15, 1930 (Machado was the secretary of the interior of Minas Gerais and Sousa Filho was Aranha's chief of staff in Rio Grande), Machado to Góis Monteiro, Barbacena, October 18, 1930, Pasta—Revolução de 1930—Telegramas Recebidos—Alagoas a Minas Gerais, AOA.

13. Távora, *Uma vida*, 1:316; Juraci M. Magalhães, *Minha vida pública na Bahia*, pp. 22–30, covers the preparations for the revolution in Paraíba; Hélio Silva, *1930—a revolução traída*, pp. 281–87; the standard work on the revolution in Paraíba is written by Vidal, *1930—história da revolução*.

14. Antônio Oliveira to Joaquim Pires, Rio, August 20, 1930, Pires to Washington Luís, n.p., n.d., Pasta—Washington Luís, AOA.

15. Vidal to Aranha, Paraíba, October 6, 1930, Pasta—Revolução de 1930—Telegramas Recebidos—Pará ao Rio Grande do Norte, AOA; Távora, *Uma vida*, 1:318.

16. Octacílio Anselmo, *A revolução de 30 no Ceará*, pp. 155–57.

Luís camp.[17] For the next two weeks, the northern revolutionary armies swelled in number and the pro–Washington Luís
governors fell one by one. On October 24, Juarez Távora, the
northern revolutionary commander, reported to Góis Monteiro,
his southern counterpart, that Bahia and Maranhão were the
only states holding out in the hands of the enemies. Tenente
Landri Sales and his unit were already approaching Belém,
obviously hoping to incorporate the federal army there for the
invasion of Maranhão, and two principal revolutionary army
groups commanded by Juraci Magalhães and Jurandir Mamede were already inside Bahia.[18]

The Legalist Defense in Bahia

The mobilization of the Bahian coronéis by the Washington
Luís government was prompt. On October 4, Geraldo Rocha,
speaking for Júlio Prestes and presumably for the president,
sent the following telegram to Coronel Horácio de Matos: "Once
again you and your brave friends' services are destined to save
the order and the Republic. State of Minas in the hands of the
seditious and friend President Júlio Prestes, through our intermediary, wants to know (1) if he can count on your support,
(2) how many men you can mobilize, (3) when can you enter the
territory of Minas—everything depends on your offers of action, (4) what resources do you need? Geraldo Rocha."[19] Horácio
accepted the assignment without any reservations.

To the legalists, the invasion of Minas Gerais by Bahian coronéis offered many attractions as a strategy for stopping the
revolution. The Gaúcho army ran into stiff resistance from São
Paulo at its frontier with Paraná. The federal army in the
Seventh Military Region in Recife had been temporarily transferred to Paraíba before the revolution, but the Távora forces
overcame the legalists on their first day.[20] In the central region,

17. Paes to Washington Luís, Maceió, October 8, 1930, Pasta—Revolução de
1930—Telegramas Recebidos—Alagoas a Minas Gerais, AOA.
18. Távora to Góis Monteiro, Aracaju, October 24, 1930, Pasta—Revolução de
1930—Telegramas Recebidos—Santa Catarina a Sergipe, AOA.
19. G. Rocha to Matos, Rio, October 4, 1930, AHQM.
20. The commanding general Lavanère Wanderley was killed in João Pessoa,
and Juraci Magalhães, one of the arresting officers, was blamed for the death.
See Silva, *1930—a revolução*, p. 286; Fontoura, *Memórias*, vol. 2, *A Aliança
Liberal e a Revolução de 1930*, p. 363.

the federal units in São João del Rei and Juiz de Fora put up valiant fights in the first week of the revolution but soon surrendered, thus opening a gap in the left flank of Rio's defense. In view of the anticipated demise of the federal army in Minas, the advisers of President Washington Luís seriously contemplated opening a second front from the north—Bahia was to attack the landlocked state. Minas had once explored the possibility of using Caravelas, the southern port of Bahia, to import arms and ammunition even before the revolution, and the Bahian authorities had been well aware that Minas abandoned such a plan only when the state of Bahia increased surveillance in that region.[21] It was therefore a fair assumption for the armchair generals that once it was cut off from the sea, Minas would exhaust its stockpile of matériel and that the invasion from Bahia would force Minas to divide its resources, thus considerably blunting its military attack on Rio. Horácio, Abílio Wolney, and Franklin had all used the São Francisco River during their campaign against the Prestes Column and had acquired intimate geographic knowledge of the backlands of Minas. Therefore, the invasion could be carried out with dispatch and success. To coordinate the operation, Francisco Rocha left Rio on October 8 for Bahia, and the following day, Pedro Lago, the governor-designate of the PRB, informed Horácio that the first payment of 600 contos for military expenses was on its way to Lençóis from Salvador.[22]

By October 11, when President Washington Luís appointed General Santa Cruz to set up the military command in Bahia to coordinate the government (legalist) defense against the growing revolutionary movement in the north, the invasion plan had suddenly been canceled. The general's assessment of the northern situation as "critical" required immediate attention, i.e., the defense plan for Salvador that was going to be the bastion for the legalist forces in the north. Paraíba, Pernambuco, Rio

21. Em homenagem ao exmo. snr. dr. Oswaldo Aranha: relatório sobre o meu trabalho, desde que fui enviado especialmente pelo exmo. snr. Oswaldo Aranha para o Rio, Pasta—Revolução de 1930—Relatórios, AOA.

22. Lago to Matos, Rio, October 9, 1930, AHQM; F. Rocha to Albuquerque, aboard the Carinhanha, April 5, 1927, Mariante to Albuquerque, Tres Lagoas (Minas), August 28, 1927, Scarecella to Albuquerque, S. Luís Cáceres (Minas), October 24, 1927, AFLA; Boletim, no. 55, March 6, 1926 (on supply of weapons to Franklin), no. 136, June 12, 1926 (minister of war's authorization for civilian participation in the campaign), no. 192, August 20, 1926 (on Geraldo Rocha Patriotic Battalion), AQG6RM.

Grande do Norte, and Piauí had already fallen to the Liberal Alliance, and Alagoas, Sergipe, and Ceará were about to fall. The two main columns of Távora's army were moving toward Bahia, while a few rebel units, especially the Landri Sales group, were fighting in Pará to overcome the Amazonian states. In the end, Santa Cruz won the politicians' support and chose the junction city of Alagoinhas as his command post. The railroads from Aracaju, Sergipe, and Juàzeiro converged in this city, a militarily strategic point for the defense of Salvador. As Santa Cruz expected, two marching columns of the revolutionaries would approach the city, one from Juàzeiro (the Mamede column) and another from Aracaju (the Magalhães group).[23] Here the revolutionaries were going to win the final victory.

CORONELISTA COUNTERPOINT: HORÁCIO AND FRANKLIN

Horácio's commitment to the Washington Luís government was to raise a total of six battalions, or three thousand men, by the end of October. The coronel was confident of arming four battalions in two weeks, and if he had plenty of money and support from coronéis, he could come up with the remaining two in another two weeks.[24] By October 18, five hundred men arrived in Cachoeira ready to join the Santa Cruz command in Alagoinhas. Horácio complained to Washington Luís about the transportation problem, but on the whole he seemed optimistic about the war preparations.[25]

As in any big venture, Horácio was held back by minor problems in his effort to raise a fighting army for the government. A political power struggle in Paramirim, one of the municípios

23. AQG6RM, Histórico de Quartel General, 1880–1962 (MS), p. 153; the October 12, 1930, entry in the log says, "Chegou ontem, a esta Capital, o sr. General de Div. Antenor Santa Cruz Pereira de Abreu, Comandante Geral das Forças em Operações no Norte do Pais."

24. Matos to Washington Luís, Lençóis, October 17, 1930, AHQM; interview with Sebastião Alves, Lençóis, July 2–3, 1968. Alves, who married a natural daughter of Horácio, served as his father-in-law's aide-de-camp in the revolution of 1930.

25. Matos to Washington Luís, Lençóis, October 17, 1930, Washington Luís to Matos, Palácio Guanabara, October 17, 1930, Sena to Matos, Bahia, October 22, 1930, AHQM. Arlindo Sena was a state deputy picked by Horácio as his personal representative in Salvador. Sena informed Horácio that Santa Cruz had dispatched two trucks for Horácio's use.

in the Lavras, turned its coronéis against each other, hampering Horácio's efforts to mobilize men there. One Coronel Miranda explained why he could not raise men for Horácio; another in the same município confided to Horácio that Miranda could easily raise at least one hundred men on the spot. The real reason for Miranda's procrastination was his uncertainty about the political situation in Paramirim (once he removed his men from the município) and the progress of the war in the São Francisco Valley where Duque and the revolutionaries seemed to be winning throughout. Others made impossible demands for mobilization. Horácio's brother-in-law asked for unlimited funds in advance and the guarantee that he would not be placed under the command of any coronel other than Horácio. Coronel Manuel Alcântara, once Horácio's state deputy (1920–24), wondered if his old chief was betting even money on both sides.[26]

One coronel who did bet on both sides was Franklin Lins of Pilão Arcado. Organizing a battalion of 630 men, he left for Juàzeiro on October 13. Information from a legalist source indicated that Franklin had been mobilized at the government's request and was on his way to Alagoinhas to join the Santa Cruz command.[27] Such a tenente conspirator as Joaquim Ribeiro Monteiro of the Sixth Military Region command continued to believe four decades later that Franklin was selling his martial services to the Washington Luís regime.[28] Tenente Monteiro was not alone in his belief. The adjutant of Franklin's battalion requested pre-combat instructions from Francisco Rocha on October 17. Horácio's state deputy Arlindo Sena in Salvador was also convinced that Franklin was on the legalist

26. Miranda to Matos, Santo Inácio (Bahia), October 21, 1930, Medrado to Matos, Mucugê (Bahia), October 17, 1930, Manuel Alcântara to Matos, Santo Inácio, October 22, 1930, ibid.

27. F. Rocha to Matos, Bahia, October 14, 1930, Rozendo Almeida to Rocha, Juàzeiro, October 17, 1930, ibid.; *A Tarde*, October 14, 1930; Boletim do Comando Geral da Força Pública do Estado da Bahia, no. 289, October 16, 1930, no. 294, October 21, 1930, no. 300, October 27, 1930, AQGPMEBa; on the sixteenth, a 230-man police group left Salvador for Bomfim, which the rebels were said to have entered from Pernambuco. The only Bahian coronel who could have come this far down from the São Francisco was Franklin. No revolutionary unit from Pernambuco had gotten down this far by that date.

28. General Joaquim Ribeiro Monteiro, "A revolução de 30 na Bahia" (MS), May 24, 1966. Professor John W. F. Dulles loaned me this paper and graciously gave permission to cite it.

side and informed his chief in Lençóis that the Pilão Arcado volunteers had arrived in Alagoinhas.[29]

Was Franklin working for both sides? He probably was. There was no doubt that he had been among the first major Bahian supporters for the candidates of the Liberal Alliance in March 1930; he was recruited by the revolutionary conspirators of Minas Gerais long before October 1930. Their strategy called for Franklin's attack on Salvador; once the capital was in the hands of the advance unit commanded by Franklin, the PRM operatives would take over the capital from the Bahian coronel. Yet in Alagoinhas, his forces did not engage in battles with the legalist army of General Santa Cruz. Franklin's strategy offered dual advantages: Had the revolutionaries won, he could point to his military occupation of Alagoinhas, as he later did, in fact; had the revolution failed, the fact that he did not attack Santa Cruz would prove that he was on the legalist side. When the revolution was over, however, the coronel was arrested as a Washington Luís sympathizer, and only the political intervention of PRM revolutionaries such as Afonso Pena Júnior, Mário Brant, and others, who testified to the unflagging loyalty of the coronel to the Liberal Alliance cause, cleared him of any antirevolutionary blemishes.[30]

HORÁCIO'S LOSS OF THE UPSTREAM VALLEY

Horácio's efforts to prop up the Washington Luís regime in Bahia were hamstrung by conflicting reports on the progress of the revolution and Duque's military success in the upstream valley on the Bahia-Minas border. On October 11, Coronel Mozart David, intendente of Caetité (the Mário Teixeira faction of this município had defected to the PRM side before October), warned Horácio of the possible invasion of Bahia by Duque and the Minas police force and advised the warlord of the Lavras to carry out the invasion of Minas first.[31] By then, the Santa Cruz

29. F. Rocha to Matos, Bahia, October 14, 1930, Sena to Matos, aboard the Comandante Capela, October 23, 1930, AHQM.

30. The Mineiro politicians who gave Franklin sworn statements were Herculano Leite, Belo Horizonte, November 7, 1931; Afonso Pena Júnior, n.p., February 9, 1931; Mário Brant, Rio, February 25, 1931, AFLA. See Lins, *O médio São Francisco*, pp. 100–101.

31. David to Matos, Caetité, October 11, 1930, Francisco Matos to Matos,

command had been set up in Alagoinhas, and, against Horácio's judgment, the first group of volunteers from the Lavras was sent to Alagoinhas. As Coronel David had predicted, Duque and a Minas state police contingent struck Carinhanha a week later. Duque probably had been on the Minas frontier after the revolution broke out but was forced to wait until the final surrender of the federal troops in Minas. That happened on the fifteenth. He was also probably informed of the surrender on the sixteenth, and two days later he and his Minas allies were in Carinhanha. After ten hours of fighting between Duque and João Alkmim, the city fell to the Duque-Minas alliance troops.[32] That same day, Mário Brant, one of the organizers of the revolution in Bahia, reported to Oswaldo Aranha that Carinhanha had fallen to Duque, adding that "our operations [in Bahia] are going well, having accomplished the objectives of the *estado maior* [general staff] by today." Incredibly, on the eighteenth, Pedro Lago informed Horácio that the federal army was winning in Minas Gerais (three days earlier, the federal regiment had surrendered), thus further confusing Horácio and his coronéis in the Lavras.[33]

Between October 18 and 24, Horácio de Matos could have changed the course of the Revolution of 1930 had he been allowed to attack Minas Gerais. He had two options: to continue obeying the orders of the Santa Cruz command in Alagoinhas (but, judging from the telegram reports of various Bahian politicians, Salvador's intelligence was not always up to date), and/or to open a lateral front west of the Lavras Diamantinas, at Xique-Xique, to stop Duque there. One report confirmed that Franklin had fought his first battle against the revolutionary army at Juàzeiro, suggesting that Távora's army from Pernambuco might have planned to rendezvous with Duque's at Juàzeiro, then attack Salvador together. Horácio independently

Livramento, October 21, 1930, AHQM. Francisco reported to Horácio that the rebels left Caetité to attack Livramento and asked for help. Later, Arlindo Sena confirmed that it was Rochinho (Francisco Rocha) and Geraldo Rocha who advised Horácio to abandon the Minas invasion plan, adding that the politicians of Minas were not happy about this decision. For details, see Sena to Matos, Bahia, December 1, 1930, ibid.

32. Alvino Pinto to Matos, São Francisco (name of a small town?), October 23, 1930, Italécio to Matos, Carinhanha, October 27, 1930, ibid.

33. Brant to Aranha, Belo Horizonte, October 18, 1930, Pasta—Revolução de 1930—Telegramas Recebidos—Alagoas a Minas Gerais, AOA; Lago to Matos, Rio; October 18, 1930 AHQM.

arrived at the same conclusion, and his analysis proved to be correct. But his strategy was never put to the test because of bad coordination between Rio-Bahia and the Lavras, the lack of time and money, and the reluctance of the backlanders to get involved.

On October 22, Santa Cruz was still waiting for the arrival of supplies from Rio.[34] The volunteer armies of Horácio and Franklin had arrived in Alagoinhas a few days earlier, and on the twenty-second, the advancing column of Juraci Magalhães entered Bahia.[35] The following day, the Mamede column crossed the São Francisco River from Petrolina, Pernambuco, to Juàzeiro, Bahia. Also on that day, a volunteer battalion organized by Federal Deputy Gileno Amado in Itabuna left the cacao country for Alagoinhas.[36]

THE OVERTHROW OF WASHINGTON LUÍS

For better or worse, the legalist forces of the coronéis in Bahia were ready to encounter the revolutionary army on October 22. Light fighting was reported. The following day, there was the first major armed confrontation. As the contending forces moved into position, the army and navy chiefs in Rio forced President Washington Luís to resign. On October 24, Francisco Rocha informed Horácio of the worst: "In Rio the Revolution victorious/Military Junta proclaimed/Generals Tasso Fragoso, Mena Barreto and Fernando Borba/Abraços/Everything in Order and Calm."[37] On the twenty-fifth, Major Franklin de

34. Sena to Matos, Bahia, October 22, 1930, AHQM. On October 22, Santa Cruz ordered the commanding officer of the Sixth Military Region and its chief of staff to proceed to Alagoinhas; for details, see AQG6RM, Histórico, p. 153.

35. Távora, Uma vida, 1:325–27; Magalhães, Minha vida, p. 31. Magalhães states that his unit entered Bahia (Barracão) on the twenty-second and by the twenty-fourth was in Alagoinhas. Távora, on the other hand, states that on the twenty-third Juraci's unit confronted the legalist forces (about 6,000 strong) in Alagoinhas.

36. Amado to Washington Luís, Itabuna, October 22, 1930, Pasta—Washington Luís, AOA.

37. F. Rocha to Matos, aboard the Comandante Capela, October 24, 1930, AHQM; on the twenty-fourth, Távora sent a telegram to Santa Cruz seeking a truce to avoid needless bloodshed. The legalist general politely pointed out that he was not taking orders from Távora but was waiting for new orders from Rio (the military junta); Távora in turn informed Santa Cruz that he was coming to Salvador to organize "a provisional government" in the name of the people. For the telegrams, see Távora, Uma vida, 1:327–29.

Queiroz, a cousin of Horácio and the commander of the Lavras Diamantinas Battalion, pledged his loyalty to the revolutionaries at the Sixth Military Region in Salvador and prepared to return to Lençóis.[38] Thus the military endeavors of Horácio de Matos ended in vain.

By November 1, Colonel Frederico Costa, the governor of Bahia, turned over the state government to the commander of the federal (now revolutionary) army. Juarez Távora and Juraci Magalhães, now both "generals" and the supreme and deputy commanders of the northern revolutionary armies, respectively, appointed Colonel Ataliba Jacinto Osório (the commander of the military region) provisional governor of Bahia. Of four key officers of the General Staff of the Revolutionary Forces in Bahia, none came from the original conspirators. Lieutenant Sousa e Melo, recovering from a broken leg, was promoted to lieutenant colonel and was made deputy commander of the Jurandir Mamede Brigade.[39]

THE DISARMAMENT OF HORÁCIO DE MATOS

The first order of business for the revolutionary governments in the northeast was the purge and exile of the supporters of Washington Luís and the disarming of the coronéis. Coronel José Pereira, chief of the Princesa revolt in Paraíba, escaped with his men during the first two weeks of October, but by the eighteenth, he was tracked down in Alagoas and his men were arrested.[40] The coronel continued to elude the closing net of the revolutionary government, and in the 1930s he lived under an assumed identity in Flores, Pernambuco, never having been brought to justice.[41] Coronel Queiroz de Pessoa, a cousin of former President Epitácio Pessoa and an ally of José Pereira, was arrested in Pernambuco and his arsenal was confiscated.[42]

38. Queiroz to Matos, Alagoinhas, October 25, 1930, AHQM.
39. Boletim das Forças Revolucionárias no Norte do Brasil, no. 31, November 24, 1930, AQGPMEBa.
40. "Correspondente" to Aranha, Olhos D'Agua, n.d., Pasta—Revolução de 1930—Telegramas Recebidos—Alagoas a Minas Gerais, AOA; *Jornal de Pernambuco*, October 18, 1930.
41. C. Nery Camelo, *Através dos sertões*, pp. 144–45; Almeida, *Memórias de José Américo*, pp. 287–88.
42. *A Tarde*, October 27, 1930.

Elsewhere in the country, potential enemies of the regime were disarmed.

The prime target for the disarmament in Bahia was Horácio de Matos and his Lavras Diamantinas. In early November, a four-man disarmament commission arrived in Lençóis. Readily agreeing to the demands of the revolutionary regime, Horácio issued a statement in his newspaper, O Sertão, advising his followers to turn in weapons and ammunition.[43] His directive to 120 coronéis and subchiefs was clear: surrender arms and do not resist. The entire task of collecting weapons in the Lavras took a little over a month, and the warlord paid for the expenses of the work.[44] Upon his return to Salvador, the chief of the commission praised Horácio for his cooperation and credited the coronel with the success of the project.[45]

Barely two weeks after the disarmament, the federal interventor in Salvador ordered Horácio's arrest. By the end of December 1930, the leading coronéis of the Lavras and the São Francisco region were detained by the revolutionary regime: Franklin of Pilão Arcado, Chico Leobas of Remanso, Abílio Wolney of Barreiras, Marcionílio of Maracás, and others were held on unspecified charges.[46] By January 1931, the initial

43. Piero Pensão Uações (?) to Matos, Bahia, November 4, 1930, Brito to Matos, Andarai, November 6, 1930, AHQM. Horácio's appeal to the citizens of the Lavras to turn over arms and munitions to the federal authorities is a document entitled "Nomes das pessoas às quais foram dirigidas cartas sobre o desarmamento," ibid.

44. Matos to General Comandante, Lençóis, December 22, 1930, Matos to Sena, Lençóis, December 23, 1930, Matos to Lima, Lençóis, n.d., December 1930, ibid.; Manifesto de Horácio de Queiroz Matos ao público do Estado da Bahia e do país, pp. 21–27.

45. A Tarde, December 13, 1930; interview with Sebastião Alves, Lençóis, July 1, 1968; Relação das armas entregues hoje pelo Cel. Horácio de Matos recebidas pelo Cel. Toscano de Brito, AHQM.

46. Sena to Matos, Bahia, December 1, 1930, AHQM. Sena stated that "no entanto Franklin Albuquerque, Marcionílio e Leobas continuam presos, e muito têm sofrido." Among others, the following Bahian politicians and businessmen provided Horácio with testimonials: Artur Fraga (former secretary general of the Bahian Commercial Association and peace negotiator of 1925), J. J. Landulfo Medrado (Seabra's secretary of justice), Antônio Seabra (Seabra's police chief), Braúlio Xavier (Bahian Supreme Court chief justice), in AHQM. Major Franklin Queiroz, Horácio's cousin and confidant, commander of the First Lavras Battalion in Alagoinhas, and editor of O Sertão (Lençóis), was also arrested for his participation on the wrong side during the revolution: VI Região Militar-1ª Sec. QG da Cidade de Salvador, January 15, 1930 [1931], Prisão de um civil, Pasta 3—Correspondência Protocolada 1930–31, SDA/AEBa.

revolutionary fervor had subsided in Bahia as the Vargas government was able to gain control of the entire country. A civilian interventor was appointed to Bahia, and by mid-January the coronéis were released. Horácio de Matos was the only one not permitted to return to his redoubt; he was ordered to remain in Salvador.[47]

The assassination of Coronel Horácio de Matos on May 16, 1931, was the final chapter of the era of the coronelista supremacy in Bahian politics. The golden age, but not coronelismo itself, died with him. The background that led to the violent death of Horácio is still a mystery. On May 14, an army officer who had arrested Horácio the previous December was gunned down by the guards of the state justice building. It was alleged that the lieutenant had attempted to kill the state secretary of justice who had signed the coronel's release order. Only two days later a policeman intercepted Coronel Horácio on a afternoon stroll with his daughter and another relative and shot him. The warlord of the Lavras carried a pistol, but there was no time to react. He died in the arms of his young daughter on the street. The two violent deaths were never linked, despite persistent suspicions. The authorities never attempted to investigate the incidents and gave a somewhat flimsy motive for the assassination of the fifty-year-old warlord: officially, the motive was private revenge.[48] With the death of Horácio, the tradition of violence in politics was gone; with the revolution, a new era of politics was ushered in.

47. Interviews with Horácio de Matos Júnior, Salvador, May 3, 1968, Horacina de Matos, Salvador, June 4, 1968, and Tácio de Matos, Mucugê, July 4–9, 1968.

48. *A Tarde*, May 16, 1931; interview with Horacina de Matos, Salvador. I was unable to locate the police (criminal) record on this case at the archives of the Secretária de Segurança Pública, Salvador. The search was made with the full approval of the state secretary, then state deputy (Horácio Júnior), and the archivist of the criminal record section.

9. The New "Old Order" in Bahian Politics, 1930–1934

T HE REVOLUTION of October 1930 was destined to fail. It was a political ménage à trois of the reformist tenentes, the urban populist groups led by the Partido Democrático of São Paulo, and the tri-state ruling parties (PRs) of conservatism. "Out" parties in various states, equally oriented to the status quo, supported the revolution in the mistaken belief that the traditional reward system of the First Republic would favor their rise to power. From the outset, the revolution lacked ideological cohesion, thus hindering its ability to accommodate the conflicting demands of its adherents. The idealistic tenentes proceeded to set up a quasi-political party of the Clube 3 de Outubro, while the seasoned political Young Turks of Rio Grande and Minas expressed their revolutionary enthusiasm by building the Legião Revolucionária.[1]

Because political, social, and philosophical differences among the revolutionary cadres and followers were accentuated in the first two years, the forging of a coherent program was doomed.

1. Peter Flynn, "The Revolutionary Legion and the Brazilian Revolution of 1930"; for a brief history of Clube 3 de Outubro, see *O Estado de São Paulo*, July 5, 1932; Hélio Silva, *1931—os tenentes no poder*.

Tenentes quarreled among themselves. Juarez Távora, "the Viceroy of the North," resigned from the Delegacia Militar in December 1931.[2] Hercolino Cascardo, a naval officer and the interventor of Rio Grande do Norte, quit his office in frustration, a political victim of opposition in early 1932. Bertino Dutra, also a naval officer and successor to Cascardo, fell victim to the same reactionary political pressures a year later. In Ceará, Interventor Carneiro de Mendonça resigned, failing to stop the return of the "old politics," and elsewhere, political and philosophical clashes between federal interventors and local politicians often resulted in the resignation or dismissal of revolutionary elites of state government.[3]

REALIGNING BAHIA'S OLD POLITICS

The civilian supporters of the Revolution were equally disenchanted with Vargas and his oscillating policies. Rio Grande, the major partner of the tri-state Liberal Alliance and the only state with political unity under the Frente Única arrangement of 1929, developed personal and philosophical fission within its leadership, and such one-time comrades-in-arms of Vargas as Borges de Medeiros, João Neves, and Flores da Cunha broke away from the revolutionary regime. In Bahia, J. J. Seabra and his Moniz followers, nominal backers of Vargas in the 1930 election, became the first and most vocal opponents of the region when their political demands were not met. By 1932, São Paulo led an abortive revolt of anti-Vargas forces in the name of constitutionalism, calling for a return to a democratic form of government.[4] By 1933, the astute Vargas was under pressure

2. Otávio Malta, *Os 'tenentes' na revolução brasileira*; Hélio Silva, *1935—a revolta vermelha*, pp. 196–97; Távora, *Uma vida*, 2: 39–42; Edgard Carone, *O tenentismo: aconcentecimentos—personagens—programas*, pp. 366–479.
3. Boris Fausto, *A revolução de 1930: historiografia e história*, p. 72.
4. Beginning in late June and early July 1932, various civic and political groups in São Paulo rallied around a new cause: a revolt against Vargas. A Liga Pro-Constituinte called a mass meeting, while Olegário Maciel, governor of Minas, offered to serve as the mediator between Vargas and Rio Grande do Sul, which was leaning toward the Paulista cause (*O Estado de São Paulo*, July 2, 1932); by July 10, São Paulo was leading the so-called Constitutional Revolt (ibid., July 10, 1932). By August 10, former president Artur Bernardes had publicly announced his support of São Paulo by stating, "Fico com São Paulo, porque para São Paulo se transportou a alma civil do Brasil." The major work on the 1932 Paulista revolt is by Paulo Nogueira Filho, *Ideais e lutas de um burguês progressista: a guerra cívica 1932*. See also Távora, *Uma vida e muitas lutas*,

and chose to construct a new foundation on which his regime could permanently place its elite and justify their legitimacy of power.

The helping hand came, interestingly enough, from both revolutionary quarters and the traditional bastion of the old regime—the coronéis and bacharéis. Juraci Magalhães in Bahia, Landri Sales in Piauí, Lima Cavalcanti in Pernambuco, Barata in Pará, and others were reconciled to the old political forces. Nevertheless, reform soon gave way to political expediency; thereby laying the groundwork for a new order. Coronel Franklin Lins of Pilão Arcado was fondly addressed as "General Franklin Albuquerque" by Juraci Magalhães. Arlindo Leoni, one-time sheik of the PRD and the gato morto of the 1924 gubernatorial election, was called "our distinguished friend."[5] In fact, it was the modality of compromise between the revolutionary and the traditional forces that produced a new "old order" in state politics.

As was the case with the advent of the First Republic in 1889, the first two and a half months after the October Revolution were chaotic. Bahia had no strong leader. Governor Frederico Costa turned over the government to the commander of the Sixth Military Region, who was replaced by another officer, and by mid-November, Leopoldo Amaral, a Seabrista politician, was appointed interventor.[6] To a politically divided state like Bahia, Amaral proved neither an able healer nor an adept administrator. His decision to release the coronéis of the backlands infuriated the revolutionary zealots. His seemingly nonpartisan approach to the administration of the state prematurely asphyxiated Seabrista hopes for a return to power. In a letter dated January 11, 1931, Seabra suggested to Vargas as Amaral's replacement some thirty-two persons considered qualified to govern Bahia: among them were João Neves, Assis Brasil, Lindolfo Color, all of Rio Grande, Francisco Campos of Minas

---

2:74–89; Hélio Silva, *1932—a guerra paulista*; for the role of Rio Grande do Sul and particularly Flores da Cunha, see Carlos E. Cortés, *Gaúcho Politics in Brazil: The Politics of Rio Grande do Sul, 1930–1964*, pp. 52–53.

5. Magalhães to Vargas, Bahia, May 22, July 2, 1934, Lata 15—Interventores Federais—Bahia, SPE/AN.

6. The complete list of the federal interventors for the period 1930–37 appears in Alzira Vargas do Amaral Peixoto, *Getúlio Vargas, meu pai*, pp. 402–14. Amaral was appointed on November 14, 1930, and served until February 12, 1931.

Gerais, and Generals Tasso Fragoso and Mena Barreto and Admiral Isaias de Noronha, the last three the military chiefs who had overthrown Washington Luís. This list conspicuously excluded any distinguished Bahian; Vargas could always appoint Seabra, if he wished a Bahian to be the interventor. But in a characteristic show of independence and contradiction, Vargas appointed Artur Neiva, a noted Bahian scientist and a long-time resident of São Paulo.[7]

THE INTERVENTORIA OF ARTUR NEIVA

If Vargas had intended to appoint someone with no strong ties and experience with Bahian politics, he did so. During Neiva's seven-month rule (February–August 1931), the soft-spoken administrator was able to bring about fifty-eight reform measures in state administration and politics. He became the prime reason for political struggle among the contending forces, and in his short tenure in power, he managed to rekindle dying political passions and flames.

The most important state reform was the Municipal Reorganization Act of July 8, 1931. Before its formal enactment, the interventor made it clear that administrative streamlining was to be one of the major objectives of the Vargas regime. The município, the traditional backwater of the coronéis, had typified their base of autonomous power and social injustice and, more important, was the chief barrier to a strong centripetal government. By assigning direct responsibility for supervising operation of the municípios to prefects, the federal interventor could bring about administrative centralization. By raising the population base of a município from 15,000 to 20,000, Neiva sought to gerrymander the political boundaries of the coronéis and their surrogates, thus weakening them considerably. In November 1930, Bahia had 155 municípios; these would be reduced to 122.[8] The reform was enacted over a storm of protest.

The core of the opposition lay in the fact that no coronel

7. Seabra to Vargas, Bahia, January 11, 1931, Lata 9—Particulares—S–T, SPE/AN. Neiva was not on Seabra's list.

8. Principais Atos da Administração do Dr. Artur Neiva na Bahia (18–II–15–VIII–1931), Lata 15, ibid.; Bahia, *Organisação municipal: Decreto no. 7.479 de 8 de julho de 1931*, outlines the basic changes in the município system imposed by Interventor Neiva.

wanted to lose município status for his territory. Many of the sparsely populated backland municípios that were most affected appealed directly to the national government to block Neiva's reform.[9] The reduction of the number of municípios could mean considerable savings to the state, but administrative efficiency did not, and does not, always elicit political support. Furthermore, the sensitivity of local chiefs was touched both favorably and unfavorably when the interventor tampered with the names of the municípios: that of Miguel Calmon was rechristened Djalma Dutra, honoring one of the tenentes of the Prestes Column who died in the revolution of October; the município of Seabra was forced to keep the name of a nonrevolutionary politician; the município of Sento Sé, which had been stripped of its historic name under Góis Calmon for punishment, was gloriously restored.

Neiva also offended both military and civilian sympathizers of the revolutionary regime by appointing politically "wrong" people to state offices. He named a renowned scholar and supporter of Vital Soares secretary of justice; in Lapa, he failed to remove the Moacir brothers and their allies from power. In Barreiras, a far western town in the São Francisco Valley, the supporters of the revolution complained that Abílio Wolney and Francisco Rocha still remained masterful coronéis of that município.[10] Perhaps not unjustly, the tenentes of Bahia and their overzealous civilian companions construed Neiva's every move to be disturbing, if not downright anti-revolutionary. The undue stress on administrative efficiency at the expense of political loyalty, the release of such old regime coronéis as Horácio de Matos, Franklin Lins, Abílio Wolney, and others on the grounds of legality, the overt appointment to state and municipal offices of coronéis and bacharéis with strong ties with the old regime were too much to bear. Slowly, the tenentes began to mount their opposition to Neiva.[11]

In such heated political passion, few were willing to recognize the contributions made by Artur Neiva. With a stroke of his pen,

9. Álvaro Marinho et al. to Aranha, Santa Cruz (Bahia), June 29, 1931. Pasta—Ministério da Justiça—Telegramas Recebidos—Bahia, AOA.
10. Osório Porto et al. to Aranha, Lapa, May 4, 1931, Durval Marinho Paes and Manuel Frederico Almeida to Aranha. Ângical (Bahia), August 26, 1931, ibid.
11. Távora, *Uma vida*, 2:38.

Neiva satisfied the long overdue dream of the cacao planters by establishing the Institute of Cacao in a decree of June 8, 1931. Cacao was the principal source of Bahia's revenue in the twentieth century, and the Bahian politicians of the First Republic had been unable to draw federal support to this vital sector. Even before the formal organization of the institute, Neiva had enthusiastically sought federal subsidies and loans for the cacao economy, just emerging from the worldwide market depression.[12] His vigorous campaign against banditry, especially against Lampião and his cohort, drew universal support. Other money-saving reform measures brought about trimming of state and city police forces, realistic tax assessment and effective collection, a requirement that judges and prosecutors in the interior live at their posts rather than in the capital, and tightening of the rules for retirement pensions for public servants.[13] These measures gave Bahia an effective government but proved to be Neiva's nemesis.

INTERVENTOR NEIVA OUT

As the interventor became unpopular, his mistakes seemed more egregious and glaring. In the first two years, the Revolutionary Legion of Oswaldo Aranha appeared to be evolving as a national political party. In many of the states in the north, federal interventors actively served as organizers for the legion.[14] In Bahia, however, Neiva showed little such leadership. The legion blossomed only in isolated regions such as Caravelas in south Bahia, not under the direction of Artur Neiva but under the auspices of the tenentes.[15] Political opposition toward

12. Neiva to Aranha, Bahia, May 20, 1931, Pasta—Ministério da Justiça—Telegramas Recebidos—Bahia, AOA, Bahia's cacao planters put pressure on Amaral also; see Sindicato dos Agricultores de Cacau to Amaral, Bahia, December 15, 1930, Ofícios e Documentos da Secretaria do Governo do Estado—Interventor Federal e Governador, Pasta 3, SDA/AEBa. Itamarati was much concerned with the British plan to "valorize" its cacao from Africa; for details, see Franco to Neiva, Rio, June 30, 1931, and Sebastião Sampaio (Brazilian consul general in New York), Plano de Defesa Imediata do Cacao, Maio 1931, Pasta 26, ibid.
13. Principais Atos da Administração do Dr. Artur Neiva.
14. Flynn, "The Revolutionary Legion"; *O Estado de São Paulo*, July 5, 10, 1932. A series of reports on the Legion movement were filed by federal interventors in the northern states; these documents are found in SPE/AN.
15. Aurelino Almeida Alcântara to Interventor Federal, Caravelas, March 23, 1931, Correspondência do Governador, no. 22, 1931, SDA/AEBa.

Neiva mounted, and by mid-August he resigned from office.[16]
The resignation presented two immediate problems. First,
the military faction, notably the tenentes led by Juarez Távora
and his northern colleagues, had to be satisfied. Regionalism
still dominated the political considerations of the Vargas regime,
and the Viceroy of the North would not favor another southerner (by either birth or upbringing) to be the interventor in a
key northern state. Second, the experiences with Leopoldo
Amaral and Artur Neiva confirmed Távora's worst fears that a
civilian was not capable of leading Bahia unless he first secured
military support. In August 1931, no civilian politician in Bahia
could draw military support. As soon as the office was vacant,
Seabra's cronies put up their old chief as the candidate.[17] One
backland chief submitted the names of Juarez Távora, Raul
Alves, and Moniz Sodré;[18] this was a politically opportunistic
gesture par excellence and an eminent expression of the coronelista instinct for survival. The viceroy proposed that Vargas
name one of three military candidates: Jurandir Mamede,
Juraci Magalhães, or Landri Sales. Távora's first choice was the
Bahian Jurandir Mamede. Sliding smoothly over the suggested
names, Vargas picked a twenty-six-year-old army lieutenant
and a native of Ceará, Juraci Montenegro Magalhães.[19]

JURACI MAGALHÃES THE HEALER

Events prior to the appointment of Magalhães to the interventor's office actually strengthened coronelismo in Bahia. Despite
the rapid administrative centralization that the Vargas regime
imposed after 1930, the decline of coronelista power did not
occur. As seen in Bahia and Minas Gerais, the traditional
coronéis of the "out" factions constituted the fighting column of
the revolution. In São Paulo, the coffee planters who were
unhappy about Washington Luís' failure to rescue the dominant
economy became the natural allies of the Liberal Alliance.[20] The

16. Neiva to Vargas, Bahia, August 15, 1931, Lata 2, SPE/AN.
17. Xavier Marques et al. to Aranha, Bahia, August 15, 1931, Pasta—
Ministério da Justiça—Telegramas Recebidos—Bahia, AOA; Avelino Fernandes Silva et al. to Vargas, Ilhéus, August 20, 1931, Lata 2, SPE/AN.
18. Barbosa to Aranha, Bahia, August 18, 1931, Pasta—Ministério da
Justiça—Telegramas Recebidos—Bahia, AOA.
19. Távora, *Uma vida*, 2:38; Peixoto, *Getúlio Vargas*, p. 403.
20. Queiroz, *O mandonismo*, p. 123.

"revolutionary" coronéis in the middle and upper valley consolidated their hold on the municípios.[21] In those municípios where the dominant coronéis had fallen from power due to their strong identification with the PRB (the Calmons and the Mangabeiras), either their rivals or the one next in line claimed power by pronouncing their support of the revolution. As the state government proved unstable prior to the advent of Juraci Magalhães, the coronéis of Bahia learned to deal directly with the Vargas regime and his immediate advisers, practicing the coronel-president politicking of the 1920s. Coronéis made myriad suggestions and recommendations that often conflicted with the objectives of Leopoldo Amaral and Artur Neiva in their attempt to override Salvador as they had done during the years of Artur Bernardes and Washington Luís.

The young interventor turned out to be a superb political tactician and pragmatist. His open attack on the former PRB and PRD bacharéis, his calculated cultivation of key state economic groups, and his clout with the Vargas regime in the gamesmanship of obtaining federal favors made him popular with the grass-root political chiefs, the coronéis. Only four months into the job, Juraci was determined to create a new power group that Vargas could depend on and draw support from. Such a power base had to be built on the município level, and to this end, the interventor sought to sever the traditional ties between the coronéis and the former PRB and PRD. In a confidential memo to Vargas, the interventor singled out the Seabras and the Monizes as the worst breed of personalistic politicians, especially Moniz Sodré, who ran the opposition press in Salvador. He was greatly concerned with the dangerous rise of the "new" Seabras and Monizes who would dominate state politics for personal gain. Calling for a mild reform of Bahian politics, Juraci Magalhães thought that the state should develop one-party politics that would allow local autonomy with min-

---

21. A handwritten letter addressed to Exmo. Snr. Dr. Leopoldo Amaral, D. D. Interventor Federal do Estado da Bahia, n.d., n.p., Ofícios Expedidos 1928–29, Gabinete do Governador, SDA/AEBa. This is a misplaced document—its content deals with Duque's activities after November 1930. On Franklin and Leobas, see Raimundo de Sousa Rocha to Secretário da Justiça, n.p.. February 24. 1931, Correspondência—1931, Pasta 4, Gabinete do Governador, ibid. The summary of the letter states, "Rocha pedindo providências contra os bandidos Franklin de Albuquerque e Francisco Leobas que há muitos anos vem assolando a zona de S. Francisco."

imal interference from the capital.[22] Magalhães was already courting the coronelista oligarchs in his war against the Seabras, the Monizes, and the like a full year before the founding of the Social Democratic Party of Bahia.

One popular policy that the interventor implemented was a campaign against banditry.[23] A by-product of the coronelista social order, banditry was a fixture in the Brazilian backlands. For over a century, bandits had roamed the backlands of the northeast, living off local merchants, cattlemen, and farmers. In the absence of a strong government, ambitious coronéis entered into agreements with bandits for survival and not uncommonly recruited them for private use as election enforcers and for personal revenge. In return, bandits were supplied with arms, provisions, or even protection from the law.[24] Banditry flourished throughout the first four decades of this century as violence became an integral part of Brazilian backland life. Lampião and his deputy Curisco were particularly active in the sertão of Pernambuco and Bahia, and repeated efforts to eradicate banditry among various states in the region proved inadequate. Taking advantage of political turmoil in the early 1930s, Lampião and his followers stepped up their activities, and Juraci Magalhães firmly committed state and federal resources to extirpate the outlaws.[25] Ironically, this campaign came to be viewed as a program that aided the traditional interests of the backlands, the coronéis.

Magalhães' energetic policy to modernize the cacao economy also proved a boon to his political strategy of culling support of the coronéis in southern Bahia. He removed the first director of the Institute of Cacao (the Neiva appointee) and named an able agronomist. He arranged loans from the Bank of Brazil and the federal government for the improvement of the economy—

22. Magalhães to Vargas, Bahia, January 11, 1932, Lata 2, SPE/AN.
23. Even before Magalhães was appointed to the federal *interventoria*, he had developed a plan to combat the raging banditry. For details, see Almir de Azevedo Gordilho to Neiva, Bahia, June 10, 1931, Correspondência—1931, Gabinete do Governador (Ofícios e Cartas Recebidos em julho de 1931), SDA/ AEBa; Magalhães to Vargas, Bahia, n.d., Lata 3A—Interventores Federais-Pernambuco, SPE/AN.
24. A protector of bandits is known as a *coiteiro*. For the workings of coiteiro-cangaceiro mutual aid, see Leonardo Mota, *No tempo de Lampião*, p. 54.
25. Gordilho to Neiva, Bahia, April 20, 1931, Pasta 23, Ofícios do Secretaria do Governo, SDA/AEBa; Gordilho et al. to Aranha, Bahia, November 6, 1931, Pasta—Ministério da Justiça—Telegramas Recebidos—Bahia, AOA.

valorization, importation of new equipment, and the development of industrial uses of cacao.[26] These policies not only benefited the state by guaranteeing more revenues but also bolstered the interventor's plans to capture support of the cacao sector. Politically, Juraci Magalhães was well liked and accepted by Bahia's backland oligarchs.

JURACI THE SUPERCORONEL OF BAHIA

The first important contact between Magalhães and the backland coronéis as allies developed in 1932. The Revolt of São Paulo threatened to spread to other regions of the country, and it was believed that Coronel João Duque and others in the São Francisco Valley were once again in collusion with the Minas politicians, especially Bernardes and his followers, who were sympathetic to the Paulista revolt. When intelligence sources reported on the mobilizing of Bernardista supporters in Bahia, Juraci Magalhães quickly activated the coronéis loyal to Salvador to rub out the threatening rebellion. The timely pre-emptive move squashed Duque and his Bernardista band, thus preventing a sympathetic revolt in São Paulo. The interventor triumphantly reported to Vargas that "our friends in the São Francisco" region had helped him keep Bahia out of the revolt, especially Carinhanha.[27] This incident strengthened further the existing bond between Salvador and the backlands.

Juraci Magalhães' reliance on the valley's coronéis to ally Bahia with Vargas in 1932 was only the first step toward political alliance. In September 1932 and January 1933, the valley's oligarchs were busily turning the working relationship into something more permanent. By evicting the supporters of the Paulista revolt and replacing them as the elite, the Juracista coronéis helped the interventor maintain his influence in the

26. Inácio Tosta Filho was Neiva's secretary of agriculture; he became the first president of the Instituto de Cacau. See Associação dos Agricultores de Ilhéus to Magalhães, Ilhéus, September 19, 1931, Correspondência—1931, Gabinete do Governador, SDA/AEBa.

27. Nelson de Sousa Carneiro, *XXII de agosto! o movimento constitucionalista na Bahia*, pp. 43–54; Magalhães to Vargas, Bahia, September 2, 10, 1932, Lata 2, SPE/AN. Magalhães reported to Vargas that the Bernardistas in Pirapora, Minas, revolted to overthrow the supporters of Olegário Maciel. Bernardes supported the Paulista revolt (*O Estado de São Paulo*, August 10, 1932).

valley against Duque. As in the First Republic, Juraci Magalhães needed the backland coronéis to prepare for his rise to power, in this case to consolidate it.

On January 9, 1933, the coronéis of twenty municípios of the São Francisco Valley and the Lavras met in Juàzeiro to pledge their loyalty to the Cearense-born federal interventor. The Backlanders' Coalition (Coligação Sertaneja) was organized by the elite of the valley's coronelato: Franklin Lins of Pilão Arcado, Abílio Wolney of Barreiras, João Sento Sé of Sento Sé, Aprígio Duarte Filho of Juàzeiro, Clemente Araújo de Castro of Santa Maria da Vitória, and many others.[28] The twenty-one coronéis declared their loyalty to Juraci Magalhães and resolved to elect him the first constitutional governor of Bahia since 1930. They also welcomed the opportunity to join the Social Democratic Party (Partido Social Democrata), still in the planning stage, and severed their ties with the former chiefs of the PRB and the PRD. Nelson Xavier, a state official for the São Francisco Navigation Company, was elected president of the Coligação Sertaneja and Franklin and Abílio Wolney vice-president and secretary, respectively.[29] By any definition, it cannot be denied that coronelismo had triumphed in the valley by surviving as the "new" elite. Juraci Magalhães emerged as the super-coronel, the chief of a new collegial oligarchy of Bahia.

THE MAKING OF A NEW "OLD ORDER"

The significance of the alliance between the interventor and the backland coronéis was to legitimize the oligarchic rule of the coronéis and to initiate reconciliation with former supporters of the PRB and the PRD. Thus began the era for the new "old order" in Bahian politics. As planned, the Social Democratic Party convention was held in Salvador on January 27 with 346 delegates representing all the state's municípios. The delegates came from various classes as well as regions—lawyers, physicians, professors, bankers, merchants, planters, ranchers,

28. Bahia—Relatório, January 1933, Anexo No. 8: Ata da Inauguração da "Coligação Sertaneja," Lata 2, SPE/AN. For details, see Pang, "The Politics of Coronelismo," pp. 315–16.

29. For an interesting but biased analysis of the development, see J. J. Seabra, *Esfola de um mentiroso*, p. 90. See also Magalhães to Vargas, Bahia, January 26, 28, 1933, Lata 2, SPE/AN.

priests, and state officials. João Pacheco de Oliveira, not Juraci, was elected symbolic chief of the party. Homero Pires, Francisco Rocha, Gileno Amado, Prisco Paraíso, Medeiros Neto, and Cônego Galrão were among those former PRB members who found a place in the new party. From the PRD, Arlindo Leoni and lesser politicians parted with Seabra and the Monizes and joined the new party. Artur Neiva, whom Juraci replaced, also found a home in the PSD of Bahia.[30] Only death or retirement prevented such political craftsmen as Frederico Costa, Antônio Pessoa, and Horácio de Matos from joining. Vital Soares, Otávio Mangabeira, and Ernesto Simões Filho were in European exile, and Antônio Moniz and Góis Calmon died in the early thirties.

The opposition, though fragmented and underfinanced, was championed by the septuagenarian José Joaquim Seabra. Joining the grand old man of Bahian politics were Moniz Sodré and João Mangabeira. The party, euphemistically called "Bahia Is Still Bahia" (*A Bahia é ainda a Bahia*), was token opposition.[31] On its side were a few minor personalist cliques, among which the Agricultural Party (Partido da Lavoura) was the second largest after the Seabristas. Even taken together, they constituted a minor ripple on the Bahian political scene.

The grand compromise of 1933 should not be dismissed as a mere political event. Like the conquest of the Aztecs by Hernán Cortéz, Juraci's strategy resulted in eliminating the top-level political princes while preserving intact the lower-level political managers. Like the *caciques* and *gamonales* of Spanish America, Bahian coronéis served as political henchmen for the PRD and the Vargas regime but with an important difference. The political system of the early 1930s was defective in trying to assert central authority over the sertão, and this weakness left room for compromise and bargaining between the indigenous forces (the coronéis) and the new conquistadores (Juraci Magalhães and Getúlio Vargas). Victor Nunes Leal aptly observed that the continuity of coronelismo depended on the mutual need for favor and compromise between the central and local governing elites. This was precisely the quintessence of the new "old order" in Bahia.[32]

---

30. Not related to the party of the same name founded in 1945 by Vargas.
31. República dos Estados Unidos do Brasil, *Anais da Assembléia Nacional Constituinte*, 1:v–xii.
32. Leal, *Coronelismo*, p. 252.

THE VICTORY OF CORONELISMO

The PSD victory in the election of 1933 was intoxicating for the Bahian elite. Of twenty-two deputies to the Constituent Assembly, the PSD elected eighteen, Seabra's party two, and the Agricultural Party one.[33] The roll call of Bahian PSD deputies had a familiar ring, the majority of them coming from the ranks of former PRB federal and state deputies of the First Republic. If coronelismo attained its first zenith in the 1920s, the second took place in 1933–37. In late September, the confident Juraci Magalhães resigned from the interventoria and ran a successful campaign in October to produce the PSD-controlled state legislature. As stipulated by the Constitution of 1934, the state legislature of Bahia elected its first post-1930 governor: Juraci Magalhães.

Thus the year 1934 closed with a peaceful transition of power. At the top in state politics, an outsider, or "a drifter" (forasteiro) as Seabra ridiculed, replaced the aristocratic Calmons and the Monizes and the bourgeois politicians of the Mangabeiras and the Seabras of the urban sector. Immediately below him, the bacharéis regained their power by embracing Juraci. Below them, at the bedrock of the political system, the coronéis not only survived the Revolution of October 1930 but also once again upheld their right to rule the sertão as familiocratic oligarchies. The system of political clientelism continued, with old clients and new patrons. The new patrons were Juraci Magalhães, Juarez Távora, and Getúlio Vargas. The revolution did not defeat the coronéis; the coronéis won.

33. The deputy of the "A Bahia é ainda a Bahia" was Seabra; the deputy of the Partido da Lavoura was Lauro Faria Santos. See Brazil, *Anais da Assembléia Nacional Constituinte*, 1:vi; Hélio Silva, *1934–a constituinte*.

10. The Twilight
of Coronelismo

THE SIGNIFICANCE of the Revolution of 1930 is not so much its impact on the decline of, or even the destruction of, coronelismo, but its role in transforming oligarchic coronelismo and integrating it into national politics. This first step toward political modernization was taken when Vargas began to forge the truly national integration of various political and social forces that at one time had stubbornly remained on the periphery of politics in the First Republic. A once highly personalistic coronel became a well-disciplined, if not willing, party cadre.

Social and economic transformations in the 1930s and 1940s added a new dimension to the modification of coronelismo. Since 1945, a coronel is seldom a personal economic czar or the social patriarch of his município. The sterotype is rapidly disappearing. Now the coronel or more respectable chefe político is often a university or faculdade graduate, frequently a lawyer or physician. Until 1964, he was a key member of one of the several political parties in his município, accepting the directorship of the local chapter. After 1964, the military dissolved parties and replaced them with a two-party system: the "in" party of the National Renovation Alliance (ARENA—Aliança Renovadora

Nacional) and the "out" party of the Brazilian Democratic Movement (MDB—Movimento Democrático Brasileiro). Former PTB (Partido Trabalhista Brasileiro), PSD (Partido Social Democrático), UDN (União Democrática Nacional), and other minor party coronéis joined one of the two authorized parties. No longer does a coronel rely on his own resources to protect and expand personal power. He skillfully utilizes the resources of his party and those of the state and federal governments—that is, the public power and resources—to promote his personal and class interests.

The decline, or, more correctly, the modification, of coronelismo can be seen in changes that have taken place principally since 1930 but more specifically since 1945. First, the system of secret balloting to some degree minimized the intervention of coronéis in elections. Prior to 1933, only the states of Minas Gerais and Ceará had a secret ballot. How well the system guarded voting freedom is another matter, but the idea of secret balloting encouraged free expression of choice, thereby undermining the personal power of coronéis.

Second, economic development—industrialization and urbanization—since 1930 has changed the traditional social order of the country, particularly of the northeast, resulting in various forms of profound social changes. Victor Nunes Leal argued that Brazilian coronelismo was the product of a decadent economic and social structure. Mass dependence on one man was reinforced by the almost total lack of social mobility, especially in northeast Brazil during the First Republic. But once Brazil began to develop gradually under Vargas, all the traditional ties and loyalties began to weaken. The rapidly expanding cobweb of highways and roads, to cite one example of changes in northeast Brazil, has effectively ended the geographical isolation of the sertão, allowing the flow of people and goods between coast and interior and between north and south. The backlanders do not now depend solely on coronéis for guidance in elections, nor are the coastal elite and parties confined to politicking in cities.

Third, post-1945 Brazil saw a proliferation of political parties of various ideological hues and regional loyalties. The return to liberal democracy after fifteen years of Vargas' centripetal rule encouraged the rise of a dozen major and minor parties, causing the coronéis to splinter into factions. None of the three major parties—Social Democratic Party, Brazilian Labor Party, and National Democratic Union—succeeded in monopolizing the partisan loyalty of former political bosses of the backlands.

Politicians of the major parties attempted to build their power bases on the município level by enticing coronéis of various importance into their parties. Family ties, business connections, and personal friendships, but seldom ideologies, were generally deciding factors in the selection of a coronel-party cadre. Factionalism developed and in the process the sacred rule of one-man power failed to survive except in remote backwaters of the sertão. As this happened, each município came to possess more than one partisan coronel. The building of a large patronage army of voters thus proved difficult, and without control of votes the power monopoly of a coronel was unviable. Such once-powerful coronelista institutions of regional power monopoly as the Coronéis Pact of 1911 in Ceará and the Sertanejo Coalition of the São Francisco Valley of Bahia in 1933 failed to reappear.

Fourth, the expanding power of state and national governments since 1945 progressively eroded the influence of a coronel. Political modernization followed by economic development and social change enlarged the role of state and federal governments in the daily activities of Brazilians, and the state simply replaced the coronel as the supreme arbiter of backland life. The dependence of the subject people, to borrow Eric Wolf's term, was further eroded as the coronel's effectiveness and legitimacy as the ruler were often undermined by partisan rivalry and slow compliance with patronage requests. The state and parties no longer have to rely on a coronel(s) for their successful operation. Once a coronel lost command of patronage, people failed to rally around him. His wards became his constituents, and the constituents became increasingly independent and recalcitrant.

Last, and least important, is the natural elimination of coronéis by death. In Bahia by 1945, the major coronéis of the First Republic had died—Horácio de Matos, Franklin Lins de Albuquerque, and Frederico Costa. Others simply retired from active politics, passing the helm to their sons and grandsons. Sons of Franklin now distinguish themselves as state and federal deputies. Sons of Horácio remain active in state and federal politics. In the 1960s, a grandson of a coronel of Casa Nova served as governor of Bahia, and he has been a federal senator since 1974. At least two sons of prominent coronéis from

the São Francisco Valley served as speakers of the state legislature. A check of the list of state and federal deputies attests to
the fact that the second- and third-generation "coronéis" continue to operate in politics, some even exploiting the names and
reputations of their illustrious fathers and grandfathers.

The twilight of coronelismo has set in. Once violence and
patronage served coronéis as complementary means of wielding
power and amassing votes. The state and at times the federal
governments resorted to equally nefarious tactics to gain control
over coronéis, but these times are gone. The state had adopted
a more sophisticated approach to taming the interior, especially the northeast: economic development through state-spon-
sored institutions such as the Northeast Development Agency
(SUDENE—Superintêndencia do Desenvolvimento do Nordeste)
and private investors from São Paulo and foreign countries.

As economic development and modernization take hold, a new
social elite will emerge. The country will retreat, and the city
will advance to the center of power. When these changes occur,
the traditional elites such as the Calmons, Mangabeiras, Seabras, and Monizes will step down from political power, and the
eventual fall of oligarchies in the littoral and the sertão will
close the era of coronelismo. The process of change is still taking
place, and soon coronéis, like cangaceiros and fanáticos, will
pass into history as relics of the First Republic.

Tables

TABLE 1
CHIEF EXECUTIVES OF BRAZILIAN MUNICÍPIOS, 1891–1920

State	Designation	Selection under State Constitution	Later Reforms
AM	Superintendente	Elected 4 yrs.	Lei 343: Feb. 14, 1906, elected 3 yrs.
PÁ	Intendente	Elected 3 yrs., served as pres. of câmara municipal	Constitution: Oct. 23, 1915, intendente elected 3 yrs.
MA	Intendente	Elected 4 yrs.	Reform: Feb. 21, 1919, prefeito elected 3 yrs.
CE	Intendente	Elected 4 yrs.	Lei 33: Nov. 11, 1892, elected by câmara annually
PI	Intendente	Not mentioned	Lei 522: June 30, 1909, intendente elected 4 yrs.
RN	Presidente	Elected 3 yrs., served as pres. of câmara municipal	Lei 108: July 28, 1898, pres. of câmara, 3 yrs.
PB		Not mentioned	Lei 424: Oct. 28, 1915, gov. nominated prefeito
PE	Prefeito	Elected 3 yrs.	Lei 1282: June 10, 1915, prefeito elected 3 yrs.
AL	Intendente	Elected 2 yrs.	Lei 8: May 13, 1892, intendente elected 2 yrs., no re-election
SE	Intendente	Elected 4 yrs.	Lei 635: Sept. 30, 1913, elected 3 yrs.
BA	Intendente	Elected 4 yrs.	Lei 1102: Aug. 11, 1915, gov. nominated; 1920: elected 2 yrs.

Continued

TABLE 1—*Continued*

State	Designation	Selection under State Constitution	Later Reforms
ES		Not mentioned	Lei 2: Nov. 18, 1913, prefeito elected 2 yrs.
RJ		Not mentioned	Lei 1620: Nov. 11, 1919, prefeito named pres. of câmara
SP		Not mentioned	Lei 1103: Nov. 26, 1907, prefeito elected by câmara 2 yrs.
PR	Prefeito	Elected 4 yrs.	Lei 761: Apr. 2, 1908, prefeito elected
SC		Not mentioned	Constitution: May 25, 1910, super'dente elected 4 yrs.
RS	Intendente	Elected 4 yrs.	No change
MG		Not mentioned	Lei 2: Sept. 4, 1891, and Lei 5: Aug. 13, 1903, pres. of câmara 3 yrs.
GO	Intendente	Elected (unspecif.)	Lei 205: Aug. 7, 1899, elected 4 yrs.
MT	Intendente	Elected 4 yrs.	Decreto 21: Jan. 29, 1892, elected 4 yrs.

Source: Castro Nunes, *As constituições estaduais.*

TABLE 2

Number of Electors in the Ten Most Coronelistic Municípios, 1905–34

Município	1905	1908	1910	1912	1934
Andaraí	608	686	686	999	939
Barreiras	715	727	1,255	1,260	1,410
Carinhanha	514	660	660	813	301
Lençóis	695	850	848	848	644
Maracás	384	442	1,053	1,071	1,353
Mucugê	626	1,185	1,185	1,185	233
Pilão Arcado	235	435	509	480	627
Remanso	377	786	878	1,007	1,000
Rio Preto	369	558	558	609	78
Sento Sé	492	492	492	702	396
Bahia (total)	73,441	91,174	99,935	108,463	153,376

Source: Brasil, Ministério da Agricultura, Indústria e Comércio, Diretoria do Serviço de Estatística, *Estatística eleitoral da República dos Estados Unidos do Brasil,* pp. 17–39; Guedes, *Anuário . . . 1934,* pp. 45–58.
Note: These figures are the number of electors who actually voted in these elections. The actual number of qualified voters should be higher.

TABLE 3

THE MAJOR TRAITS OF THE FOUR BRAZILIAN OLIGARCHIC TYPES, 1889–1930

	Familiocratic	Tribal	Collegial	Personalistic
Membership	consanguine members nonconsanguine members socioeconomic dependents confined to a smaller region, i.e., comarca or município closely organized/centralized	cluster of related families drawn from statewide, mostly rural, sector organized by alliance or compact decentralized setup	families and clans economic interest groups individual followers drawn from statewide rural and urban regions decentralized with clearly defined chiefs of subgroups	cluster of related, unrelated families, clans individual followers of charismatic leader drawn from statewide heavily urban sector highly centralized organized and held by leader's charisma
Objectives	preservation of familial economic interests monopoly of political power desire to command social respect	perpetuation of the status quo or the ruling elite group monopoly of political offices: municipal, state, federal	expansion of collegial members' economic interests preservation of the group's monopoly of state and federal politics control of federal presidency	preservation of the status quo for the members personal control of state or federal politics by the leader arbitrary use of public resources for the group by the leader
Means of Control	economic supremacy dependency tie ability to dispense favors use of private armed forces	promotion of nepotism/patronage usurpation of public resources for tribal interests use of tribal armed forces and state militia	personal, state, federal armies organization of party or a college of interest groups equitable share of "spoils" of state, federal gov'ts	promotion of nepotism and patronage use of state militia party of *personalistically* loyal members electoral alliances, compacts
Loyalty	directed to the head of family permanent, inalienable	directed to elected or recognized tribal chief temporary or for leader's lifetime	directed to factional (tribal) leader of the PR	directed toward charismatic leader for the leader's lifetime

TABLE 4
NUMBER OF RURAL ESTABLISHMENTS IN TEN STATES

State	Total	Under 100 Hectares	Over 100 Hectares
Alagoas	8,840	6,107 (69.1%)	2,733 (30.9%)
Bahia	65,181	53,443 (82.0%)	11,738 (18.0%)
Ceará	16,223	7,594 (46.8%)	8,629 (53.2%)
Distrito Federal	2,088	2,051 (98.2%)	37 (1.8%)
Goiás	16,634	5,187 (31.2%)	11,447 (68.8%)
Minas Gerais	115,655	70,025 (60.5%)	45,630 (39.5%)
Paraná	30,951	24,560 (79.4%)	6,391 (20.6%)
Pernambuco	23,336	11,219 (48.1%)	12,117 (51.7%)
Rio de Janeiro	23,699	18,080 (76.3%)	5,619 (23.7%)
Rio Grande do Sul	124,990	104,529 (83.6%)	20,461 (16.4%)
São Paulo	80,921	59,600 (73.7%)	21,321 (26.3%)

SOURCE: Brasil, Ministério da Agricultura, Industria e Comércio, *Recenseamento do Brasil—1920*: *Agricultura*, vol. 3, part 1, p. xiii.

TABLE 5
Types of Partidos Republicanos in Brazil: Chain of Communications

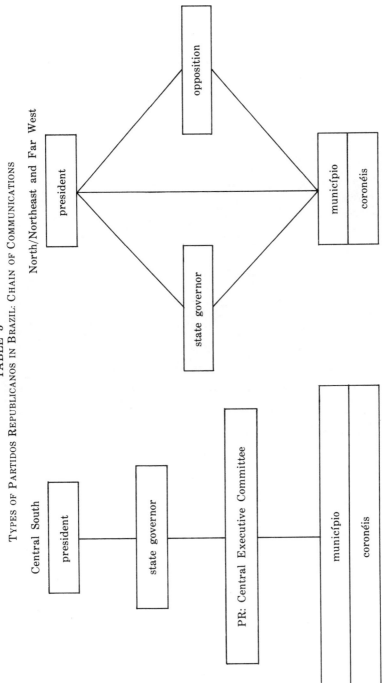

Appendixes

President	State	Year
Prudente José de Morais Barros	São Paulo	1894–98
Manuel Ferras de Campos Sales	São Paulo	1898–1902
Francisco de Paula Rodrigues Alves	São Paulo	1902–6
Afonso Augusto Moreira Pena	Minas Gerais	1906–9
Nilo Peçanha	Rio de Janeiro	1909–10
Hermes Rodrigues da Fonseca	Rio Grande do Sul	1910–14
Wenceslau Brás Pereira Gomes	Minas Gerais	1914–18
Francisco de Paula Rodrigues Alves[a]	São Paulo	1918
Epitácio da Silva Pessoa	Paraíba	1919–22
Artur da Silva Bernardes	Minas Gerais	1922–26
Washington Luís Pereira de Sousa	São Paulo	1926–30
Júlio Prestes de Albuquerque[b]	São Paulo	1930–

a. Rodrigues Alves, the only president elected twice during the First Republic, died before he could assume office for the second term.

b. The victors of the 1930 election never assumed office due to the Revolution, which overthrew the First Republic.

APPENDIX 2
VICE-PRESIDENTS OF BRAZIL, 1894–1930

Vice-President	State	Year
Manuel Vitorino Pereira	Bahia	1894–98
Francisco de Assis Rosa e Silva	Pernambuco	1898–1902
Francisco Silviano de Almeida Brandão	Minas Gerais	1902–3
Afonso Augusto Moreira Pena	Minas Gerais	1903–6
Nilo Peçanha	Rio de Janeiro	1906–9
Wenceslau Brás Pereira Gomes	Minas Gerais	1910–14
Urbano Santos da Costa Araújo	Maranhão	1914–18
Delfim Moreira da Costa Ribeiro	Minas Gerais	1918–20
Francisco Álvaro Bueno de Paiva	Minas Gerais	1920–22
Urbano Santos da Costa Araújo [a]	Maranhão	1922
Estácio de Albuquerque Coimbra	Pernambuco	1922–26
Fernando de Melo Viana	Minas Gerais	1926–30
Vital Henriques Batista Soares [b]	Bahia	1930–

a. Urbano Santos, the only vice-president elected twice during the First Republic, died before he could assume office for the second term.
b. The victors of the 1930 election never assumed office due to the Revolution, which overthrew the First Republic.

APPENDIX 3
APPOINTED AND ELECTED GOVERNORS OF BAHIA, 1889–1937

Name	Birthplace	Previous Office	Years Served
Virgílio Clímaco Damásio	Salvador	Professor of medicine	1889
Manuel Vitorino Pereira	Salvador	Physician	1889–90
Hermes Ernesto da Fonseca	Alagoas (?)	General	1890
José Gonçalves da Silva	Salvador	State senator	1890–91
Joaquim Ferreira Leal [a]	Salvador	State senator	1891–92
Joaquim Manuel Rodrigues Lima [b]	Caetité–LD	State senator	1892–96
Luís Viana	Casa Nova–SFO	State senator	1896–1900
Severino dos Santos Vieira	São Francisco do Conde–CR	Federal minister	1900–1904
José Marcelino de Sousa	Nazaré–CR	State senator	1904–8
João Ferreira de Araújo Pinho [c]	Santo Amaro–CR	Banker	1908–11
Aurélio Viana [a]	Salvador (?)	State deputy	1911–12
Braúlio Xavier da Silva Pereira	Mucugê–LD	State chief justice	1912
José Joaquim Seabra	Salvador	Federal minister	1912–16
António Ferrão Moniz de Aragão	Salvador	Federal deputy	1916–20
José Joaquim Seabra	Salvador	Federal senator	1920–24
Francisco Marques de Góis Calmon	Maragogipe–CR	Banker	1924–28
Vital Henriques Batista Soares [d]	São Francisco do Conde–CR	Federal deputy	1928–30
Frederico Augusto Rodrigues da Costa		President of state senate	1930
Leopoldo Amaral [e]	Salvador	Engineer	1930–31
Artur Neiva [e]	Salvador	Scientist	1931
Juraci Montenegro Magalhães [f]	Ceará	Army officer	1931–37

NOTE: LD, Lavras Diamantinas; CR, Capital and Recôncavo; SFO, São Francisco.

a. Interim.
b. Rodrigues Lima was the first popularly elected governor.
c. Araújo Pinho resigned in December 1911.
d. Vital Soares was elected to the federal vice-presidency in 1930.
e. Federal interventor.
f. Juraci Magalhães was a federal interventor August 1931–April 1935 and was the elected governor April 1935–November 1937.

APPENDIX 4
Fifty Most "Active" Coronéis of Bahia, 1889–1937

Name	Occupation [a]	Region [b]	Party [c]	Highest Office [d]	Period of Rule [e]
Franklin Lins de Albuquerque [f]	Merchant	Pilão Arcado–SFO	4, 5, 7, 8	Intendente	1918–37
Francisco Leobas de França Antunes [f]	Rancher	Remanso–SFO	4, 5, 7	Intendente	1916–30
Abílio Rodrigues de Araújo [f]	Rancher	Rio Preto–SFO	2, 4–6	Intendente	1902–25
Bernardino da Silva Bahia	Merchant	Feira de Santana–CR	3, 5, 7	Intendente	1915–30
Olímpio Antônio Barbosa	Rancher	Palmeira–LD	4–7	State deputy	1920–37
Antônio Balbino de Carvalho	Rancher	Barreiras–SFO	2, 3, 5, 7	Intendente	1900–1930
Manuel Alcântara de Carvalho	Merchant	Lençóis–LD	2, 4–7	State deputy	1920–37
Anfilófio de Castelo Branco [f]	Rancher	Remanso–SFO	2, 4–6	Councilman	1912–24
Antônio Honorato de Castro	Rancher	Casa Nova–SFO	1, 2, 4–8	Intendente	1900–1937
Clemente de Araújo Castro	Rancher	Sta. Maria da Vitória–SFO	4, 5, 7	Intendente	1920–30
Ramiro Ildefonso de Araújo Castro	Planter	Ilhéus–CS	1, 2, 4, 5	Substitute judge	1890–1924
Pedro Levino Catalão	Planter	Ilhéus–CS	1, 2, 4	Councilman	1890–1920
Francisco Dias Coelho	Merchant	Morro do Chapéu–LD	1–4	Councilman	1890–1920
Militão Rodrigues Coelho	Rancher	Brotas–LD	1–3	Intendente	1880–1920
José Abraham Cohim	Rancher	Morro do Chapéu–LD	2, 3, 5	State senator	1900–1924
Frederico Augusto Rodrigues da Costa [f]	Politician	Salvador–CR	1–3, 5–7	State senator	1910–30
Aprígio Duarte Filho	Merchant	Juàzeiro–SFO	3, 5–8	Intendente	1916–37
João Correia Duque [f]	Rancher	Carinhanha–SFO	2, 4, 5, 7	Intendente	1912–37
Francisco Borges de Figueiredo Filho	Rancher	Macaúbas–SFO	4, 5, 7	Intendente	1920–30
Francisco Joaquim Flores	Rancher	Sta. A Brejos–SFO	2–7	Intendente	1900–1930
Manuel Leôncio Galrão [f]	Priest	Areia–CR	1–3, 5–8	Federal deputy	1892–1937
Aureliano de Brito Gondim	Rancher	Andaraí–LD	2, 3, 5, 7	Intendente	1910–30
José Kruschewsky	Planter	Itabuna–CS	2, 3, 5, 7	Intendente	1910–28
Eugênio José Correia de Lacerda	Rancher	Remanso–SFO	2, 3	State deputy	1908–20
José Pedreira Lapa	Rancher	Mundo Novo–LD	2–4, 5, 7	Police delegate	1910–30

Name	Occupation	Location	Terms	Office	Years
Hermelino Marques de Leão[f]	Priest	Macaúbas-LD	1–3	State senator	1890–1920
Rodolfo Martins de Sousa	Merchant	Salvador-CR	2, 4, 6, 7	Unknown	1910–28
Clementino Pereira de Matos[f]	Rancher	Chapada Velha-LD	1, 2	Unknown	1880–1910
Horácio de Queiroz Matos[f]	Merchant	Lençóis-LD	4, 5, 7	State senator	1920–31
Antônio Landulfo da Rocha Medrado[f]	Rancher	Mucugé-LD	1–3, 5, 7	State deputy	1880–1928
Alfredo de Queiroz Monteiro	Merchant	Salvador-CR	1–3	State senator	1880–1920
Agostinho Froes da Mota	Merchant	Feira de Santana-CR	2, 3	Intendente	1908–20
José de Sousa Nogueira	Rancher	Xique-Xique-SFO	2, 4, 5, 7	Intendente	1910–28
Tranquilino José Nogueira	Merchant	Curralinho-CR	1–3	Substitute judge	1890–1920
Aristides Novis	Merchant	Salvador	1, 2	Unknown	1880–1910
Manuel Duarte de Oliveira	Politician	Salvador-CR	2, 3, 5–7	Secretary of the treasury (state)	1900–1930
Manuel Fabrício de Oliveira	Rancher	Campestre-LD	1–3	Intendente	1880–1920
Otávio Passos	Merchant	Lençóis-LD	7, 8	Intendente	1925–37
Antônio Pessoa da Costa e Silva[f]	Planter (Lawyer)	Ilhéus-CS	1–3, 5–7	State senator	1880–1930
Carlos Pinto	Merchant (Lawyer)	Salvador-CR	2, 3, 5	State senator	1912–24
Henrique Alves dos Reis	Planter	Itabuna-CS	1, 2, 4, 6, 7	Intendente	1880–1930
Francisco Joaquim da Rocha[f]	Lawyer (Rancher)	Barreiras-SFO	5, 6–8	Federal deputy	1920–37
Domingos Adami de Sá	Planter	Ilhéus-CS	1, 2, 4	Intendente	1880–1924
César de Andrade Sá[f]	Merchant	Lençóis-LD	2, 3, 5, 7	State senator	1910–30
Felisberto Augusto de Sá[f]	Rancher	Lençóis-LD	1	Intendente	1870–97
João Nunes de Sento-Sé[f]	Rancher	Sento-Sé-SFO	3, 5, 7, 8	Intendente	1916–37
Antônio Pereira da Silva Moacir	Physician	Lapa-SFO	5–7	Federal deputy	1920–37
Marcionílio Antônio de Sousa[f]	Planter	Maracás	1, 2, 4–7	President, município council	1900–1930
Manuel Misael da Silva Tavares	Planter	Ilhéus	1–3, 5, 7	Intendente	1890–1930
Abílio Wolney[f]	Rancher	Barreiras-SFO and Goiás	4–8	State deputy (Goiás)	1920–37

Continued

APPENDIX 4—*Continued*

Note: The rule of the coronéis of the First Republic extended to 1937.

a. Many coronéis had more than one economic activity. Many merchants owned ranches and plantations, and some planters and ranchers were lawyers. For simplicity, the best known occupation of each is listed.

b. The first name appearing is the município, the second the region. CR, Capital and Recôncavo; SFO, São Francisco Valley; LD, Lavras Diamantinas, central west; CS, Central South.

c. The codes are: (1) Federal Republican Party (1893–98); (2) Bahian Republican Party (1901–12); (3) Republican Democratic Party (1912–24); (4) Popular Convention Party (1919–20); (5) Republican Democratic Party—second phase (1920–24); (6) Republican Concentration Party (1923–27); (7) Bahian Republican Party (1927–30); (8) Social Democratic Party of Bahia (1933–37).

d. The highest office held by the coronéis. Those coronéis who were state deputies, state senators, and federal deputies had been município councilmen, presidents of the council, and/or intendentes.

e. The period of rule is used as the approximate period of a coronel's political influence. After this period, if a coronel was not deceased, he continued to remain a coronel in the social sense, even though not actively engaged in politics.

f. These coronéis were the outstanding political bosses—warlords and party cadres.

Glossary

afilhado: godson
agregado: farm hand, rural employee
arrendatário: tenant, renter

bacharel: university graduate, generally a lawyer; *bacharéis* (pl.)
bancada: state congressional delegation
barão: baron, the lowest-ranking grade of Brazilian nobility
batalhões patrióticos: citizens' volunteer groups in a federal military campaign
beata: pious one, a follower of religious fanaticism
bico de pena: writing-in of nonexistent votes

cabo eleitoral: election enforcer who gathers and even buys votes
cacique: local political chieftain in Spanish America, especially in the Caribbean and Mexico. See *gamonal*
café com leite: "coffee with cream," a political alliance that bridged the interests of São Paulo and Minas Gerais
café contra leite: "coffee against cream," a political rivalry that characterized the relationship between São Paulo and Minas Gerais after 1910
cangaceiro: bandit, social bandit, who steals for the poor and seeks restoration of justice; *cangaço* or *cangacerismo* for social banditry
capanga: ruffian or gunsel, generally a follower of a bandit or a rural potentate
capitão-mor: captain-major, the highest military rank in colonial times, equivalent to colonel
cabra: see *capanga*
coligados: the coalitioned; the political alliance of various factions in Pernambuco in 1920–22
colono: European colonist, immigrant settler

comarca: judicial district, comprised of two or more counties
comissão de reconhecimento: election verification committee in state or national legislature
conde: count, the third highest ranking grade of Brazilian nobility
coronel: colonel, political boss in interior and urban towns; *coronéis* (pl.)
coronelato: status of being a coronel
coronelismo: coronel's rule; an institution of one-man domination in politics, especially between 1850 and 1950
coronelista: of a coronel; coronelistic
corpo fechado: closed body; person with a bullet-proof body; myth held by the follower of a coronel

degola: throat-cutting; refusal to grant a congressional seat
delegado (regional): county police chief
diploma: diploma, electoral certification with votes collected
doutor: holder of doctorate, medical school graduate, university graduate in politics; *doutores* (pl.)
duplicata: situation in which two winners claim electoral victory; election stalemate
duque: duke, the highest-ranking grade of Brazilian nobility

engenho central: sugar refinery, first founded in Brazil in 1877; more advanced and capable of handling bigger loads than an *engenho de açúcar*; also known as *usina*
engenho de acucar: sugar mill/plantation
Exército da 2ª Linha: army reserve, successor to the National Guard in 1918

fanático: religious fanatic
fantasma: ghost voter
fazenda de gado: cattle ranch; fazenda also means a plantation or farm
fazendeiro: planter or rancher
feitor: plantation manager, administrator of a trading post during the early sixteenth century
forasteiro: outsider, political carpet-bagger
fósforo: voter bought by a political faction

gamonal: local political boss in the Andean countries, especially in Peru
gato morto: victim, political scapegoat

intendente: prefect, chief executive of county until 1930

jagunço: gunman loyal to one particular master, follower of a religious fanatic leader or a bandit
jornaleiro: journeyman, rural or urban wage-earner paid by the day
juiz municipal: county judge, generally elected
junta de apuração: county commission that reviews election results; also *comissão de apuração*
junta de classificação: classification committee for slave registration in the 1870s and 1880s; county voter registration board

latifúndio: large rural estate, characterized by uneconomic use of land
lavrador: a middle- or small-sized farm owner, generally ill equipped farmer

major: major, minor political boss
marquês: marquis, the second highest ranking grade of Brazilian nobility

mesa eleitoral: election board

mestre de açúcar: sugar master, sugar mill technician

município: county, the lowest administrative-legislative unit in the Brazilian federation, subdivided into districts; state (province under the monarchy) was divided into municípios

novos ricos: the new rich

padrinho: godfather; *padrinho influente*, political protector

parceiro: sharecropper

parecer: opinion, generally pertaining to governmental decision or action; legislative committee review, judicial or executive review of specific issue(s)

parentesco carnal: relatives of marriage between two sets of siblings

parentesco espiritual: relatives of religious or social ritual

parentesco de aliança: relatives by marriage

partido republicano: Republican party, first founded in Brazil in 1870

paz e concórdia: peace and harmony, the 1920–22 political reconciliation arrangement by Pernambuco's key factions

política da salvação: salvationist politics of 1910–14, an anti–Pinheiro Machado political movement to rescue state politics from the hands of the traditional oligarchies allied to the Gaúcho federal senator

prefeito: prefect

promotor público: county prosecutor

roçado: small plot cleared of brush and wood for subsistence or small-scale cash crop farming

senhor de engenho: sugar planter/mill owner; in São Paulo, also known as *engenheiro*, literally an engineer

sertanejo: backlander

sertão: backlands, hinterlands

superintendente: county chief executive in Amazonas under the First Republic

suplente de juiz (juiz suplente): substitute judge

tenente: lieutenant; *tenente-coronel*: lieutenant colonel

tenentismo: social-political reformist movement of the 1920s instigated by a group of army junior officers

vaqueiro: cowboy

visconde: viscount, the fourth highest ranking grade of Brazilian nobility

zona colonial: area settled by European colonists, generally in southern Brazil

Bibliography

PAPERS

Private

Afonso Augusto Moreira Pena (Rio)
The Araújo Pinho Family Papers (Rio)
Barão de Cotegipe (Rio)
Barão do Rio Branco (Rio)
Epitácio da Silva Pessoa (Rio)
Floriano Peixoto (Rio)
Francisco Marques de Góis Calmon (Salvador)
Franklin Lins de Albuquerque (Salvador)
Gonçalo Moniz (Salvador)
Horácio de Queiroz Matos (Mucugê)
José Antônio Saraiva (Rio)
Nilo Peçanha (Rio)
Oswaldo Aranha (Rio)
Otávio Mangabeira (Rio)
Rui Barbosa (Rio)
Severino dos Santos Vieira (Salvador)
Virgílio Clímaco Damásio (Salvador)

Public

Arquivo da Associação Comercial da Bahia
Arquivo do Instituto Geográfico e Histórico da Bahia
Arquivo do Instituto Histórico e Geográfico Brasileiro

NOTE: At the publisher's request, all names and titles have been revised to conform to the latest Brazilian orthography in use.

Arquivo do Ministério do Exército
Arquivo do Museu Republicano "Convenção de Itu"
Arquivo do Quartel General da Polícia Militar do Estado da Bahia
Arquivo do Quartel General da 6ª Região Militar
Arquivo Histórico do Ministério das Relações Exteriores (Itamarati)
Arquivo Histórico do Museu Imperial
Arquivo Nacional
United States National Archives

JOURNALS

Anais do Museu Paulista (AMP)
Hispanic American Historical Review (HAHR)
Revista Brasileira de Estudos Políticos (RBEP)
Revista de História (RH)
Revista do Instituto do Ceará (RIC)
Revista do Instituto Genealógico da Bahia (RIGBa)
Revista do Instituto Geográfico e Histórico da Bahia (RIGHBa)
Revista do Instituto Histórico e Geográfico Brasileiro (RIHGB)
Revista do Instituto Histórico e Geográfico de São Paulo (RIHGSP)

NEWSPAPERS

A Bahia (Salvador)
O Democrata (Salvador)
Diário da Bahia (Salvador)
Diário de Notícias (Salvador)
Diário Oficial (Salvador)
O Estado de São Paulo (São Paulo)
O Imparcial (Salvador)
Jornal de Notícias (Salvador)
Jornal de Pernambuco (Recife)
A Tarde (Salvador)

PUBLISHED AND UNPUBLISHED OFFICIAL DOCUMENTS

AQGPMEBa. Boletins, 1925–30 (MS).
AQG6RM. Boletins, 1920–30 (MS).
———. Histórico da Quartel General, 1880–1962 (MS).
Bahia. *Fala dirigida à Assembléia Legislativa Provincial da Bahia, na abertura da sessão ordinária do ano de 1845, pelo presidente da província Francisco de Sousa Soares d'Andrea.* Bahia: n.p., 1845.
———. *Fala com que o Ilm. e Exm. Sr. Dez. Experidião Eloi de Barros Pimentel abriu a 2ª sessão da 25ª legislatura da Assembléia Provincial da Bahia em 1 de maio de 1885.* Bahia: Tip. do Diário da Bahia, 1885.
———. *Leis do Estado da Bahia no ano de 1920.* Bahia: Imprensa Oficial do Estado, 1922.
———. *Mensagem e Relatórios apresentados à Assembléia Geral Legislativa pelo Chefe de Divisão Reformado Joaquim Ferreira Leal Vice Governador do Estado.* Bahia: Tip. do Diário da Bahia, 1892.

——. *Mensagem e Relatórios apresentado à Assembléia Geral Legislativa pelo Dr. Joaquim Manuel Rodrigues Lima Governador do Estado.* Bahia: Tip. do Diário da Bahia, 1894.

——. *Mensagem apresentada à Assembléia Geral Legislativa pelo Exm. Sr. Dr. Luís Viana Governador da Bahia em 7 de abril de 1897.* Bahia: Tip. do Correio de Notícias, 1897.

——. *Mensagem apresentada à Assembléia Geral Legislativa pelo exm. sr. dr. Severino Vieira Governador do Estado em 11 de abril de 1901.* Bahia: Tip. do Diário da Bahia, 1901.

——. *Mensagem apresentada à Assembléia Geral Legislativa na abertura da 1ª sessão ordinária da 7ª legislatura por Severino Vieira Governador do Estado.* Bahia: Oficinas do Diário da Bahia, 1903.

——. *Mensagem apresentada à Assembléia Geral Legislativa do Estado da Bahia na abertura da 1ª sessão ordinária da 9ª legislatura pelo Dr. José Marcelino de Sousa Governador do Estado.* Bahia: Oficinas do Diário da Bahia, 1907.

——. *Mensagem apresentada à Assembléia Geral Legislativa do Estado da Bahia na abertura da 2ª sessão ordinária da 9ª legislatura pelo Dr. José Marcelino de Sousa Governador do Estado.* Bahia: Oficinas da Empresa "A Bahia," 1908.

——. *Mensagem apresentada à Assembléia Geral Legislativa do Estado da Bahia na abertura da 2ª sessão ordinária da 11ª legislatura pelo Dr. J. J. Seabra Governador do Estado.* Bahia: Seção das Obras da "Revista do Brasil," 1912.

——. *Mensagem apresentada à Assembléia Geral Legislativa do Estado da Bahia na abertura da 2ª sessão ordinária da 14ª legislatura pelo Dr. Antônio Ferrão Moniz de Aragão Governador do Estado.* Bahia: Imprensa Oficial do Estado, 1918.

——. *Mensagem apresentada pelo Exm. Snr. Dr. Francisco Marques de Góis Calmon Governador do Estado da Bahia à Assembléia Geral Legislativa por ocasião da abertura da 1ª reunião ordinária da 18ª legislatura em 7 de abril de 1925.* Bahia: Imprensa Oficial do Estado, 1925.

——. *Organisação municipal: Decreto no. 7.479 de 8 de julho de 1931.* Bahia: Imprensa Oficial do Estado, 1931.

——. *Relatório apresentado à Assembléia Legislativa da Bahia pelo excelentíssimo senhor Barão de S. Lourenço, Presidente da mesma provincia, em 6 de marco de 1870.* Bahia: Tip. do Jornal da Bahia, 1870.

——. *Relatórios apresentados à Assembléia Geral Legislativa pelo Dr. Joaquim Manuel Rodrigues Lima Governador do Estado em 7 de abril de 1895.* Bahia: Wilcke, Picard e C., 1895.

——. *Relatórios apresentados à Assembléia Geral Legislativa pelo Dr. Joaquim Manuel Rodrigues Lima Governador do Estado em 7 de abril de 1896.* Bahia: Tip. do Correio de Notícias, 1896.

——. *Relatório apresentado ao Exmo. Sr. Dr. José Marcelino de Sousa Governador do Estado da Bahia pelo Dr. João Pedro dos Santos Secretário do Tesouro e Fazenda.* Feira de Santana: Foto-Tip. e Enc. d' "O Propulsor," 1905.

Brasil. *Anais da Assembléia Nacional Constituinte.* 22 vols. Rio: Imprensa Nacional, 1934–37.

——. Documentos Parlamentares. *Intervenção nos estados.* 16 vols. Paris and Rio: various publishers, 1913–26.

——. [Calógeras, João Pandiá]. *Relatório apresentado ao Presidente da República dos Estados Unidos do Brasil.* Rio: Imprensa Militar do Estado Maior do Exército, 1920.

———. Ministério da Agricultura, Indústria e Comércio. Diretoria do Serviço de Estatística. *Estatística eleitoral da República dos Estados Unidos do Brasil.* Rio: Imprensa Nacional, 1914.

———. *Recenseamento do Brasil—1920: Agricultura.* 5 vols. Rio: Imprensa Nacional, 1923.

———. Ministério da Justiça e Negócios Interiores. *Notícia histórica dos serviços, instituições e estabelecimentos pertencentes a esta repartição, elaborada por ordem do respectivo ministro, Dr. Amaro Cavalcanti.* Rio: Imprensa Nacional, 1898.

———. Tribunal Superior Eleitoral. *Dados estatísticos: eleições federais e estaduais.* Rio: Imprensa Nacional, 1952.

Pernambuco. *Mensagem apresentada ao congresso legislativo do estado em 6 de março de 1899 pelo Governador Dr. Joaquim Correia de Araújo.* Pernambuco: Imprensa Oficial, 1899.

———. Arquivo Público Estadual. *Documentos do Arquivo Público Estadual e da Biblioteca do Estado sobre a Comarca do São Francisco, selecionados, coordenados e publicados pelo Exmo. Snr. Barbosa Lima Sobrinho.* Vols. 4, 5. Recife: Arquivo Estadual, 1950.

United States National Archives. Records of the Department of State Relating to Internal Affairs of Brazil, 1910–29 (823.00/51–823.5067), 54 rolls.

BOOKS, MONOGRAPHS, ARTICLES, AND THESES

Abranches, [João] Dunshee de. *Governos e congressos da República dos Estados Unidos do Brasil 1889–1917.* 2 vols. São Paulo: n.p., 1918.

Aguiar, Alberto Cardoso de. *A intervenção na Bahia.* Rio: Tip. Batista de Sousa, 1920.

Aguiar, Durval Vieira de. *Descrições práticas da Província da Bahia com declaração de todas as distâncias intermediárias das cidades, vilas e povoações.* Bahia: Diário da Bahia, 1888.

Albuquerque, Ulisses Lins de. *A luta dos Pereiras e Carvalhos.* Rio: José Olympio, 1953.

———. *Um sertanejo e o sertão (memórias).* Rio: José Olympio, 1957.

———. *Moxotó brabo (aspectos históricos-sociológicos de uma região sertaneja-Pernambuco).* Rio: Organização Editora, 1961.

Alden, Dauril. *Royal Government in Colonial Brazil.* Berkeley: University of California Press, 1968.

———, ed. *Colonial Roots of Modern Brazil.* Berkeley: University of California Press, 1973.

Almeida, José Américo de. *Memórias de José Américo (o ano de Nêgo).* Rio: José Olympio, 1968.

Amado, Jorge. *O cavaleiro de esperança (vida de Luís Carlos Prestes).* 10th ed. Rio: Novos Horizontes, 1956.

———. *O país do carnaval, cacau, suor.* 15th ed. São Paulo: Martins, 1966.

Amaral, Araci. *Artes plásticas na semana de 22.* São Paulo: Perspectiva, 1970.

Amaral, Brás do. *Historia da Bahia do império à república.* Bahia: Imprensa Oficial, 1923.

———. "Memória histórica sobre a proclamação da república na Bahia." *RIGHBa* (1904):4–67.

Andrade, Delmiro Pereira de. *Evolução histórica da Paraíba do norte.* Rio: Minerva, 1946.

Andrade, Gilberto Osório de. *Montebelo, os males e os mascates.* Recife: UFPe, 1969.

Andrade, Manuel Correia de. *A terra e o homem no nordeste*. 3d ed. São Paulo: Brasiliense, 1973.

Andreski, Stanislav. *Parasitism and Subversion: The Case of Latin America*. New York: Schocken, 1969.

Anselmo, Octacílio. *Padre Cícero: mito e realidade*. Rio: Civilização Brasileira, 1968.

——— . *A revolução de 30 no Ceará*. Fortaleza: UFCe, 1970.

Aragão, Antônio Ferrão Moniz de. *A Bahia e os seus governadores na república*. Bahia: Imprensa Oficial, 1923.

Araripe, J. C. Alencar. *A glória de um pioneiro: a vida de Delmiro Gouveia*. Rio: Cruzeiro, 1965.

Arraes, Montes. *Decadência e redenção no nordeste (a política dos grandes estados)*. Rio: n.p., 1962.

Associação Comercial da Bahia. *Relatório da Diretoria da Associação Comercial da Bahia, 1881–1930*. 41 vols. Titles vary.

———. *Representação dirigida ao congresso legislativo federal contra a aprovação do Convênio de Taubaté sobre valorização do café e fixação do valor da moeda*. Bahia: n.p., 1912.

Audrin, Frei José M., O.P. *Os sertanejos que eu conheci*. Rio: José Olympio, 1963.

Azevedo, Aroldo de. *Arnolfo Azevedo, parlamentar da primeira república*. São Paulo: Nacional, 1968.

Azevedo, Fernando de. *Canaviais e engenhos na vida política do Brasil*. 2d ed. São Paulo: Melhoramentos, n.d.

Azevedo, Luís Viotti de. "Evolução dos partidos políticos no município de São João Evangelista." *RBEP* 6 (1959):183–94.

Azevedo, Miranda. "Baianos ilustres." *RIGHBa* 30 (1904): 219–22.

Barbosa, Mário Ferreira. *Anuário estatístico da Bahia—1923*. Bahia: Imprensa Oficial do Estado, 1924.

———. *Economia e finanças: cifras e notas do Estado da Bahia*. Bahia: Imprensa Oficial do Estado, 1932.

Barbosa, Olímpio Antônio. *Album de Lençóis no seu primeiro centenário 1845–1945*. Lençóis: n.p., 1946.

———. *Horácio de Matos, sua vida e suas lutas*. Salvador: Era Nova, 1953.

Barbosa, Rui. *O Art. 6º da constituição e a intervenção de 1920 da Bahia*. Rio: Castilho, 1920.

———. *Uma campanha política: a successão governamental na Bahia 1919–1920*. São Paulo: Saraiva, 1932.

Barros, Francisco Borges de. *Dr. J. J. Seabra, sua vida, sua obra na república*. Bahia: Imprensa Oficial do Estado, 1931.

———. *Memória sobre o município de Ilhéus*. Bahia: Tip. Bahiana, 1915.

Barros, João Alberto Lins de. *Memórias de um revolucionário*. Rio: Civilização Brasileira, 1954.

Bartolomeu, Floro. *Juàzeiro e o Padre Cícero (depoimento para a história)*. Rio: Imprensa Nacional, 1927.

Basbaum, Leôncio. *História sincera da república*. 3 vols. 2d ed. São Paulo: Edições LB, 1962.

Batista, Bolívar Sant'Ana. *Discurso de despedida*. Salvador: Imprensa Oficial, 1967.

Belo, José Maria. *A History of Modern Brazil 1889–1964*. Translated by James L. Taylor. Stanford: Stanford University Press, 1966.

Bendix, Reinhard. *Max Weber: An Intellectual Portrait*. Garden City, N.Y.: Anchor, 1962.

Benício, Manuel. *O rei dos jagunços*. Rio: n.p., 1899.

Blondel, Jean. *As condições da vida política no Estado da Paraíba*. Rio: Fundação Getúlio Vargas, 1957.

Boehrer, George C. A. *Da monarquia à república: história do Partido Republicano do Brasil (1870–1889)*. Rio: MEC/Imprensa Nacional, 1954.

Boxer, Charles R. *The Golden Age of Brazil 1695–1750. Growing Pains of a Colonial Society*. Berkeley: University of California Press, 1969.

———. *Portuguese Society in the Tropics: The Municipal Councils of Goa, Macao, Bahia, and Luanda, 1510–1800*. Madison: University of Wisconsin Press, 1965.

Braga, Leopoldo. *Uma sinistra história de roubos, saques, e homicídios*. Bahia. n.p., 1943.

Brito, Lemos. *A cisão: páginas de crítica*. Bahia: Tip. Baiana, 1908.

Brito, Manuel Tomás de Carvalho. *Concentração Conservadora de Minas Gerais*. Rio: Oficinas Gráficas, 1929.

Bulcão Sobrinho, Antônio de Araújo de Aragão. "A Bahia não se dá e não se vende." *RIHGB* 265 (October–December 1964):238–40.

———. *Famílias baianas*. 3 vols. Salvador: IGBa, 1961.

———. "O homem do norte—Luís Viana." *RIHGB* 261 (October–December 1963):6–32.

———. "O pregoeiro da república: Virgílio Clímaco Damásio." *RIHGB* 264 (July–September 1964):274–81.

———. "A proclamação da república na Bahia." *RIHGB* 257 (October–December 1962):6–15.

———. "Relembrando o velho senado baiano." *RIHGB* 218 (January–March 1953):183–203.

———. "Representantes da Bahia na Câmara Federal da primeira república." *RIHGB* 263 (April–June 1964):55–86.

Calasans, José. *Lulu Parola e os acontecimentos políticos de 1891*. Salvador: Centro de Estudos Baianos, 1967.

———. "A primeira fase de conspiração no norte: abril–maio 1930." *Universitas: Revista de Cultura da Universidade Federal da Bahia* 5 (January–April 1970):41–61.

———. "A revolução de 1930 na Bahia." *Porto de Todos os Santos* 1 (April 1968):5–18.

———. *No tempo de Antônio Conselheiro*. Salvador: Progresso, 1959.

Camelo, C. Nery. *Através dos sertões*. Rio: A Noite, 1939.

Campos, [Jôao da] Silva. *Crônica da Capitania de São Jorge dos Ilhéus*. Bahia: Vitória, 1947.

Cardoso, Fernando Henrique, and Faletto, Enzo. *Dependência e desenvolvimento na América Latina: ensaio de interpretaçáo sociológica*. 2d ed. Rio: Zahar, 1973.

Carneiro, Glauco. *O revolucionário Siqueira Campos*. 2 vols. Rio: Cruzeiro, 1966.

Carneiro, J. Fernando. *Imigração e colonização no Brasil*. Rio: Universidade do Brasil, 1950.

Carneiro, Nelson de Sousa. *XXII de agosto! o movimento constitucionalista na Bahia*. São Paulo: Nacional, 1933.

Carone, Edgard. *A primeira república (1889–1930): texto e contexto*. São Paulo: DIFEL, 1969.

———. *A república velha (instituições e classes sociais)*. São Paulo: DIFEL, 1969.

———. *A república velha II (evolução política)*. São Paulo: DIFEL, 1971.

———. *O tenentismo: aconcentecimentos—personagens—programas*. São Paulo: DIFEL, 1975.

Carvalho, Antônio Gontijo de. *Raul Fernandes, um servidor do Brasil*. Rio: AGIR, 1956.

Carvalho, Daniel de. *Francisco Sales, um político de outros tempos.* Rio: José Olympio, 1963.

Carvalho, Fernando Setembrino de. *Memórias: dados para a história do Brasil.* Rio: n.p., 1950.

Carvalho, José Murilo de. "Elite and State-Building in Imperial Brazil." Ph.D. dissertation, Stanford University, 1974.

Carvalho, M. Balbino de. *A luta no Graças.* Rio: Jacinto Ribeiro dos Santos, 1926.

Carvalho, Orlando M. *Política do município (ensaio histórico).* Rio: AGIR, 1946.

——. *O rio da unidade nacional: o São Francisco.* São Paulo: Nacional, 1937.

Casanta, Guerino, ed. *Correspondência de Bueno Brandão.* Belo Horizonte: Imprensa Oficial, 1958.

Cascudo, Luís Câmara. *Dicionário do folclore brasileiro.* 2 vols. Rio: Instituto Nacional de Livros, 1962.

Castro, Sertório de. *A república que a revolução destruiu.* Rio: Freitas Bastos, 1932.

Chagas, Américo. *O cangaceiro Montalvão.* 2d ed. São Paulo: n.p., 1962.

——. *O chefe Horácio de Matos.* São Paulo: n.p., 1961.

Cohen, Ronald, and Middleton, John, eds. *Comparative Political Systems: Studies in the Politics of Pre-Industrial Societies.* Garden City, N.Y.: The Natural History Press, 1967.

Correia, Edgard Simões. *As cartas falsas atribuídas ao snr. dr. Artur Bernardes e a prova da verdade.* N.p., 1922.

Correia Filho, Virgílio. *Pedro Celestino.* Rio: Zélio Valverde, 1945.

Cortés, Carlos E. *Gaúcho Politics in Brazil: The Politics of Rio Grande do Sul, 1930-1964.* Albuquerque: University of New Mexico Press, 1974.

Costa, Afonso. "Genealogia baiana." *RIHGB* 191 (April–June 1946):3–279.

Costa, Emília Viotti da. *Da monarquia à república: momentos decisivos.* São Paulo: Editorial Grijalbo, 1977.

——. "A proclamação da república." *AMP* 19 (1965):169–207.

——. "Sobre as origins da república." *AMP* 18 (1964):63–120.

Coutinho, Lourival. *O general Góis depõe. . . .* Rio: Coelho Branco, 1955.

Cova, José Álvaro. *Relatório apresentado ao Exmo. Sr. Dr. Antônio Ferrão Moniz de Aragão.* Bahia: Imprensa Oficial do Estado, 1917.

Cruz, Levy. "Função do comportamento político numa comunidade do São Francisco." *RBEP* 5 (1959):126–60.

Cunha, Euclides da. *Os sertões.* 27th ed. Rio: Francisco Alves, 1968.

Dantas Júnior, J. C. Pinto. *O Barão de Jeremoabo (Dr. Cícero Dantas Martins) 1838-1938.* Bahia: Imprensa Oficial, 1939.

Debes, Célio. *O partido republicano na propaganda (1872-1889).* São Paulo: n.p., 1975.

della Cava, Ralph. "Brazilian Messianism and National Institutions: A Reappraisal of Canudos and Joaseiro." *HAHR* 48 (August 1968):402–20.

——. *Miracle at Joaseiro.* New York: Columbia University Press, 1970.

Derby, Orville A. "Os primeiros descobrimentos de diamantes no Estado da Bahia." *RIGHBa* 31 (1906):143–51.

Diégues Júnior, Manuel. *População e açúcar no nordeste do Brasil.* São Paulo: Comissão Nacional de Alimentação, 1954.

Dulles, John W. F. *Anarchists and Communists in Brazil, 1900-1935.* Austin: University of Texas Press, 1973.

——. *Vargas of Brazil: A Political Biography.* Austin: University of Texas Press, 1967.

Eisenstadt, S. N., ed. *Max Weber on Charisma and Institution Building.* Chicago: University of Chicago Press, 1968.

Facó, Rui. *Cangaceiros e fanáticos: gênese e lutas.* 2d ed. Rio: Civilização Brasileira, 1965.

Faoro, Raymundo. *Os donos do poder.* 2 vols. 2d ed. São Paulo: Globo/USP, 1975.

Fausto, Boris. *A revolução de 1930: historiografia e história.* São Paulo: Brasiliense, 1972. [See also *História geral da civilização brasileira.*]

Fernandes, Heloísa Rodrigues. *Política e segurança: Força Pública do Estado de São Paulo: fundamentos histórico-sociais.* São Paulo: Alfa-Omega, 1974.

Flugel, Felix, "Coffee Valorization in Brazil." Master's thesis, University of California, Berkeley, 1917.

Flynn, Peter. "The Revolutionary Legion and the Brazilian Revolution of 1930." In *Latin American Affairs,* edited by Raymond Carr, pp. 71–105. London: Oxford University Press, 1970.

Fontoura, João Neves da. *Memórias.* 2 vols. Porto Alegre: Globo, 1958.

Franco, Afonso Arinos de Melo. *A alma do tempo.* Rio: José Olympio, 1961.

———. *Um estadista da república (Afrânio de Melo Franco e seu tempo).* 3 vols. Rio: José Olympio, 1955.

———. *Rodrigues Alves: apogeu e declínio do presidencialismo.* 2 vols. Rio: José Olympio, 1973.

Franco, Virgílio de Melo. *Outubro, 1930.* 3d ed. Rio: Schmidt, 1931.

Frank, André Gunder. *Capitalism and Underdevelopment in Latin America: Historical Studies of Chile and Brazil.* Rev. ed. New York: Monthly Review, 1969.

Freyre, Gilberto. *The Masters and the Slaves (Casa Grande e Senzala): A Study in the Development of Brazilian Civilization.* Translated by Samuel Putnam. 2d ed. rev. New York: Alfred Knopf, 1966.

———. *Nordeste: aspectos da influência da cana sobre a vida e a paisagem do nordeste do Brasil.* Rio: José Olympio, 1937.

Fried, Morton, H. *The Evolution of Political Society: An Essay in Political Anthropology.* New York: Random House, 1967.

Friedrich, Carl J. *Man and His Government: An Empirical Theory of Politics.* New York: McGraw-Hill, 1963.

Gabaglia, Laurita Pessoa Raja. *Epitácio Pessoa (1865–1942).* 2 vols. Rio: José Olympio, 1951.

Galvão, Walnice Nogueira. *No calor da hora: a Guerra de Canudos nos jornais—4ª expedição.* São Paulo: Ática, 1974.

Gama, A. B. See Sousa, Afonso Rui de.

Gerth, H. H., and Mills, C. Wright, eds. *From Max Weber: Essays in Sociology.* New York: Oxford University Press, 1958.

Góis, Raul de. *Um sueco emigra para o nordeste.* 2d ed. Rio: José Olympio, 1961.

Gomes, Ordival Cassiano. *Manuel Vitorino Pereira: médico e cirurgião.* Rio: AGIR, 1957.

Graham, Richard. *Britain and the Onset of Modernization in Brazil 1850–1914.* Cambridge: At the University Press, 1968.

Guedes, Antônio Peixoto. *Anuário estatístico da Bahia—1934.* Bahia: Imprensa Oficial, 1936.

História geral da civilização brasileira. 9 vols. São Paulo: DIFEL, 1960–77. (This is a continuing series on Brazilian history with nine volumes to date. The first seven—two on the colonial period and five on the empire—were edited by Sérgio Buarque de Holanda and the last two on the First Republic were edited by Boris Fausto.)

Holloway, Thomas H. *The Brazilian Coffee Valorization of 1906: Regional*

Politics and Economic Dependence. Madison: University of Wisconsin Press, 1975.

Hsu, F. L. K. *Clan, Caste, and Club*. Princeton: D. Van Nostrand, 1963.

Ianni, Octavio, et al. *Política e revolução social no Brasil*. Rio: Civilização Brasileira, 1965.

Imaz, José Luís de. *Los que mandan (Those Who Rule)*. Translated by Carlos A. Astiz. Albany: State University of New York Press, 1970.

Jackle, Frank Robert. "John Casper Branner and Brazil." Ph.D. dissertation, Stanford University, 1967.

José, Oiliam. *A propaganda republicana em Minas*. Belo Horizonte: RBEP, 1960.

Kennedy, John Norman. "Bahian Elites, 1750–1822." *HAHR* 53 (August 1973): 415–39.

Lambert, Jacques. *Os dois brasís*. Rio: INEF, 1959.

Leal, Victor Nunes. *Coronelismo, enxada e voto (o município e o regime representativo no Brasil)*. 2d ed. São Paulo: Alfa-Omega, 1975.

———. *Coronelismo: The Municipality and Representative Government in Brazil*. Translated by June Henfrey. Cambridge: Cambridge University Press, 1977.

Leite, Manuel da Costa. *Apontamentos históricos sobre o exército nacional de 2ª linha*. Porto Alegre: Globo, 1926.

Lima, Lourenço Moreira. *A Coluna Prestes (marcha e combate)*. 2d ed. São Paulo: Brasiliense, 1945.

Lima Júnior, Felix. *Delmiro Gouveia—o Mauá do sertão alagoano*. Maceió: n.p., 1963.

Lima Sobrinho, Barbosa. *A verdade sobre a revolução de outubro*. São Paulo: Unitas, 1933.

Lins, Wilson. *Os cabras do coronel*. Rio: GRD, 1964.

———. *O médio São Francisco: uma sociedade de pastores e guerreiros*. Salvador: Progresso, 1952; 2d ed., 1960.

———. *O reduto*. São Paulo: Martins, 1965.

———. *Remanso da valentia*. São Paulo: Martins, 1967.

Lipson, Leslie. "Government in Contemporary Brazil." *The Canadian Journal of Economics and Political Science* 22 (May 1966):183–98.

Lourenço Filho. *Juàzeiro do Padre Cícero*. 3d ed. São Paulo: Melhoramentos, n.d.

Love, Joseph L. *Rio Grande do Sul and Brazilian Regionalism 1882–1930*. Stanford: Stanford University Press, 1971.

Luz, Nícia Vilela. "O papel das classes médias brasileiras no movimento republicano." *RH* 28 (January–March 1964):13–27.

Macaulay, Neill. *The Prestes Column: Revolution in Brazil*. New York: Quadrangle, 1974.

Macedo, Nertan. *O bacamarte dos Mourões*. Fortaleza: Instituto do Ceará, 1966.

———. *Floro Bartolomeu: o caudilho dos beatos e cangaceiros*. Rio: Cruzeiro, 1970.

———. *Abílio Wolney, um coronel da serra geral*. Goiânia: Legenda, 1975.

Machado Neto, Brasílio. *O município no Brasil*. Rio: Confederação Nacional do Comércio, 1958.

Machado Neto, Zahidé, ed. *O coronelismo na Bahia*. Bahia: UFBa, 1972.

Magalhães, Bruno de Almeida. *Artur Bernardes, estadista da república*. Rio: José Olympio, 1973.

Magalhães, F. *Delmiro Gouveia: pioneiro e nacionalista*. Rio: Civilização Brasileira, 1962.

Magalhães, Juraci M. *Minha vida pública na Bahia.* Rio: José Olympio, 1957.
Magalhães Júnior, R[aimundo]. *Deodoro: a espada contra o império.* 2 vols. São Paulo: Nacional, 1957.
———. *Rui, o homem e o mito.* 2d ed. Rio: Civilização Brasileira, 1965.
Malta, Otávio. *Os "tenentes" na revolução brasileira.* Rio: Civilização Brasileira, 1969.
Mangabeira, João. *Rui, o estadista da república.* Rio: José Olympio, 1943.
Manifesto de Horácio de Queiroz Matos ao público do Estado da Bahia e do país. Lençóis: n.p., 1930.
Manifesto político: o Dr. Manuel Vitorino, vice presidente da república à nação. Bahia: n.p., 1898.
Menezes, Francisco da Conceição. "Geofísica baiana: superfície, limites e aspectos físicos do Estado da Bahia." *RIGHBa* 61 (1935):63–67.
Menezes, Jaime de Sá. *Vultos que ficaram. os irmãos Mangabeira (Francisco, João e Otávio).* Salvador: Editora MF, 1977.
Monteiro, Joaquim Ribeiro. "A revolução de 30 na Bahia." MS.
Montenegro, Abelardo F. "José Antônio do Fechado e o banditismo político." *RBEP* 1 (1956):159–69.
Moraes, Aurino. *Minas na Aliança Liberal e na revolução.* Belo Horizonte: Pindorama, 1933.
Moraes, Maria Augusta Sant'Ana. *História de uma oligarquia: os Bulhões.* Goiânia: Oriente, 1974.
Moraes, Walfrido. *Jagunços e heróis.* Rio: Civilização Brasileira, 1963.
Morazé, Charles. *Les trois âges du Brésil.* Paris: Armand Colin, 1954.
Morel, Edmar. *Padre Cícero: o santo do Juàzeiro.* 2d ed. Rio: Civilização Brasileira, 1966.
Mosca, Gaetano. *The Ruling Class (Elementi di scienza politica).* New York: McGraw-Hill, 1939.
Mota, Leonardo. *No tempo de Lampião.* 2d ed. Fortaleza: UFCe, 1967.
Mourão, João Martins de Carvalho. "Os municípios, sua importância política no Brasil-colônia e no Brasil-reino. situação em que ficaram no Brasil imperial pela Constituição de 1824 e pelo Ato Adicional." *Anais do Primeiro Congresso de História Nacional* 3 (1916):299–318.
Murdock, George P. *Social Structure.* New York: Macmillan, 1949.
Nabuco, Joaquim. *Um estadista do império: Nabuco de Araújo.* 4 vols. São Paulo: Instituto Progresso, 1949.
Nascimento, Francisco Fernandes do. *Milagre na terra violenta: Padre Cícero, o santo rebelde.* Rio: Gráfica Record, 1968.
Nóbrega, Apolônio. *História republicana da Paraíba.* João Pessoa: Imprensa Oficial, 1950.
Nogueira, Ataliba. *Antônio Conselheiro e Canudos: revisão histórica.* São Paulo: Nacional, 1974.
Nogueira Filho, Paulo. *Ideais e lutas de um burguês progressista: a guerra cívica 1932.* 4 vols. Rio: José Olympio, 1965–71.
———. *Ideais e lutas de um burguês progressista: o Partido Democrático e a revolução de 1930.* 2 vols, 2d ed. Rio: José Olympio, 1965.
Nunes, Castro. *As constituições estaduais do Brasil (comentadas e comparadas entre si e com constituição federal).* 2 vols. Rio: Leite Ribeiro, 1922.
Oates, Ernest Donald. "Washington Luís and the Brazilian Revolution of 1930." Ph.D. dissertation, Brigham Young University, 1974.
Pang, Eul-Soo. "The Changing Roles of Priests in the Politics of Northeast Brazil, 1889–1964." *The Americas* 30 (January 1974):341–72.
———. *"Coronelismo* in Northeast Brazil." In *The Caciques: Oligarchical Politics*

and the System of Caciquismo in the Luso-Hispanic World, edited by Robert Kern, pp. 65–88. Albuquerque: University of New Mexico Press, 1973.

———. *O Engenho Central do Bom Jardim na economia baiana: alguns aspectos de sua história, 1875–1891*. Rio: Arquivo Nacional and Instituto Histórico e Geográfico Brasileiro, forthcoming.

———. "The Politics of *Coronelismo* in Brazil: The Case of Bahia, 1889–1930." Ph.D. dissertation, University of California, Berkeley, 1970.

———. "The Revolt of the Bahian *Coronéis* and the Federal Intervention of 1920." *Luso-Brazilian Review* 8 (December 1971):3–25.

———, and Seckinger, Ron L. "The Mandarins of Imperial Brazil." *Comparative Studies in Society and History* 14 (March 1972):215–44.

Payne, James L. "The Oligarchy Muddle." In *Latin American Politics*, edited by Robert D. Tomasek, pp. 38–54. Garden City, N.Y.: Anchor, 1970.

Peixoto, Afrânio, et al. *Góis Calmon in memoriam*. Rio: Irmãos Pongetti, 1933.

Peixoto, Alzira Vargas do Amaral. *Getúlio Vargas, meu pai*. Porto Alegre: Globo, 1960.

Pereira, Gonçalo Ataíde. *Memória histórica e descritiva do município dos Lençóis*. Bahia: "A Bahia," 1910.

Pessoa, Epitácio. *João Pessoa—Aliança Liberal—Princesa*. Rio: Instituto Nacional de Livros, 1965.

———. *Pela verdade*. 2 vols, 2d ed. Rio: Instituto Nacional de Livros, 1957.

———. *Revolução de outubro de 1930 e república nova*. Rio: Instituto Nacional de Livros, 1965.

Pierson, Donald. *O homem no vale do São Francisco*. 3 vols. Rio: MI/SUVALE, 1972.

Pinheiro, Irineu. *O Juàzeiro do Padre Cícero e a revolução de 1914*. Rio: Pongetti, 1938.

Pinho, [José] Wanderley [de Araújo]. *História de um engenho do Recôncavo. Matoim–Novo Caboto–Freguezia. 1552–1944*. Rio: Z. Valverde, 1946.

———. "Uma escolha senatorial no fim da monarquia: a questão Moura–Carneiro da Rocha na correspondência do Conselheiro Saraiva." *RIHGB* 185 (October–December 1944):184–212.

Pinho, Pericles Madureira de. "Luís Tarqüínio." *RIGHBa* 43 (1908):167–70.

———. *Luís Tarqüínio: pioneiro da justiça social no Brasil*, Bahia: Vitória, 1944.

———. *Orientação e prática da polícia na Bahia: relatório de 1929*. Bahia, 1930.

———. *São assim os baianos*. Rio: Fundo de Cultura, 1960.

Pinto, Adélia. *Um livro sem título (memórias de uma provinciana)*. Rio: Pongetti, 1962.

Pinto, L. A. Costa. *Lutas de famílias no Brasil (introdução ao seu estado)*. São Paulo: Nacional, 1949.

———. *Recôncavo: laboratório de uma experiência humana*. Rio: Centro Latin-Americano de Pesquisas em Ciências Sociais, 1958.

Pompeu Sobrinho, Th. "O homem do nordeste." *RIC* 51 (1937):337–48.

———. "Povoamento do nordeste brasileiro." *RIC* 51 (1937):107–62.

Ponce Filho, Generoso. *Generoso Ponce, um chefe*. Rio: Pongetti, 1952.

Pontes, Antônio Barroso. *Mundo dos coronéis*. Rio: Cruzeiro, 1970.

Porto, João da Costa. *Os tempos de Dantas Barreto*. Recife: UFPe, 1973.

———. *Os tempos de Rosa e Silva*. Recife: UFPe, 1970.

Prado Júnior, Caio. *The Colonial Background of Modern Brazil*. Translated by Suzette Macedo. Berkeley: University of California Press, 1969.

Quadros, Consuelo Novais Soares de. "Os partidos políticos da Bahia na primeira república." Master's thesis, Universidade Federal da Bahia, 1973.

Queiroz, Maria Isaura Pereira de. *O campesinato brasileiro*. São Paulo: Vozes/USP, 1973.

———. "O coronelismo numa interpretação sociológica." In *HGCB* 8:155–90.

———. *O mandonismo local na vida política brasileira (da colônia à primeira república): ensaio de sociológica-política*. São Paulo: IEB/USP, 1960.

———. *O mandonismo local na vida política brasileiro e outros ensaios*. São Paulo: Alfa-Omega, 1976.

———. *O messianismo no Brasil e no mundo*. São Paulo: Dominus, 1965; 2d ed. rev., São Paulo: Alfa-Omega, 1977.

Ramos, Guerreiro. *A crise do poder no Brasil (problemas da revolução nacional brasileira)*. Rio: Zahar, 1961.

"Relação dos cidadãos que têm governado o Estado de São Paulo desde 1889 até 1938." *Publicações do Arquivo Nacional* 36 (1939):27–31.

Ribeiro, Edson. *Juàzeiro na estreira do tempo*. Salvador: Mensageiro da Fé, 1968.

Rocha, Geraldo. *Nacionalismo político e econômico*. Rio: A Nota, 1937.

———. *O Rio São Francisco: fator precípuo de existência do Brasil*. 2d ed. São Paulo: Nacional, 1946.

Rodrigues, José Honório. *Conciliação e reforma no Brasil*. Rio: Civilização Brasileira, 1965.

Russell-Wood, A. J. R. *Fidalgos and Philanthropists: The Santa Casa da Misericórdia of Bahia, 1550–1755*. Berkeley: University of California Press, 1968.

Sá, José de. *O bombardeio da Bahia e seus efeitos*. Bahia: Diário da Bahia, 1918.

Sá, M. Auxiliadora Ferraz de. *Dos velhos aos novos coronéis*. Recife: PIMES/ UFPe, 1974.

Saes, Décio. *Classe média e política na primeira república brasileira (1889–1930)*. Petrópolis: Vozes, 1975.

Sales, Joaquim de. *Se não me falha a memória (políticos e jornalistas do meu tempo)*. Rio: São José, 1960.

Sales, [Manuel Ferraz de] Campos. *Da propaganda à presidência*. São Paulo: A Editora, 1908.

Sampaio, Nelson de Sousa. *O diálogo democrático na Bahia*. Belo Horizonte: Faculdade de Direito da UFMG, 1960.

———. "Méio século de política baiana." *RBEP* 20 (1966):105–24.

Sampaio, Teodoro. *O Rio de São Francisco: trechos de um diário de viagem e a Chapada Diamantina 1878–1880*. São Paulo: Escolas Profissionais Salesinas, 1905.

Santos, José Maria dos. *Os republicanos paulistas e a abolição*. São Paulo: Martins, 1942.

Santos Filho, Lycurgo. *Uma comunidade rural do Brasil antigo (aspectos da vida patriarcal no sertão da Bahia nos séculos XVIII e XIX)*. São Paulo: Nacional, 1956.

Seabra, J. J. *Esfola de um mentiroso: estudo documentado da ação política e administrativa do interventor Juraci Magalhães, na Bahia, contendo um esclarecimento completo em torno do assassinato do general Lavanère Wanderley, na Paraíba, em outubro de 1930*. Rio: n.p., 1936.

Seligsohn, Otto. *Bahia-kakao*. Hamburg: n.p., 1959.

Schwartz, Stuart B. *Sovereignty and Society in Colonial Brazil: The High Court of Bahia and its Judges, 1609–1751*. Berkeley: University of California Press, 1973.

Silva, Celson José da. *Marchas e contramarchas do mandonismo local*. Belo Horizonte: RBEP, 1975.

Silva, Hélio. *1889—a república não esperou amanhecer*. Rio, 1972.

——. *1922—sangue na areia de Copacabana*. Rio: Civilização Brasileira, 1964.

——. *1926—a grande marcha*. Rio: Civilização Brasileira, 1965.

——. *1930—a revolução traída*. Rio: Civilização Brasileira, 1966.

——. *1931—os tenentes no poder*. Rio: Civilização Brasileira, 1966.

——. *1932—a guerra paulista*. Rio: Civilização Brasileira, 1967.

——. *1934—a constiuinte*. Rio: Civilização Brasileira, 1969.

——. *1935—a revolta vermelha*. Rio: Civilização Brasileira, 1969.

Silva, Simoens da. *O Padre Cícero e a população do nordeste*. Rio: Imprensa Nacional, 1927.

Skidmore, Thomas E. *Politics in Brazil, 1930–1964: An Experiment in Democracy*. New York: Oxford University Press, 1969.

Smith de Vasconcelos, Rodolfo Smith de Vasconcelos, 1⁰ Barão, and Smith de Vasconcelos, Jaime Luís Smith de Vasconcelos, 2⁰ Barão. *Arquivo nobiliárquico brasileiro*, Lausanne, Switzerland: La Concorde, 1918.

Soares, Glauco Ary Dillon. *Sociedade e política no Brasil*. São Paulo: DIFEL, 1973.

Sobral, Lívio. "Padre Cícero Romão." *RIC* 54 (1940):135–40.

——. "Padre Cícero Romão." *RIC* 56 (1942):110–14.

——. "Padre Cícero Romão." *RIC* 57 (1943):285–96.

Sobreira, Azarias, Pe. "Floro Bartolomeu—o caudilho baiano." *RIC* 64 (1950): 193–202.

Sodré, Nelson Werneck. *História militar do Brasil*. Rio: Civilização Brasileira, 1965.

Sousa, Afonso Rui de (pseud. Gama, A. B.). *Coluna Prestes (2 anos da revolução)*. Salvador: Gráficas Fonseca Filho, 1927.

Sousa, Maria Mercedes Lopes de. *Um estadista quase desconhecido*. Bahia: Imprensa Oficial, 1948.

——. *José Marcelino de Sousa e sua obra administrativa no São Francisco*. Rio: AGIR, 1946.

Távora, Fernandes. "O Padre Cícero." *RIC* 57 (1943):268–81.

Távora, Juarez. *Uma vida e muitas lutas*. 3 vols. Rio: José Olympio, 1973–77.

Teofilo, Rodolfo. *Libertação do Ceará (queda da oligarquia de Acioli)*. Lisboa: n.p., 1914.

Tinoco, Brígido. *A vida de Nilo Peçanha*. Rio: Civilização Brasileira, 1962.

Torres, Camilo. *Revolutionary Priest: The Complete Writings and Messages of Camilo Torres*. New York: Vintage, 1971.

Torres, João Camilo de Oliveira. *Estratificação social no Brasil*. São Paulo: DIFEL, 1965.

——. *História de Minas Gerais*. 5 vols. Belo Horizonte: Difusão Pan-Americana de Livros, 1962.

Tosta, Joaquim Inácio. *Renúncia de mandato: discurso proferido na Câmara dos Deputados na sessão de 29 de dezembro de 1907*. Rio: Imprensa Nacional, 1907.

Tourinho, João Gonçalves. *História da sedição na Bahia em 24 de novembro de 1891*. Bahia: Tip. João Gonçalves Tourinho, 1893.

O treze de novembro de 1899 da capital da Bahia (subsídios para a história). Bahia: Diário da Bahia, 1900.

Tricart, Jean; Santos, Milton; Silva, Teresa Cardoso da; and Carvalho, Ana Dias da Silva. *Estudos de geografia da Bahia*. Salvador: Progresso, 1958.

Vianá, Oliveira. *O ocaso do império*. 3d ed. Rio: José Olympio, 1959.

Victoria, João da Costa Pinto. "Família Costa Pinto." *RIGBa* 11 (1959):17–115.

Vidal, Ademar. *1930—história da revolução na Paraíba*. São Paulo: Nacional, 1932.

Vieira, Romualdo Leal. *Sento-Sé rico e ignoto.* Bahia: Imprensa Oficial, n.d.

Vilaça, Marcos, and Albuquerque, Roberto C. de. *Coronel, coronéis.* Rio: Tempo Brasileiro, 1965.

Vilhena, Luís dos Santos. *Cartas de Vilhena: notícias soteropolitanas e brasílicas.* Annotated by Brás do Amaral. Bahia: Imprensa Oficial, 1922.

———. *A Bahia no século XVIII.* 3 vols. Salvador: Itapuã, 1969. (A reprint of the 1922 edition under a new title.)

Willems, Emílio. *Uma vila brasileira: tradição e transição.* São Paulo: DIFEL, 1961.

Zenha, Edmundo. *O município no Brasil (1532-1700).* São Paulo: Instituto Progresso, 1948.

Index

237

LATIN AMERICAN MONOGRAPHS—SECOND SERIES

NUMBER 1 (1965): *Fidel Castro's Political Programs from Reformism to "Marxism-Leninism"* by Loree Wilkerson

NUMBER 2 (1966): *Highways into the Upper Amazon Basin* by Edmund Eduard Hegen

NUMBER 3 (1967): *The Government Executive of Modern Peru* by Jack W. Hopkins

NUMBER 4 (1967): *Eduardo Santos and the Good Neighbor, 1938–1942* by David Bushnell

NUMBER 5 (1968): *Dictatorship and Development: The Methods of Control in Trujillo's Dominican Republic* by Howard J. Wiarda

NUMBER 6 (1969): *New Lands and Old Traditions: Kekchi Cultivators in the Guatemalan Lowlands* by William E. Carter

NUMBER 7 (1969): *The Mechanization of Agriculture in Brazil: A Sociological Study of Minas Gerais* by Harold M. Clements, Sr.

NUMBER 8 (1971): *Liberación Nacional of Costa Rica: The Development of a Political Party in a Transitional Society* by Burt H. English

NUMBER 9 (1971): *Colombia's Foreign Trade and Economic Integration in Latin America* by J. Kamal Dow